THE CAMBRIDGE
ANCIENT HISTORY

PLATES TO VOLUME III

THE CAMBRIDGE
ANCIENT HISTORY.

PLATES TO VOLUME III

The Middle East,
the Greek World and the Balkans
to the Sixth Century B.C.

NEW EDITION

Edited by
JOHN BOARDMAN F.B.A.

*Lincoln Professor of Classical Archaeology and Art
in the University of Oxford*

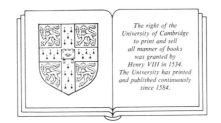

The right of the
University of Cambridge
to print and sell
all manner of books
was granted by
Henry VIII in 1534.
The University has printed
and published continuously
since 1584.

CAMBRIDGE UNIVERSITY PRESS

CAMBRIDGE

LONDON   NEW YORK   NEW ROCHELLE
MELBOURNE   SYDNEY

Published by the Press Syndicate of the University of Cambridge
The Pitt Building, Trumpington Street, Cambridge CB2 1RP
32 East 57th Street, New York, NY 10022, USA
296 Beaconsfield Parade, Middle Park, Melbourne 3206, Australia

© Cambridge University Press 1984

First published 1984

Printed in Great Britain by
The University Press, Cambridge

Library of Congress catalogue card number: 75–85719

British Library Cataloguing in Publication Data
The Cambridge ancient history.—New ed.
Plates to volume III
1. History, Ancient
I. Boardman, John
930   D57

ISBN 0 521 24289 4

CONTENTS

v

MAPS

ACKNOWLEDGEMENTS

Acknowledgement is due to the following for their permission to reproduce the photographs indicated.

M. Andronikos: 326; Athens, American School of Classical Studies, Agora Excavations: 273, 301; Athens, American School of Classical Studies, Corinth Excavations: 288, 336; Athens, British School of Archaeology: 321; Athens, French School of Archaeology: 282, 310a, b, 335, 348, 357; Athens, German Archaeological Institute: 281, 292, 297, 304c, 307, 308a, b, 316, 317a, b, 318, 319, 320, 332c, 333, 344, 345, 349, 352, 355a, b, 384, 385; Athens, National Museum: 275, 329, 346; O. Aytuğ Taşyürek: 124; Baghdad, National Museum of Antiquities: 30, 77, 78, 83, 84, 85; Basel, Antikenmuseum: 353, 360; Beirut, Institut Français d'Archéologie: 130a; Berlin (East), Staatliche Museen: 32, 37, 47, 51, 59, 64, 71, 95, 97, 102, 103, 113 (left-hand figure), 115, 121; Berlin (West), Staatliche Museen: 263, 284, 332a, 375; John Boardman: 141a–c, 267, 270, 274a, b, 306, 364; Boston, Museum of Fine Arts: 181, 195b, 332b; A. Cambitoglou: 266; Cambridge, Fitzwilliam Museum (courtesy of the Syndics): 240; Châtillon-sur-Seine: 373a, b; Chicago, Oriental Institute: 174; D. Collon: 136a, 129; J. M. Cook: 313, 380; Copenhagen, National Museum: 379b; Corfu Museum (courtesy of G. Dontas): 283; Corinth Museum: 290; Cyprus (courtesy of the Department of Antiquities): 196, 197a, b, 198, 199, 200, 201, 202, 203, 204, 205, 206, 207, 208, 209, 210, 211, 212, 213, 214, 215, 216, 217, 218, 219, 220, 222, 223; Peter Dorrell: 117; Vl. Dumitrescu: 2a–f, 7a, b, 11, 12, 13, 15, 18b, 19a, b, d, 20, 21, 24, 25, 26b, c, 27; Florence, Soprintendenza Antichità d'Etruria: 377; Hatice Gonnet: 111b; Hamburg, Museum für Kunst und Gewerbe: 99, 300b, 338b; Harvard, Sardis Archaeological Exploration: 236a, b, 237a, b; C. H. E. Haspels (courtesy of J. M. Hemelrijk): 228a, b; J. D. Hawkins: 106, 107, 109b, 125; Hirmer Verlag, Munich: 109a, 111a, 114, 123, 126, 305, 311, 327, 341, 342, 356, 359, 368, 372; B. S. J. Isserlin: 137a, b; Izmir Museum: 242; T. G. H. James: 183, 184, 185; L. H. Jeffery: 381; Jerusalem, Israel Museum: 147, 148, 149, 150, 153, 154, 155, 156, 165, 166, 167, 170, 171, 172; Kahia, Tunis: 138c; Karlsruhe, Badisches Landesmuseum: 134; J. J. Klein: 363; N. Kontos: 331; Lisbon, Gulbenkian Foundation: 178; London, British Museum (courtesy of the Trustees): 28, 29, 33, 34, 35, 40, 41, 42, 43, 44, 46, 50, 52, 53, 54, 55, 56, 57, 58, 60, 61, 62, 63, 65, 66, 67, 68, 70, 73, 74, 75, 76a, b, 79, 80, 81, 82, 86, 87, 88, 91, 92, 93, 94, 96, 98, 100, 118, 120b, 127a, 128a–e, 130b, 132a–d, 133a–b, 139a, 140a, 142a, 145, 161, 162a, b, 163, 164, 173, 175, 176a, 187, 188, 189, 191a, b, 192, 194a, b, 195a, c, 294, 298, 371, 383; London, Egypt Exploration Society: 193; M. Lowe: 286; Lycia, French Archaeological Mission: 243; Madrid, Museo Arqueologico Nacional: 142b, 144a; H. Metzger: 238, 239; P. Micha: 158; Munich, Antikensammlungen: 295; O. Muscarella: 256a–f; New York, Brooklyn Museum: 177, 182a, b; New York, Hispanic Society of America: 143; New York, Metropolitan Museum of Art: 108 (Gift of Mrs Henry Marden, 1890), 257a–c (Gift of Khalil Rabenou 1958), 280, 332a; Oxford, Ashmolean Museum: 14a, b, 38, 72, 101, 293, 322; Paestum Museum: 369; Paris, Cabinet des Médailles, 224; Paris, Caisse Nationale des Monuments Historiques et des Sites: 176b; Paris, Louvre: 31, 36, 39a–d, 49, 131a, 135a, b, 146, 179, 180, 221, 370; Philadelphia, University Museum: 225, 226, 227, 229, 230, 231, 233, 300a; M. R. Popham: 265, 325b–g, 343, 379a; F. Prendi: 2g, 5, 6, 7c–d, 9, 10, 16c, 18a, 19c, 22, 23, 26a; Rome, Conservatori Museum: 367; Rome, German Archaeological Institute: 378; Rome,

Soprintendenza alle Antichità dell' Etruria Meridionale – Roma II: 324; N. Schimmel: 338a, c; R. V. Schoder, SJ: 268a, b, 269, 271, 272, 304a, 309c, 365, 366; Sofia, Museum of the History of Sofia: 251; Rosa Staneva: 1a–c, 3, 4, 8, 16a, b, 17, 246, 247, 248, 249a–d, 250; Tehran, Iran Bastan Museum: 258, 262; Tel-Aviv, Institute of Archaeology, Tel-Aviv University: 157, 159, 160, 168, 169; Tübingen, Archaeological Institute: 296; Warsaw, State Archaeological Museum: 257e–j; R. L. Wilkins: 289, 302, 303, 376d; G. Xylouris: 276, 279; G. M. Young: 330.

PREFACE

This volume, which accompanies the publication of the new edition of *Cambridge Ancient History* Volume III, has been designed in a different manner to that of the Plates Volumes of the earlier editions, and to the one Plates Volume which serves the new edition of Volumes I and II. The choice of illustration has not been determined solely by the contents of the chapters in the text volumes (Volume III is being published in three parts) although their authors have been invited to make suggestions and some references to illustrations will be found in *CAH* III².2. The sections here correspond only roughly with the text chapters and although many have been compiled by the text authors, many others have not, and within some of the longer sections the material is presented in an order which bears no relationship to that in the text volume. We have tried to include a good range of illustrations of the material evidence of historical (in the broadest sense of the word) relevance for the places, peoples and periods dealt with in *CAH* III². This therefore both supplements that volume and stands as an independent survey of surviving physical evidence. For this reason brief introductory notes and bibliographies have been provided to each section for the general reader, and in many items the description and commentary goes on to discuss other matters which the subject suggests. This volume appears before the publication of the new edition of *CAH* III².2, to which the reader would have been referred for further information on subjects considered here in Sections 6, 10, 11, 12 and for the later parts of periods illustrated in Sections 2, 3, 7, 8.

For Section 1 Dr Sherratt has been able to use photographs kindly provided by authors of the text chapters, Professors Vl. Dumitrescu, M. Garašanin and F. Prendi. In Section 13 Mervyn Popham kindly provided the illustrations and narrative for 325.

The maps have been drawn by David Cox of Cox Cartographic Ltd; and many of the line drawings have been prepared by Marion Cox. The authors and editor are deeply grateful to the many museums, institutes and scholars who have provided photographs and given permission for their publication here.

Oxford, 1982   J.B.

ABBREVIATIONS

AAA	*Athens Annals of Archaeology*
AJA	*American Journal of Archaeology*
ANET	J. B. Pritchard (ed.), *Ancient Near Eastern Texts* (ed. 3; Princeton, 1969)
Ant. K.	*Antike Kunst*
Arch. Anz.	*Archäologischer Anzeiger*
Arch. viv.	*Archéologie vivante: Carthage* (Paris, 1968–9)
Arias–Hirmer	P. Arias and M. Hirmer (trans. B. B. Shefton), *A History of Greek Vase Painting* (London, 1962)
AS	*Anatolian Studies*
AS Atene	*Annuario della Scuola Archeologica di Atene*
Ath. Mitt.	*Mitteilungen des Deutschen Archäologischen Instituts. Athenische Abteilung.*
BASOR	*Bulletin of the American Schools of Oriental Research*
BCH	*Bulletin de correspondance hellénique*
Beazley, *ABV*	J. D. Beazley, *Attic Black-Figure Vase-Painters* (Oxford, 1956)
Beazley, *ARV*	idem, *Attic Red-Figure Vase-Painters* (ed. 2; Oxford, 1963)
Beazley, *Para*	idem, *Paralipomena* (Oxford, 1971)
BICS	*Bulletin of the Institute of Classical Studies, London*
Boardman, *GO*	J. Boardman, *Greeks Overseas* (London, 1980)
Boardman, *GSAP*	idem, *Greek Sculpture. Archaic Period* (London, 1978)
Bothmer	B. V. Bothmer, *Egyptian Sculpture of the Late Period* (New York, 1960)
BSA	*Annual of the British School at Athens*
CAH	*Cambridge Ancient History*
Coldstream, *GG*	J. N. Coldstream, *Geometric Greece* (London, 1977)
Cook, *GPP*	R. M. Cook, *Greek Painted Pottery* (ed. 2; London, 1972)
CVA	*Corpus Vasorum Antiquorum*
Fittschen	K. Fittschen, *Untersuchungen zum Beginn der Sagendarstellungen bei den Griechen* (Berlin, 1969)
Genge, *NSR*	H. Genge, *Nordsyrisch-südanatolische Reliefs* (Copenhagen, 1979)
Harden	D. B. Harden, *The Phoenicians* (London, 1962)
IEJ	*Israel Exploration Journal*
JdI	*Jahrbuch des Deutschen Archäologischen Instituts*
JEA	*Journal of Egyptian Archaeology*
Jeffery, *LSAG*	L. H. Jeffery, *Local Scripts of Archaic Greece* (Oxford, 1961)
JHS	*Journal of Hellenic Studies*
Kurtz–Boardman	D. C. Kurtz and J. Boardman, *Greek Burial Customs* (London, 1971)
Layard, *Monuments*	A. H. Layard, *The Monuments of Nineveh* (London, 1849, 1853)
Lefkandi i	M. R. Popham and L. H. Sackett, edd., *Lefkandi* i (London, 1979–80)

Meriggi, *Manuale* P. Meriggi, *Manuale di Eteo Geroglifico* (Rome, II/1, 1967; II/2–3, 1975)

Orthmann, *USK* W. Orthmann, *Untersuchungen zur Späthethitischen Kunst* (Bonn, 1971)

RA *Revue d'Assyriologie et d'Archéologie orientale*

Richter, *Korai* G. M. A. Richter, *Korai* (London, 1968)

Schefold I K. Schefold, *Myth and Legend in Early Greek Art* (London, 1966)

Schefold II idem, *Götter- und Heldensagen der Griechen in der spätarchaischen Kunst* (Munich, 1978)

Simon–Hirmer E. Simon and M. & A. Hirmer, *Die griechischen Vasen* (Munich, 1976)

Snodgrass, *EGAW* A. M. Snodgrass, *Early Greek Armour and Weapons* (Edinburgh, 1964)

SSEAJ *Society for the Study of Egyptian Antiquities, Journal*

Top. Bibl. B. Porter, R. L. B. Moss and J. Málek, *Topographical Bibliography of Ancient Egyptian Hieroglyphic Texts, Reliefs and Paintings* (Oxford, 1927–)

ZA *Zeitschrift für Assyriologie und vorderasiatische Archäologie*

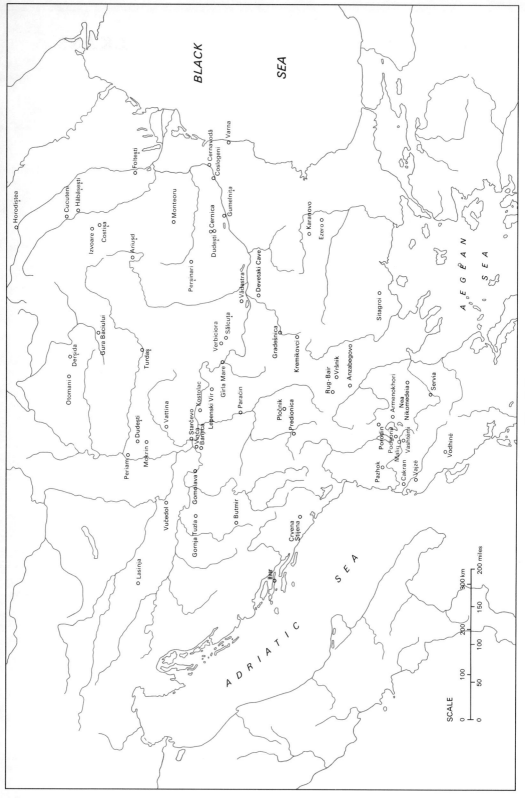

1. The Balkans

1. THE PREHISTORY OF THE BALKANS TO 1000 B.C.

A. G. SHERRATT

The earliest traces of human occupation in south-east Europe go back some half a million years to the stage of human evolution represented by *Homo erectus*. This discontinuous occupation during the warmer phases of the Ice Age was followed by permanent settlement of the region in the last glacial phase (75,000–10,000 years ago), represented by finds from upland caves. The critical transitional period around 40,000 years ago (which saw the appearance of modern man and more advanced stone industries) is not well represented in this region, but during the later part of this glacial period there are abundant traces of the reindeer- and mammoth-hunting groups related to those of the wider province covering the south Russian steppes.

With the advance of forests in the milder climate that began to prevail some 10,000 years ago, these animals retreated to the open steppe areas which persisted to the north of the Black Sea. They were replaced by wild cattle, pig or deer from further south, and the rivers were recolonized by fish. Sites from this early post-glacial period are best preserved in the Iron Gates region, where communities gained a living from fishing in the Danube and hunting in the forests nearby. This local development reached a climax around 6000 B.C., when it began to be replaced by an intrusive economy, based on cereal cultivation and livestock rearing, that had developed in the Near East.

The earliest farming communities in the Balkans show a clear relationship to contemporary cultures in Anatolia/Asia Minor, and the groups which penetrated into the lowland plains of Thrace and the lower Danube used a handmade pottery decorated with designs in red and white paint. The permanent villages established at this time were sometimes occupied more or less continuously for the next 4,000 years, creating substantial settlement-mounds that provide a clear picture of the subsequent development of farming cultures. During the sixth millennium B.C. farming spread into the Middle Danube area, Transylvania and Moldavia, where less substantial sites are especially plentiful along the rivers of the lowland loess areas.

The contacts maintained between these groups are evident from the changes in pottery style which can be traced over the whole of this area. The early painted wares gave way some time around 5000 B.C. to darker pottery, often decorated by incised ornament picked out in white paste. Experiments with new materials produced pigments in different colours, such as the silvery graphite which was used in Romania and Bulgaria to paint the elegant spiral decoration that is one of the striking achievements of Neolithic art. This style of decoration also appears on the pottery figurines that were characteristic products of these cultures.

Among the materials with which these peasant farmers became familiar were the ores of copper that are plentifully represented in the Balkan and Carpathian mountains. Simple objects of smelted copper occur from the mid-fifth millennium onwards, and by 4000 B.C. the scale of production is indicated by the occurrence of mining sites such as the shafts for the extraction of malachite at Rudna Glava in north-east Yugoslavia. Using simple casting techniques this material was made into flat axes and shafthole tools that were occasionally exported beyond the Carpathians to Central Europe and the west Pontic steppes. The wealth of these Copper Age cultures has recently been demonstrated by the discovery of a cemetery on the Black Sea coast at Varna, where graves contain not only copperwork but elaborate items in sheet gold.

During the fourth millennium B.C. a fundamental transformation occurred in the cultures of south-east Europe that reflects the increasing importance of the steppe areas to the east. One

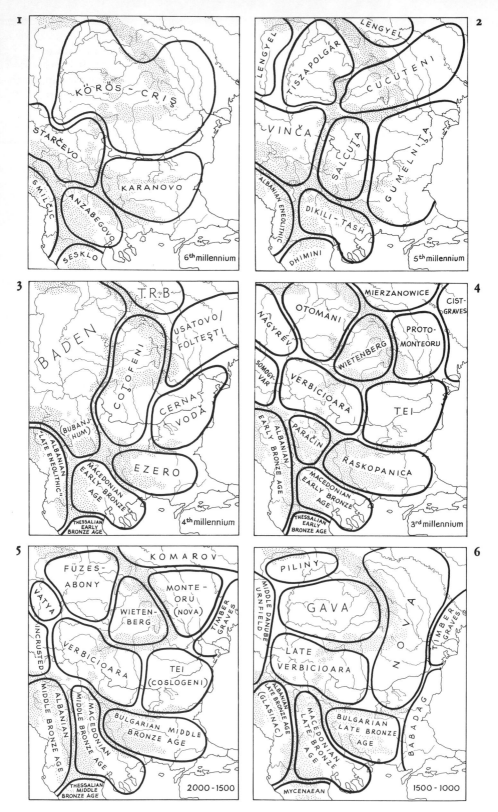

1

KÖRÖS – CRIŞ

STARČEVO

SMILČIĆ

ANZABEGOVO

KARANOVO

SESKLO

6th millennium

2

LENGYEL

LENGYEL

LENGYEL

TISZAPOLGÁR

CUCUTENI

VINČA

SALCUŢA

GUMELNIŢA

ALBANIAN ENEOLITHIC

DIKILI – TASH

DHIMINI

5th millennium

3

T.R.B.

BADEN

USATOVO/ FOLTEŞTI

COŢOFENI

CERNA VODĂ

(BUBANJ- HUM)

ALBANIAN "LATE ENEOLITHIC"

MACEDONIAN EARLY BRONZE AGE

EZERO

THESSALIAN EARLY BRONZE AGE

4th millennium

4

NAGYRÉV

OTOMANI

MIERZANOWICE

CIST- GRAVES

PROTO- MONTEORU

SOMOGY- VAR

WIETENBERG

VERBICIOARA

TEI

ALBANIAN EARLY BRONZE AGE

PARAČIN

RASKOPANICA

MACEDONIAN EARLY BRONZE AGE

THESSALIAN EARLY BRONZE AGE

3rd millennium

5

KOMAROV

FÜZES- ABONY

VATYA

MONTE- ORU (NOVA)

WIETEN- BERG

INCRUSTED

TIMBER GRAVES

VERBICIOARA

TEI (COSLOGENI)

ALBANIAN MIDDLE BRONZE AGE

MIDDLE BRONZE AGE

MACEDONIAN MIDDLE BRONZE AGE

BULGARIAN MIDDLE BRONZE AGE

THESSALIAN MIDDLE BRONZE AGE

2000 – 1500

6

PILINY

MIDDLE DANUBE URNFIELD

GAVA

VATYA

LATE VERBICIOARA

TIMBER GRAVES

ALBANIAN LATE BRONZE AGE (GLASINAC)

MACEDONIAN LATE BRONZE AGE

BULGARIAN LATE BRONZE AGE

BABADAG

MYCENAEAN

1500 – 1000

aspect of this is the abandonment of many of the long-occupied settlement mounds and a phase of renewed colonization that extended the settled area from the edges of the plains which had been the foci of earlier settlement. The elaborate styles of painted decoration disappeared, and a new range of pottery forms, including jugs and cups, made their appearance. The metalworking tradition was radically altered by the adoption of the two-piece mould and the use of alloying – initially with arsenic rather than tin – that indicate connexions with the Caucasian metallurgical school. These developments were contemporary with the Early Bronze Age in the Aegean but there are no indications in the Balkans of the more sophisticated forms of social organization implied by the craftsman-made jewellery of the Troy treasures or the seal-impressions of the House of Tiles at Lerna.

Whereas the core area of Neolithic and Copper Age development had been the southern plains such as lowland Thrace, the focus of change in the third and second millennia B.C. shifted northwards to Transylvania and adjacent areas. The wealth of copper and gold in this region, and the successful livestock-raising economy of its inhabitants, provided the basis for a series of powerful chiefdoms centred on the lower valleys of the Carpathians. Access to the tin sources of Bohemia provided an essential element in the growth of an impressive local bronze industry that produced decorated weaponry known both from local hoards and along a trade route that reached northwards as far as Scandinavia. Gold was also worked, not only for ornaments but also for metal vessels, the first in temperate Europe. Large quantities of these materials, and even an iron dagger, have been recovered from fortified centres in the north east of the Carpathian Basin.

Another new element at this time was the chariot, whose use is demonstrated by models of spoked wheels. These are associated with elements of horse-gear such as bone cheek-pieces whose compass-work decoration resembles that on similar objects from the Mycenae Shaft Graves (*c.* 1600 B.C.). It is possible that these techniques of horsemanship, derived ultimately from the steppes, entered Greece from this area.

Further contacts with the Aegean world are evident during the closing phases of Mycenean civilization in the thirteenth century B.C. The recession and political unrest in the east Mediterranean at this time coincided with further expansion and the achievement of new levels of industrial production by the communities of Transylvania and the lower Danube, and fresh contacts with the steppes. Weapons of Central European type appeared in the Mediterranean, and the technology of sheet-bronzeworking, previously confined to palatial workshops, came into use further north. The great expansion in population in the following two centuries had its effects both in the north Aegean (Troy VII B) and in Central Europe, where it is represented by the spread of the Urnfield cultures. The events of this period set the pattern for the succeeding millennium, when the peoples of the Balkans emerged into the historical record as the Thracians and Illyrians.

GENERAL BIBLIOGRAPHY

J. M. Coles and A. Harding, *The Bronze Age in Europe* (London, 1979)
R. Hoddinott, *The Thracians* (London, 1981)
S. K. Kozłowski, *The Mesolithic in Europe* (Warsaw, 1973)
J. Mellaart, *The Neolithic of the Near East* (London, 1975)
N. Sandars, *The Sea Peoples* (London, 1978)
H. Todorova, *The Eneolithic Period in Bulgaria* (Oxford, British Archaeological Reports, Int. Ser. 1978)
R. Tringham, *Hunters, Fishers and Farmers of eastern Europe, 6000–3000 BC* (London, 1971)

B.C.*	Albania	Greece	Macedonia	Šumadija	Thrace
6000	Early Neolithic	Sesklo	Nea Nikomedia	Starčevo	Karanovo I & II
5000	Middle Neolithic	Larisa Dhimini	Sitagroi II	Vinča	Karanovo III (Veselinovo)
4000	Eneolithic	Rachmani	Dikili-Tash	Salcuţa	Karanovo IV & V Gulmeniţa (Karanovo VI)
3000	Late Eneolithic	Early Helladic I	Macedonian Early Bronze Age	Bubanj Hum	Ezero (Karanovo VII)
	Albanian Early Bronze Age	Early Helladic II & III		Paraćin	Raskopanica
2000	Albanian Middle Bronze Age	Middle Helladic	Macedonian Middle Bronze Age		Bulgarian Middle Bronze Age
1000	Albanian Late Bronze Age	Late Helladic (Mycenaean)	Macedonian Late Bronze Age		Bulgarian Late Bronze Age

(*All dates are based on the tree-ring calibration of radiocarbon)

Lower Danube	Moldavia	Transylvania	Eastern Hungary	Maps
Criş	Criş	Criş	Körös	1
Vinča/ Dudeşti	Linear Pottery Precucuteni	Alföld Linear Pottery Petreşti	Tisza	2
Boian/ Vădastra Salcuţa	Cucuteni	Tiszapolgár Bodrogkeresztúr		
Cernavodă	Usatovo-Folteşti	Coţofeni	Baden	3
Verbicioara/ Tei	Monteoru	Wietenberg	Nagyrév Otomani	4
Verbicioara/ Coslogeni	Noua	Wietenberg	Füzesabony	5
Late Verbicioara	Noua	Gava	Suciu–Piliny	6

1a

1b

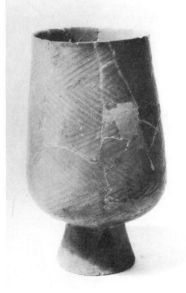

1c

1. The pottery of the first farming groups (*c.* 6000–5000 B.C.) in Bulgaria was already quite advanced, and shows similarities with the early painted wares of Greece and western Anatolia (e.g. Hacilar). Characteristic shapes were vessels with ring-bases, either tulip beakers or open bowls. The bowl (a), decorated with white paint on a red ground, is from Kremikovci near Sofia. The tulip beakers are from Karanovo in central Bulgaria, showing (b) the white paint typical of Karanovo I and (c) the channel decoration of Karanovo II.

2. Pottery decorated in light paint is typical of the earliest farming groups throughout the Balkans. Sherds (a)–(c) are from Podgorie, (d)–(e) from Vashtëmi, and the vessel (f) is from Burini, Albania. The bowl (g) is from Gura Baciului in Transylvania (Romania).

3. Around 5000 B.C. new forms of dark-burnished pottery became common in many parts of the Balkans. In Bulgaria this is represented by the Veselinovo culture, whose attractive ring-base and polypod vessels with knob handles are characteristic of Karanovo III.

4. Some of the most attractive products of Balkan Neolithic potters are the theriomorphic vases such as this stag-vessel from Muldava in Bulgaria.

5. The great diversity of ceramic traditions that developed in the fifth millennium B.C. is shown by these four vessels from Romania, characteristic of (a) the Dudeşti culture, (b) the Vinča culture, (c) the Vădastra culture and (d) the Boian culture. Shallow channel decoration is typical of the earlier phases, though more deeply-incised lines that could be filled with white paste became more common. Each area emphasized its cultural distinctiveness through a typical repertoire of patterns.

6. Small figurines and cult objects are common finds from the fifth millennium. Among the most famous are the pair (a) from a cemetery at Cernavodă in the Romanian Dobruja. They belong to the Hamangia culture, whose pottery (b) is found along the Black Sea Coast. Some plastic ornament was applied to pottery, as in the case of the Vădastra handles (c) or the later example of a bowl in the shape of a quadruped (d) from the Gumelniţa culture.

a   b   c   d   e 2

2f

2g

3a

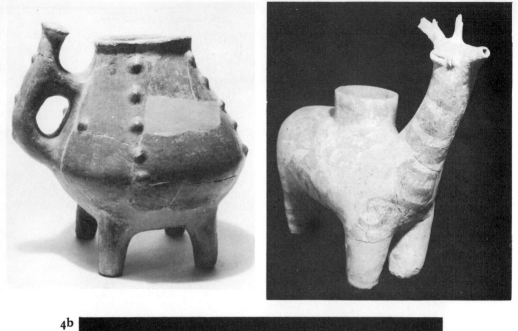

5a

5c

5b

5d

6a

6b

6d

6c

7a

7. Representations of the human body were usually schematic, and are hard to interpret in detail. The rod-head figurine fragments (**a, b**) are from the middle Neolithic settlement of Dunavec (Korçë) in Albania. Finely incised ornament (**c**) is characteristic of figurines of the Cucuteni culture, though it is uncertain whether they represent tattoos or details of clothing. The large hollow figurine (**d**) of the Gumelniţa culture is almost 40 cm high, and decorated with painted curvilinear ornament in silvery graphite paint.

8. As well as baked clay figurines, some examples are known in marble, such as the female with folded arms (**a**) from Bulgaria. Plastic ornament on pottery occasionally shows human figures (**b**) in an attitude of prayer, also from Bulgaria.

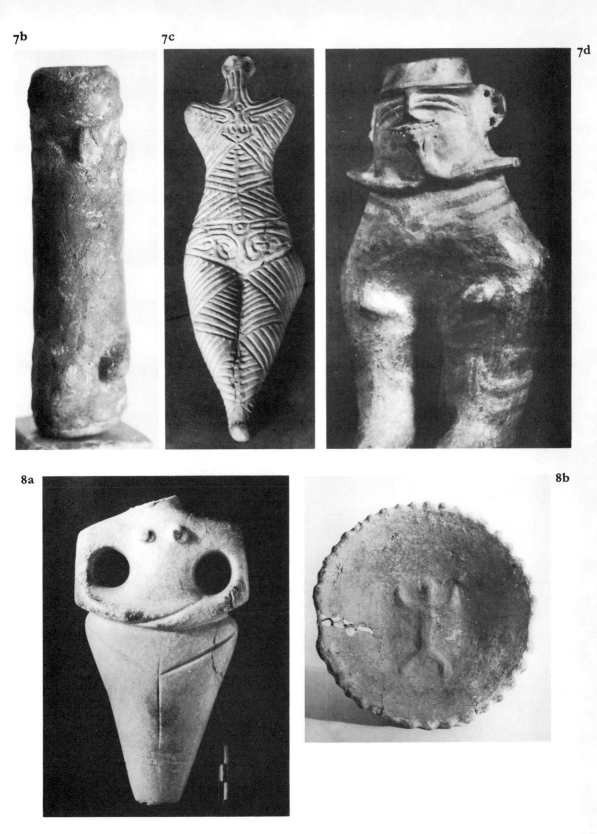

7b

7c

7d

8a

8b

9. Some of the finest Neolithic painted pottery from Romania is associated with the fourth-millennium Cucuteni culture in the north east of the country (Moldavia) and adjacent parts of the U.S.S.R. The earliest stage used the incised and white-filled decoration typical of Boian and related groups (**a**), but under the influence of the Transylvanian Petreşti culture (**b**) there developed a tradition first of bichrome painting (**c**) and then trichrome (**d**) with paints based on both iron and manganese.

10. The ornament used on pottery (**a**) was also employed architecturally for buildings of special importance such as cult houses. Fragments of painted wall plaster from the Boian levels at Căscioarele on the Danube in Romania decorated a room with special fittings that included a pair of painted columns (**c**). From a later level on the same site came a model (**d**) of four houses on a perforated base, some 24 cm high.

10a

10c

10d

5

12. Among the more imaginative products of the Eneolithic inhabitants of Albania in the fourth millennium were anthropomorphic vessels like one from Kamnik (**a**) 14 cm high, or elaborate vessels perhaps with a ceremonial function, as (**b**), some 30 cm high with ball handles.

13. Female figurines played a prominent part in religious ritual and some were set in small shrines, but most of these figurines would have had a domestic setting, in household cults. They are usually fairly schematically rendered as in (**a**), (**b**). Baked clay was also used to make 'seals' either in stamp form (**c**), 3 cm wide, or cylinders, some 7 cm long (**d, e**), which were more probably used as stamps for paint (or even simply as beads) since no sealings have been found. Some archaeologists, however, have seen in them a reflection of the true seals which were in use at this time in the Near East.

11. Polychrome pottery with lattice- or curvilinear painted designs was characteristic of the fourth millennium cultures in many parts of the Balkans. In Albania the closest stylistic connexions are with Thessaly, via the Adriatic coast and the Corinthian gulf. These painted pots are from the site of Kamnik (Kolonjë).

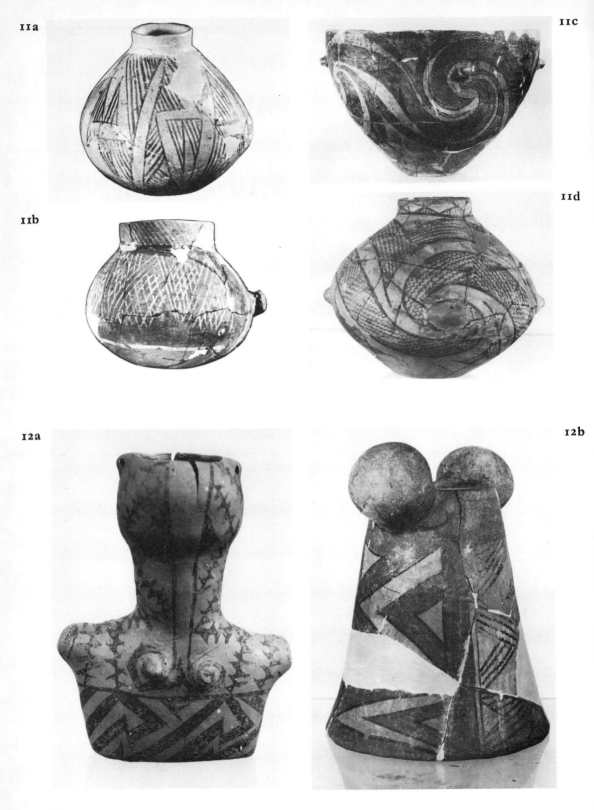

11a

11b

11c

11d

12a

12b

14

13a

13b

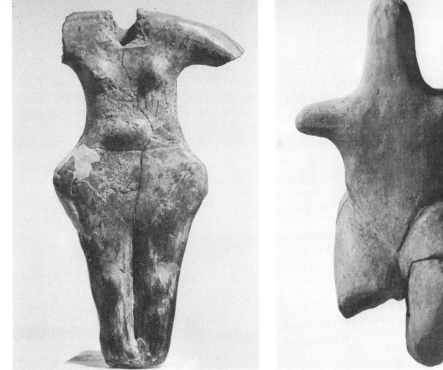

13c

13d

13e

14. Some of the most elaborate figurines are shown seated on stools or chairs, and are carefully decorated by incised and painted ornament. This example (a) is from Vinča in Yugoslavia, and may be wearing a mask. The holes were for the insertion of feathers or other organic plumes. A major feature of this period was the development of a local south-east European tradition of copper-casting, shown in its most advanced form in this (b) shafthole axe-adze from Romania. It was made from a blank of pure copper cast in a one-piece mould, and subsequently shaped by hammering. Such forms disappeared with the introduction of Near Eastern traditions of metalworking using alloying and the two-piece mould.

(Oxford, Ashmolean Museum 1939.68 (a), 1927.1541 (b).)

15. During the later fourth millennium the great variety of earlier painted wares declined, and well-made plain wares became more common. These examples are from Albania (Maliq II and III).

14a

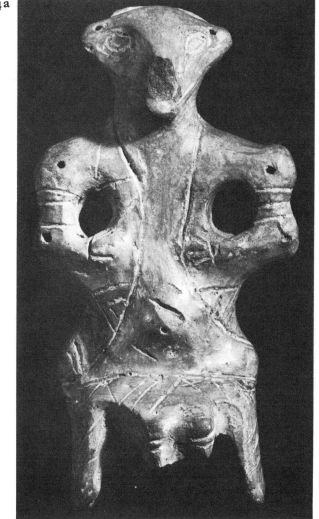

14b

15b

15a

15c

16. During the fourth millennium figurines became more schematic, and these examples, (**a, b**), which are typical of the Gumelniţa culture of Bulgaria and Romania, are pieces of flat bonework with incised and bored decoration. Some have been found with gold rings in the perforations. Although schematized, they are still clearly female. A particular class of zoomorphic sceptres that belong to this period, such as the example from Casimcea (**c**), have a distribution from Romania round the Black Sea on to the Pontic steppes, and indicate growing contacts with that area.

17. One of the most spectacular discoveries of recent years has been the cemetery at Varna in Bulgaria, which, as well as copper objects, contains large quantities of goldwork, much in forms not seen before. Manufacturing techniques were mostly simple as with the sheet-gold bovid (3 cm high) and winged pendants (**a, b**); but more elaborate sheet-gold fittings for axes and sceptres (**c**) also occur.

(Varna, Archaeological Museum.)

15d

15e

16a

16b

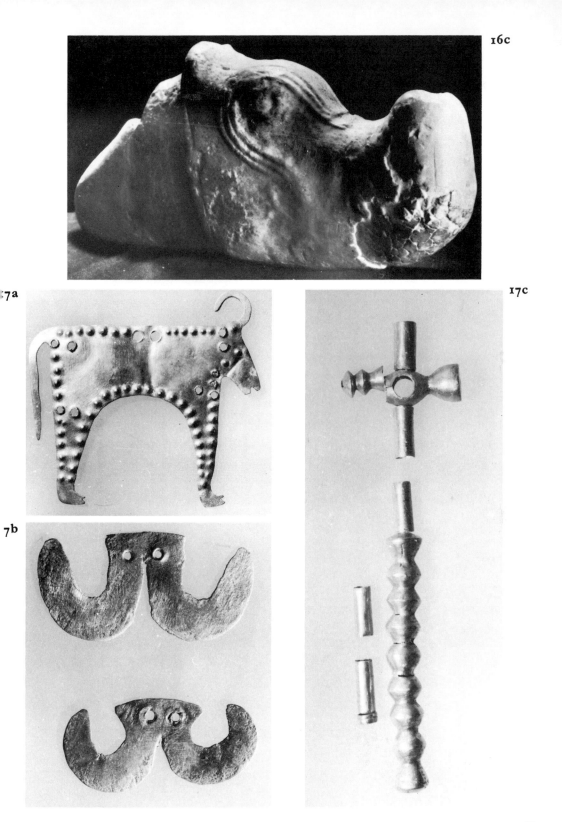

16c

17a

17c

17b

19

18. During the later fourth and third millennia B.C., important developments were taking place on the steppes, where expanding pastoral populations formed a bridge between southeast Europe and the Caucasus, introducing new features of animal husbandry and technology. The expansion of steppe populations is marked by the characteristic standing stones (**a**) with pecked representations of axes and other items like this from Hamangia in the Dobruja, that occur in Romania and adjacent steppe areas. One of the most important features introduced by these new contacts was the Near Eastern tradition of alloy metallurgy, using two-piece moulds to cast shafthole axes (**b**) of a new long-bladed type that rapidly superseded the native copper axe-adzes.

18b

19a

18a

19b

19c

19d

20a

20c

20b

20d

19. A new range of shapes appeared in the later fourth and third millennia, probably reflecting changes in diet, which in some areas included wine and olive oil for the first time. Drinking cups are especially prominent, either in local forms, as from Maliq in Albania (**a**), or occasionally (**b**) of north-west Anatolian type (the *depas amphikypellon* of Schliemann) from Baa Dere in Bulgaria. These assemblages also contain amphorae (**c**) and bowls (**d**) as shown by these examples from Romania and Albania.

20. This group of simple handled bowls, jugs and cups is characteristic of large areas of the Balkans in the third millennium. The examples are from Maliq IIIa (Albanian Early Bronze Age).

21. The growth of metallurgical industries is reflected both in the increasing sophistication of metal objects and in certain pottery shapes such as the high-flung strap handles (**a**) from Maliq IIIc that appear in Greece and the Balkans. By contrast the flat, ogival bronze dagger (**b**) from the Vajzë tumulus (Albania) is one of the forms characteristic of metal industries related to those of Central Europe. Simpler pottery shapes persisted, such as the handled jug from Maliq IIIc, Albania (**c**).

22. The Bronze Age cultures of the Balkans are distinguished by local styles within a broadly similar ceramic repertoire. These examples show profuse incised and encrusted decoration of the Tei culture (**a**); the simple balance of the Verbicioara culture (**b**); the powerful, swinging curves of the Otomani culture (**c**); the baroque elaboration of the Monteoru culture (**d**).

21a

21b

21c

23. The wealth of Romania and adjacent parts of the Carpathian basin in the Bronze Age was partly based on the gold sources of the area. Local workshops achieved a considerable degree of craftmanship. The curvilinear ornament of Otomani pottery (**22c**) is reflected in the gold sheet buttons (**a**) with repoussé decoration from Ostrovu Mare; the gold dagger (**b**) from Perşinari recalls details of early Mycenaean weapons of the Shaft-Grave period. The bracelets from Tirgu Mureş (**c**) show a control of three-dimensional modelling. The figurine from Cîrna (**d**) shows the ornaments worn with female costume.

24. Shapes of vessels in the areas around Greece were heavily influenced by metal prototypes. These pottery forms remained in use for centuries, and ultimately provided the basic shapes for some Classical vases. These examples are from the Late Bronze Age levels of Maliq IIId, Albania.

25. The metal industry in Albania in the Bronze Age included both local types and imported forms. Shafthole axes of Scutarine type (**a, b**) had a characteristically sinuous outline, and ribbed decoration. These examples are from Schelcon and Lezhë. Swords include both Central European (**c**) and Mycenaean (**d**) types (both these examples from Rrethe Bazje in the Mati valley). Socketed spearheads were also made in Central European forms, as with this flame-shaped example from Maliq IIId(**e**).

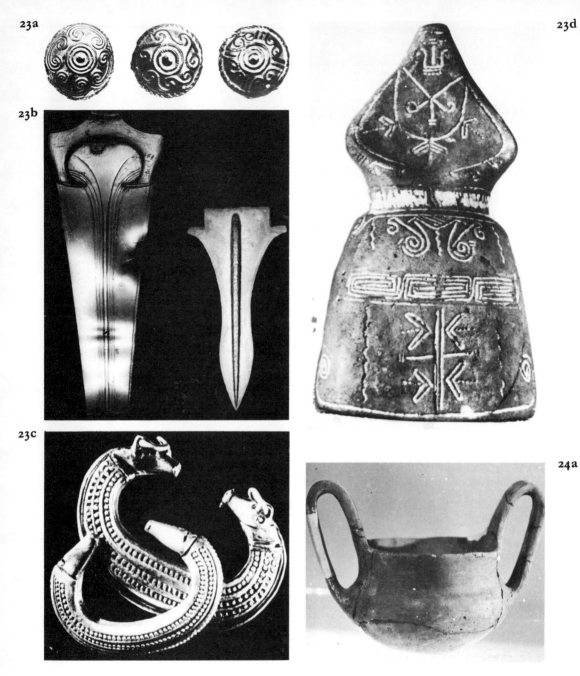

23a

23b

23c

23d

24a

25c

25d

25e

26a

26b

26c

27a

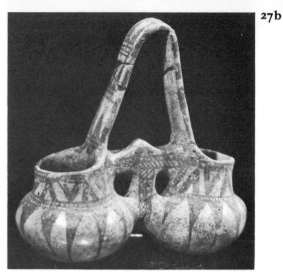

27b

27c

27d

26. In the final centuries of the second millennium, iron gradually came into use beside bronze. In Central Europe the variety of Bronze Age cultures gave way to a remarkable ceramic uniformity, typified by the cylinder-necked urn with channel decoration, as in this example from Romania (**a**). Bronze was still used for weapons, as shown by these finds from Albanian tumuli: the socketed violin-shaped arrowhead from Vodhinë (**b**) and the spearhead of Vajzë type from Pazhok (**c**).

27. In Albania, the pottery of the Early Iron Age still carried painted decoration, and elaborate forms with complex shapes for social rituals are often found as grave goods with important burials in tumuli. A group of three vessels (**a, b, c**) came from a tumulus at Barç (Korçë); the biconical jug (**d**) came from a tomb at Bulçar (Elbasan).

2. BABYLONIA

P. R. S. MOOREY

Any attempt to describe the material culture of Babylonia, the region south of Baghdad in modern Iraq, from *c.* 1200–600 B.C. is heavily handicapped by the absence of coherent archaeological sequences at the major excavated sites: Babylon, Kish, Nippur, Sippar, Ur and Uruk. All too often the massive building operations of later centuries obliterated vestiges of this whole period. No major building complex, no substantial archive of tablets, no major works of art (and relatively few minor ones) are yet known. Even at the best of times in a region where the primary raw material was clay, surviving examples of mudbrick architecture and sculpture are mere shadows of contemporary achievement. The fine work in precious metals or semi-precious stones, the mural paintings and the glazed brick friezes have long since gone, through decay or plunder. The main evidence is provided by a few indifferently carved stone stelae (*kudurrus*), permanent records of land grants or privileges to high officials, with repetitive iconography. Scenes cut on cylinder seals, not so common in this period as earlier and less easily identified, extend the range of information; but there is nothing here to compare with the panorama of contemporary life provided by the monumental Assyrian palace reliefs. With the advent of the Neo-Babylonian dynasty in the last quarter of the seventh century B.C. our knowledge of mudbrick architecture and of polychrome glazed-brick mural decoration, notably at Babylon itself, increases and with it the range of pottery and other objects from excavations. But still it is very restricted. Babylonian cultural life, which had considerable impact in Assyria, was deeply conservative and, even when it was not consciously archaizing, her art used age-old themes and motifs throughout the first half of the first millennium B.C. So far as may be assessed at present it did not have much impact at this time outside Mesopotamia.

For general bibliography see under Assyria.

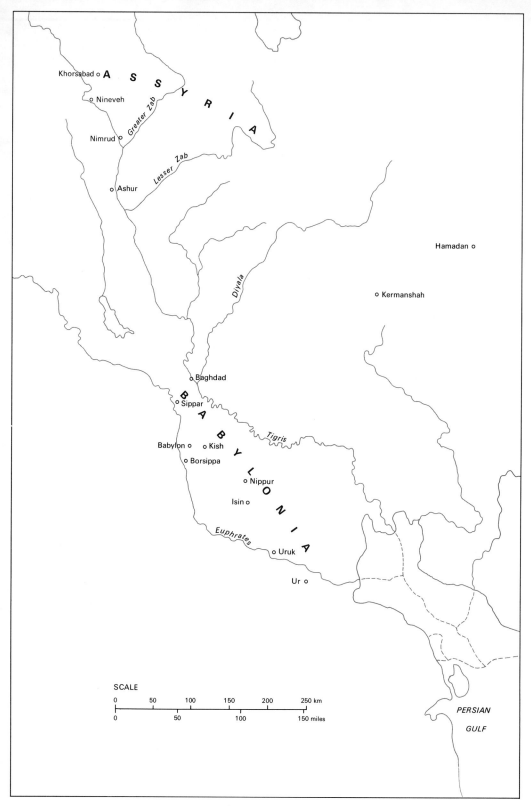

2. Babylonia and Assyria

28. Limestone *kudurru* from the reign of Nabu-mukin-apli, king of Babylon (*c.* 979–944 B.C.), recording the title deeds of an estate and family feuds over its ownership. The two figures well illustrate the commonplace style and execution of so many of these monuments.

(British Museum WA 90835. Width 25.5 cm.)
    L. W. King, *Babylonian boundary stones and memorial tablets in the British Museum* (London, 1912) no. 9; J. A. Brinkman, *A Political History of Post-Kassite Babylonia, 1158–722 B.C.* (Chicago, 1968) 173.

29. Greystone tablet with an inscription of Nabu-apla-iddina, king of Babylon (*c.* 877–855 B.C.), recording the recent history and restoration of the temple of the Sun God (Shamash) at Sippar. The god is shown seated in a shrine holding the rod and ring of authority; above his head are symbols of the Moon God (Sin),

the Sun God and Ishtar. Two servants are shown manipulating a sun-disk on a stool – a unique glimpse of Babylonian temple 'machinery'. A priest leads the king, followed by a minor goddess, into the divine presence. The whole scene is set on wavy lines probably representing the heavenly ocean. The style of this relief is archaizing, strongly reminiscent of much earlier Babylonian art.

(British Museum WA 91004. Height 29.5 cm., width 17.8 cm.)
    King, *op. cit.* no. 36; J. A. Brinkman, *RA* 70 (1976) 183–4.

30. Panel of relief sculpture carved on the front of the limestone throne-base from Fort Shalmaneser at Nimrud in Assyria in or about 845 B.C. The Assyrian king, Shalmaneser III, on the right, greets Marduk-zakir-shumi of Babylon, whom he had assisted in suppressing a rebellion by his younger brother. This rare representation of two kings as equals in Assyrian art may

be instructively compared with a local 'portrait' of this Babylonian king in the next
illustration.

(Baghdad, National Museum of Antiquities ND
11,000; 2.28 m × 3.82 m full size of throne base.)
    P. Hulin, *Iraq* 25 (1963) 48–69; M. E. L. Mallo-
wan, *Nimrud and its Remains* (London, 1966) 446–7.

31. A limestone *kudurru* recording a royal
grant of property and income to a *kalu* priest of
Ishtar of Uruk, dated in the second year of
King Marduk-zakir-shumi (*c.* 854–819 B.C.). In
the upper panel the king, on the left, faces the
recipient priest, who has a lamp set on a table
behind him. Behind the king are a series of
divine symbols, in traditional Babylonian guise,
denoting the gods who, as it were, guaranteed
the gift.

(Paris, Louvre AO 6684. Height 33 cm.)
    F. Thureau-Dangin, *RA* 16 (1919) 117–41;
Brinkman, *op. cit.* 201–2.

32. This basalt *kudurru* from the reign of King
Marduk-apla-iddina (Merodach-Baladan) II
(reigned *c.* 721–710 and 703 B.C.) is one of the
finest of its kind. The inscription records a land
grant to the governor of Babylon shown, in
suitably diminished scale, facing his royal
master. Although the execution is finer than
usual, the iconography is traditional.

32

33

(Berlin, Staatliche Museen (East) VA 2663. Height 46 cm.)

W. F. Leemans, *Jaarbericht 'Ex Oriente Lux'* 10 (1945) 444–9; J. A. Brinkman, *Studies Presented to A. Leo Oppenheim* (Chicago, 1964) 6–53.

33. A limestone foundation tablet showing the Assyrian king Ashurbanipal (668–627 B.C.) carrying a basket of earth to symbolize his restoration and adornment of *Esagila*, the ancient temple of Marduk at Babylon, to whose throne he had appointed his twin brother. The iconography is again traditional, in a style more Babylonian than Assyrian.

(British Museum WA 90864. Height 36.8 cm.)

British Museum: *A Guide to the Babylonian and Assyrian Antiquities* (London, 1922) 74, no. 300; D. D. Luckenbill, *Ancient Records of Assyria and Babylonia* II (Chicago, 1927) §974ff.

34. The upper part of a trachyte stela showing Nabonidus, king of Babylon (555–539 B.C.), in traditional pose with an ornamental staff topped by the moon-crescent of the god Sin, whom the king particularly revered. In the upper register are symbols of the Moon God, the Sun God (Shamash) and Ishtar, no longer depicted in the old Babylonian *kudurru* style.

34

(British Museum WA 90837. Height 58.5 cm.)

King, *op. cit.* no. 37; C. J. Gadd, *AS* 8 (1958) 35ff.; W. Röllig, *ZA* 22 (1964) 247ff.

35. White limestone lion's head from Sippar, perhaps a furniture terminal, one of the rare pieces of sculpture in the round from Babylonia in this period. It was originally inlaid and has been dated to the eighth or seventh centuries B.C.

(British Museum WA 91678. Height 10.2 cm.)

British Museum: A Guide to the Babylonian and Assyrian Antiquities (1922) 188 with figure.

35

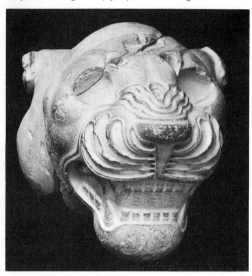

36

36. Bronze terminal cast as a dragon's head for fitting to a composite statue or a piece of furniture. It was originally inlaid. Such creatures, sacred to Marduk, were shown in polychrome glazed bricks on the walls flanking the great processional way leading to the Ishtar Gate at Babylon in the Neo-Babylonian period (c. 625–539 B.C.), to which this head probably belongs.

(Paris, Louvre. Length 14.5 cm.)

M. Rutten, *Encyclopédie photographique de l'art* II (Paris, 1936) pl. 39.

37. A sardonyx sceptre that may once have been held by one of the many deity statues in Babylon (where it was found in the German excavations) in the sixth century B.C.

(Berlin, Staatliche Museen (East) VA Bab. 1625. Length 38.4 cm.)

G. R. Meyer, *Altorientalische Denkmäler im Vorderasiatischen Museum zu Berlin* (Leipzig, 1965) pl. 175.

38. Clay statuette (restored) of Ninshubur, messenger of the gods, found in a foundation deposit in room 1 of the Neo-Babylonian Temple on Tell Ingharra, part of ancient Kish.

(Oxford, Ashmolean Museum 1928.527. Height 17.2 cm.)

Ch. Watelin, *Excavations at Kish* III (Paris, 1930) pl. 6.

39. Four bronze arrowheads inscribed for Babylonian kings: **(a)** and **(c)** Mar-biti-apla-usur (c. 985–980 B.C.); **(b)** Nabu-mukin-apli (c. 979–944 B.C.); **(d)** Eulmash-shakin-shumi (c. 1005–989 B.C.). Such inscribed arrowheads, and also daggers, have frequently been reported from western Iran, where they indicate Babylonian relations with local tribesmen.

(Paris, Louvre.)

P. Amiet, *Revue du Louvre* (1973) 224, fig. 29.

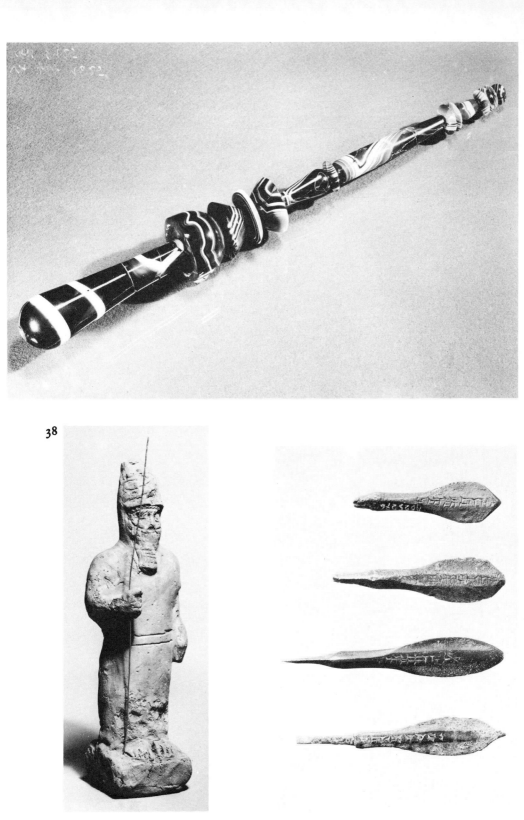

37

38

39

40. Syenite or basalt duck weight of 30 mina (40 lb 4 oz; 18.25 kg), from the palace of Eriba-Marduk, king of Babylon (*c.* 769–761 B.C.), found in the North-West Palace at Nimrud in Assyria.

(British Museum WA 91433. Length 3.2 cm.)

A. H. Layard, *Discoveries among the Ruins of Nineveh and Babylon* (London, 1853) 600; *British Museum: A Guide to the Babylonian and Assyrian Antiquities* (1922) 213.

41. Hard greenstone weight of one mina (978.3 gr), the property of a certain Marduk-shar-ilani. The text states that it is an exact copy of a weight made by Nebuchadrezzar II (604–562 B.C.) after a standard fixed by Shulgi, king of Ur (*c.* 2094–2047 B.C.); a neat illustration of the strength of tradition in Babylonian life and culture.

(British Museum. WA 91005. Height 9.5 cm.)

British Museum: A Guide to the Babylonian and Assyrian Antiquities (1922) 213.

42. Cylinder Seal of Marduk-shakin-shumi, a minor Chaldaean prince of the early eighth century B.C., who may have been the father of King Eriba-Marduk (*c.* 769–761 B.C.). The owner is represented as on *kudurrus*.

(British Museum WA 129532. Height 3.4 cm.)

H. Carnegie (ed.), *Catalogue . . . Collection . . . Earl of Southesk* II, 82–3, QB39; Brinkman, *op. cit.* (**28**) 215–16.

43. Jasper cylinder seal showing a Babylonian king with attendants and a variety of deity symbols in the upper field; ninth or eighth century B.C.

(British Museum WA 89590. Height 5.1 cm.)

D. J. Wiseman, *Cylinder Seals of Western Asia* (London, 1959) no. 81.

45a

45b

45c

44. Agate cylinder seal showing a bare-headed priest before divine symbols on altars: the crescent of the Moon God Sin and the star of Ishtar: a scene typical of Neo-Babylonian cylinder and stamp seals; sixth century B.C.

(British Museum WA 89813. Height 3.7 cm.)
  Wiseman, *op. cit.* no. 96.

45. *Zikkurats* were the distinctive form of temple tower used, in variant forms, throughout Mesopotamia. None has survived to its full height, so they are reconstructed (**b, c**) from views carved on Assyrian reliefs (**a**) and the description of the *zikkurat* at Babylon, given by the Greek historian Herodotus (I. 181). The tower rose in rectangular stages of steadily diminishing size. The number of stages varied and some, if not all, *zikkurats* had a small shrine on top. The meaning and purpose of these structures have been much debated. The names by which they were known suggest that they were conceived as 'mountains', though little credence is now given to the idea that this must indicate builders who originally came from a mountainous region. This apparently simple description embraces a complex religious concept evoking the cosmic mountain of Sumerian mythology which symbolized life-giving forces and was the setting in which superhuman powers were made manifest. In this context men and gods were brought into closest contact. At Babylon, Herodotus tells us, the upper shrine was equipped 'with a fine couch in it, richly covered, and beside it a golden table . . . The Chaldaeans also say (though I do not believe them) that the god enters the temple in person and takes his rest upon the couch' (I. 182). See A. Parrot, *Ziggurats et Tour de Babel* (Paris, 1949).

((**a**) Drawing of a relief in the North Palace at Kuyunjik (Nineveh) showing a *zikkurat*, perhaps at Der in Babylonia, seventh century B.C. After C. J. Gadd, *The Stones of Assyria* (London, 1936) 206, no. 73, pl. 28.)
((**b**) Reconstruction of the *zikkurat* at Ur as it might have appeared in the sixth century B.C. After C. L. Woolley, *Ur Excavations* v, pl. 88.)
((**c**) Reconstruction of the *zikkurat* and surrounding area of Babylon in the sixth century B.C. After E. Unger, *Babylon* (Berlin and Leipzig, 1931) pl. 7.)

3. ASSYRIA

P. R. S. MOOREY

The daily life and culture of Assyria, the nor-thern part of modern Iraq, from about 1000 B.C. to the fall of its empire in 612 B.C., have been very largely reconstructed from the evidence of monumental stone relief sculptures, a few mural paintings, and small finds found in royal palaces. Archaeological excavation has concen-trated on the great cities of Ashur, Nimrud (Calah) and Nineveh (Kuyunjik), and on Sargon's palace complex at Khorsabad; of small towns and villages at this time we know virtually nothing save what little may be gleaned from textual evidence. Apart from royal palaces and arsenals, only temples have been excavated in sufficient numbers to estab-lish the main traditions of architecture and decoration. Provincial buildings, notably at Til Barsib (Tell Ahmar), and a few other monu-ments in Syria illustrate something of Assyria's impact outside her homeland. Her legacy in art was not conspicuous and much of her enduring tradition drew its strength from the age-old Babylonian scribal schools.

The monumental stone reliefs, which lined the lower part of walls in the mudbrick cere-monial apartments of royal palaces, were designed to extol the king, vicegerent of the gods (above all Ashur) on earth. They concen-trated almost exclusively on triumphs in war, for such best indicated the power of Assyria's gods. Regular royal campaigns served the vital needs of a state without natural frontiers and primary raw materials. Occasional glimpses of the king as hunter or high priest emphasized his role as hero and dutiful servant of the gods. Much is made explicit in a wealth of detail and incident that provide an invaluable guide as much to costume and equipment, to architec-ture and furniture, as to the conduct of battles, of sieges, of lion-hunts, and of fertility rites. Each of the major Assyrian kings over a period of two hundred years added to the series. The most famous groups are those of Ashurnasirpal II from the North-West Palace at Nimrud, of Sennacherib and Ashurbanipal from the South-West Palace at Nineveh, and of Ashurbanipal in the North Palace, also at Nineveh.

GENERAL BIBLIOGRAPHY

R. D. Barnett, *Assyrische Palastreliefs* (Artia, Prague, n.d.)

H. Frankfort, *The Art and Architecture of the Ancient Orient* (Harmondsworth, 4th revised impres-sion, 1970)

B. Hrouda, *Die Kulturgeschichte des assyrischen Flach-bildes* (Bonn, 1965)

T. A. Madhloom, *The Chronology of Neo-Assyrian Art* (London, 1970)

A. Moortgat, *The Art of Ancient Mesopotamia* (London, 1969)

A. Parrot, *Nineveh and Babylon* (London, 1961)

E. Strommenger and M. Hirmer, *The Art of Meso-potamia* (London, 1964)

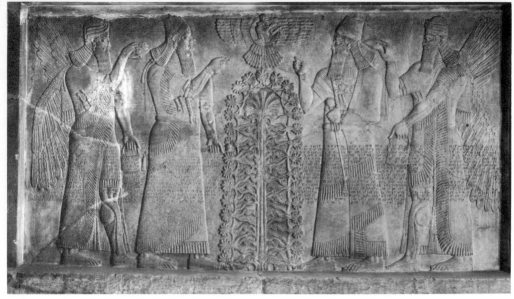

The Assyrian king, his court and army

46. Mosul-marble relief set in a recess immediately behind the throne-base in the ceremonial reception room (B) of the North-West Palace at Nimrud built by Ashurnasirpal II (883–859 B.C.). It epitomizes the king's place as vicegerent of the state god, Ashur, and his responsibility for the prosperity of his realm. The king is shown twice, wrapped tightly in a great cloak, flanking a sacred tree above which hovers Ashur in a winged disk. The scene is flanked by protective winged genii holding cones and buckets: propitious fertility symbols (cf. **66**).

(British Museum WA 124531. Height 1.7 m.)
Layard, *Monuments* I, 25; C. J. Gadd, *The Stones of Assyria* (London, 1936) 131–2.

47. Mosul-marble relief from the north-east side of the outer court of King Sennacherib's (704–681 B.C.) palace at Nineveh. It shows the crown prince, followed by two high officials, and servants pulling the king on his wheeled throne (only the front of the pole is shown here). The prince is distinguished by his rosetted tiara, with back pendants, his richly embroidered robe, his fine bracelets, his long side tassel and the lions on his sword chape. Early seventh century B.C.

(Berlin, Staatliche Museen (East) VA 955.)
Gadd, *op. cit.* pl. 23; J. E. Reade, *Iraq* 29 (1967) 45–8.

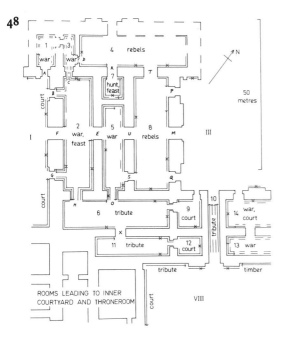

48. Restored plan of part of the Palace of Sargon II at Khorsabad, indicating the subjects of the reliefs in the various rooms.

(After J. E. Reade, *Baghdader Mitteilungen* 10 (1979) 79, fig. 6.)

49. Mosul-marble relief from Khorsabad of King Sargon II (721–705 B.C.) facing a senior member of his court, possibly the grand vizier

(*turtān*) rather than the crown prince, though there are similarities with the prince in **47**.

(Paris, Louvre AO 19874. Height 2.98 m.)
  M. Rutten, *Encyclopédie* 1, pl. 311 (B).

50. Mosul-marble relief from Room S¹ of the North Palace at Nineveh showing King Ashurbanipal (668–627 B.C.) feasting in a garden with his queen – one of the very rare representations of this member of the court. This small scene is particularly rich in information on costume, furniture and utensils; a macabre note is provided by the head of the vanquished king of Elam in the tree near the harpist. Although many scenes of 'banquets' survive from the Near East, on seals and to a lesser extent in monumental art, the participants almost invariably sit on stools or chairs with upright backs, as does the queen here. The reclining king is a unique representation in Neo-Assyrian art.

(British Museum WA 124920. Width 1.35 m.)
  R. D. Barnett, *Sculptures from the North Palace of Ashurbanipal at Nineveh (668–627 B.C.)* (London, 1976) pls. 63, 65.

51. Dolerite stela of King Esarhaddon (680–669 B.C.) of Assyria from Zincirli in south-east Turkey, symbolizing the king as conqueror. Ropes secure the diminutive figures of the kneeling, shackled, ruler of Egypt or his son, with negroid features, and the standing king of Tyre(?) with Semitic features. In the upper field four deities appear riding upon their respective animals, with others represented just by symbols, patrons of the king's triumph.

(Berlin, Staatliche Museen (East) VA 2708. Height 3.22 m.)
  F. von Luschan, *Ausgrabungen in Sendschirli* I (Berlin, 1893) 11–29, pl. 1.

52. Mosul-marble relief of King Ashurnasirpal II (883–859 B.C.) from the throne-room (B) of the North-West Palace at Nimrud showing a royal lion-hunt. This was a traditional theme in ancient Near Eastern art used here to highlight the king's heroic character in a hazardous sport.

(British Museum WA 124534. Height 86.4 cm.)
  Layard, *Monuments* I, 10; Gadd, *op. cit.* p. 133.

53. Mosul-marble relief from Room S¹ of the North Palace at Nineveh showing at top: King Ashurbanipal (669–627 B.C.), well protected, shooting at a springing lion; in centre: the king twisting a rampant lion's tail; below: the king pouring a libation of wine over dead lions. Part of the inscription in the centre reads, 'I seized a lion of the plain(?) by its tail, and at the command of Ninurta and Nergal, the gods in whom I trust, I smashed its skull with my own

mace.' The contrast between this relief and that of Ashurnasirpal II in **52** indicates the changes in Assyrian relief sculpture over two hundred years.

(British Museum WA 124886–7. Height 16 cm.)
  Barnett, *op. cit.* 54, pl. 57.

54. Mosul-marble relief from room C of the North Palace at Nineveh showing the citizens of Nineveh climbing a wooded hill to watch the royal lion-hunt. King Ashurbanipal, hunting from a chariot, is glimpsed through a

garden pavilion on the hill. To the right a wall of guards and archers enclose spearmen with hunting hounds and wounded lions, illustrating how the hunt was staged in a royal park with careful control of the lions. Artistically this is one of the most adventurous of Assyrian reliefs, normally so stereotyped.

(British Museum WA 120863–4. Height *c*. 15.5 cm.)
   Barnett, *op. cit.* 37, pl. 6.

55. Mosul-marble relief of King Ashurnasirpal II from the throne-room (B) of the North-West Palace at Nimrud. It extols the king as heroic warrior, whilst offering the modern scholar interesting information on siege tactics.

(British Museum WA 124536. Height *c*. 98 cm.)
   Layard, *Monuments* 1, 17; Gadd, *op. cit.* 133.

56. Mosul-marble relief from room M of the North Palace at Nineveh showing the army of Ashurbanipal (667–627 B.C.) storming a walled Egyptian city in 667 B.C. Prisoners in local costume are led away.

(British Museum WA 124928. Height 1.14 m.)
   Barnett, *op. cit.* 47, pl. 36.

57. Mosul-marble relief from the Central Palace of Tiglath-pileser III (745–727 B.C.) at Nimrud showing the evacuation of a captured city, to judge by the palm tree probably Baby-

lonian. The most interesting detail is in the centre, where an officer dictates a list of spoils to two scribes. One scribe holds a clay tablet in his left hand, a stylus in his right, to record in Akkadian in the cuneiform script, whilst the other scribe is writing on a leather roll in Aramaic.

(British Museum WA 118882.)

R. D. Barnett and M. Falkner, *The Sculptures of Tiglath-Pileser III (747–725 B.C.)* (London, 1962) 11–12, pls. 3, 4.

58. Mosul-marble relief from the throne-room (B) of the North-West Palace of Ashurnasirpal II at Nimrud showing domestic scenes in the

58

59

king's tent as his evening meal is prepared and horses groomed. The scene is rich in detail and though schematic, full of life and activity.

(British Museum WA 124548. Height *c*. 89 cm.)
Layard, *Monuments* 1, 30; Gadd, *op. cit.* 135.

59. Mosul-marble relief of the reign of Ashurbanipal showing an officer entering his tent, where refreshment and a bed are prepared for him; in the adjoining tent a butcher is at work.

(Berlin, Staatliche Museen (East) VA 965. Height 39 cm.)
Gadd, *op. cit.* 218, pl. 29a.

60. Fragmentary Mosul-marble relief from Room S¹ of the North Palace of Ashurbanipal at Nineveh showing captives under guard preparing their meal.

(British Museum WA 124788. 29 × 70 cm.)
Barnett, *op. cit.* 59, pl. 66.

Assyrian religion: state cults

61. Limestone stela of Ashurnasirpal II (883–859 B.C.) found at the entrance of the temple of the god Ninurta at Nimrud. The king is shown in the traditional posture of worship before deity symbols (cf. **51**). A long historical inscription covers the back, sides and front.

(British Museum WA 10885. Height 2.92 m.)
H. R. Hall, *Babylonian and Assyrian Sculpture in the British Museum* (Paris and Brussels, 1928), pl. 13.

62. Limestone altar found in front of the stela of Ashurnasirpal II shown in **61**.

(British Museum WA 108806.)
   Hall, *op. cit.* pl. 13.

63. A section of relief on the bronze covering for temple doors at Balawat, showing an expe-

dition by King Shalmaneser III (858–824 B.C.) to the source of the Tigris. In the upper register animals are sacrificed and a mason appears to be carving an inscription guided by a scribe with stylus and tablet. Below, more animals are led to sacrifice and masons carve a relief of the king in the rock near the flowing river.

65

65. One of two limestone statues from the Temple of Nabu at Nimrud, dedicated to the god by the governor of the city 'for the life of Adad-nirari, King of Assyria (810–783 B.C.), his lord, and Sammuramat, the queen, his lady'. Although the figure wears the horned headdress of a god, it is unlikely to be Nabu. The position of the hands suggest instead a divine servant.

(British Museum WA 118889. Height 1.77 m.)
   Gadd, *op. cit.* 150–1.

66. Mosul-marble relief, from Room I (perhaps a bathroom) in the North-West Palace at Nimrud, showing bare-footed, eagle-headed winged genii flanking a sacred tree. The role of such creatures is not precisely understood; but they commonly care for the sacred tree, as here, where they appear with cones and buckets to symbolize the necessary manual fertilization of the female flowers of the date palm with male efflorescence.

(British Museum WA 124583. Height *c.* 1.117 m.)
   Gadd, *op. cit.* 142.

67. Mosul-marble slab from the south-west side of the entrance into room XXXII of Sennacherib's palace (704–681 B.C.) at Nineveh. The figure wears the horned headdress of a deity; his companion, brandishing a mace and a dagger, has a lion's head and the feet of a predatory bird. Such genii traditionally guarded the entrances to rooms against the intrusion of evil spirits.

(British Museum WA 118932.)
   Gadd, *op. cit.* 174–5, pl. 17.

(British Museum WA. Height *c.* 28 cm.)
   L. W. King, *Bronze Reliefs from the Gates of Shalmaneser* (London, 1915) 30–1, pl. 59.

64. A roughly finished limestone relief of a god from the city of Ashur. He stands on a creature combining features of a lion, a bull and a predatory bird.

(Berlin, Staatliche Museen (East) VA 8750. Height *c.* 50 cm.)
   W. Andrae, *Das Wiedererstandene Assur* (Leipzig, 1938) pl. 22b.

68. Limestone model of a sphinx supporting a column base (her legs should have been restored as those of a lioness, not a bull). Such bases alternated with lion-supports in palace porticoes, where, like the genii in **67**, the sphinx was a guardian spirit. Eighth to seventh century B.C.

(British Museum WA 90954. 9.5 × 7.5 cm.)
   Barnett, *op. cit.* 36, pl. 1.

66

67

68

90954

69. A bird's-eye view (**a**) from the east of the Citadel at Khorsabad at the end of the eighth century B.C., with (**b**) a restoration of the Nabu Temple as seen from the top of the *zikkurat*.

(After G. Loud and C. B. Altman, *Khorsabad* II (Chicago, 1938) frontispiece and pl. 2.)

Popular religion and magic

70. Five baked clay statuettes of hounds, placed in a recess under a sculptured slab in the entrance to Room S of the North Palace, Nimrud, in the earlier seventh century B.C. They are painted different colours and their names are inscribed on them, such as 'Enemy-catcher', painted red (30002) and 'Biter of his enemy', painted green (30004).

(British Museum WA 30001–5.)
   Barnett, *op. cit.* 36, pl. 1.

71. A bronze bell used to drive out evil spirits by being rung in an exorcism ritual; eighth or seventh century B.C. The top bears a tortoise and two lizards in relief; round the side are lion-headed demons, a human figure and a

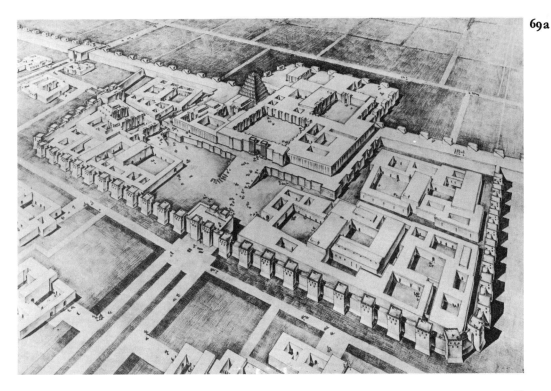

69a

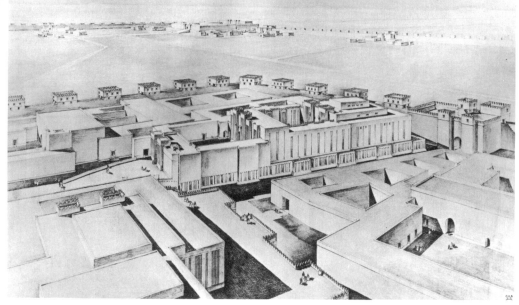

priest wearing a fish-skin and carrying a pail. The ends of the handle and the clapper are cast as serpent-heads.

(Berlin, Staatliche Museen (East) VA 2517. Height 30 cm.)

B. Meissner, *Babylonien und Assyrien* i (Heidelberg, 1920) fig. 142.

72. Pendent bronze statuette of the Assyrian demon Pazuzu, who protected women in childbirth against the demon Lamashtu; seventh century B.C.

(Oxford, Ashmolean Museum 1892.43. Height 10.8 cm.)

P. R. S. Moorey, *Iraq* 27 (1965) 33–41.

72

Objects of daily life

73. Detail from a Mosul-marble relief from Nineveh, of the reign of Sennacherib (704–681 B.C.), showing an irrigation system with a *shadūf*. The men above are dragging an unfinished sculpture of a bull uphill.

(British Museum WA 124820.)
Layard, *Monuments* II, 15 (drawing).

74. Fragment from a basalt obelisk of King Ashurnasirpal II (883–859 B.C.) showing the weighing of tribute on a balance.

(British Museum WA 118800. Width 73.6 cm.)
Gadd, *op. cit.* 128–9, pl. 6 (upper part).

74

73

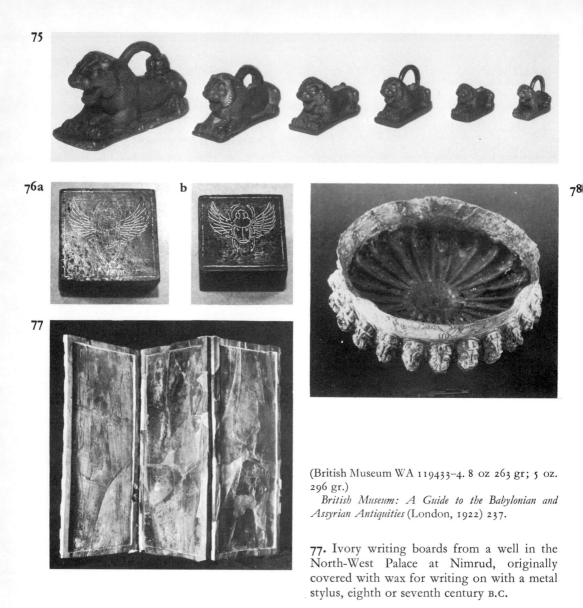

75

76a   b   **78**

77

(British Museum WA 119433–4. 8 oz 263 gr; 5 oz. 296 gr.)

British Museum: A Guide to the Babylonian and Assyrian Antiquities (London, 1922) 237.

77. Ivory writing boards from a well in the North-West Palace at Nimrud, originally covered with wax for writing on with a metal stylus, eighth or seventh century B.C.

(Baghdad, National Museum of Antiquities ND 3557. 33.8 cm × 15.6 cm.)

M. E. L. Mallowan, *Nimrud and its Remains* I (London, 1966) 152, pl. 90.

75. A selection of lion-shaped bronze weights; from Nimrud, eighth century B.C. The weight is indicated by vertical strokes cut on the animal's side.

(British Museum WA 91220ff.)

British Museum: A Guide to the Babylonian and Assyrian Antiquities (London, 1922) 170–1.

76. Bronze weights inlaid with beetles in gold, possibly indicating an Egyptian or Phoenician origin, from Nimrud, eighth century B.C.

78. Silver bowl decorated with repoussé lion-heads found in a cache under the floor of Room C.6 of Fort Shalmaneser at Nimrud, later eighth or seventh century B.C. One of the very few known pieces of Assyrian silver plate.

(Baghdad, National Museum of Antiquities ND 7844. Diameter 12.5 cm.)

Mallowan, *op. cit.* II (1966) 430, pl. 357.

79. Spouted sheet bronze strainer-bowl with cast zoomorphic handle; stylistically this vessel may be attributed to a late eighth-century Assyrian source, though it is reported to be from Italy. It is so far unparalleled from an excavation.

(British Museum WA 124591 (Temple Collection). Width 19.6 cm.)

R. D. Barnett, *Rivista di Studi Fenici* 2 (1974) 29–30; P. R. S. Moorey, *Iranica Antiqua* 15 (1980) 188ff., figs. 2–4, pl. 3b.

80. Green glass jar inscribed for King Sargon II (722–705 B.C.); from Nimrud. Such vessels

80

79

81

82

**85**

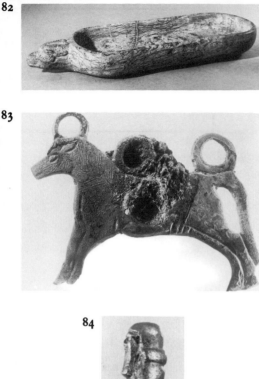**83**

**86**

**84**

as this were carved from solid blocks of glass worked as if they were stone. Blown glass was not invented until the first century B.C.

(British Museum WA 90952. Height 8.8 cm.)
A. von Saldern in A. Leo Oppenheim, *Glass and Glassmaking in Ancient Mesopotamia* (Chicago, 1970) 218, fig. 17.

81. Two views of a stone dish showing a hero between two rampant lions: a motif of great antiquity in Mesopotamia; eighth or seventh century B.C.; source unknown.

(British Museum WA 135450. Length 16 cm.)
Unpublished.

82. Stone dish with a handle carved in the shape of a deer's head; eighth or seventh century B.C. from Sherif Khan.

(British Museum WA 135451. Length 32.5 cm.)
Unpublished.

83. Electrum(?) cheekpiece for a horse-bit found in a well in the North-West Palace at Nimrud. Only on royal vehicles between about 700 and 650 B.C. are horses shown wearing such cheekpieces.

(Baghdad, National Museum of Antiquities ND 2180. Length 10.5 cm.)
Mallowan, *op. cit.* 1 (1966) 127, pl. 70.

84. Bronze linch-pin from the hub of a chariot wheel found in the 'Burnt Palace' at Nimrud in the upper rubbish of room 32, eighth century B.C. The kneeling man is in a gesture of adoration for a god or king.

(Baghdad, National Museum of Antiquities ND 2136. Height 13.5 cm.)
Mallowan, *op. cit.* 1 (1966) 208, pl. 142.

85. Oval pendant of pale blue chalcedony (22 mm × 12 mm) set in a gold frame with a chain from a seventh-century B.C. grave in room DD of the North-West Palace at Nimrud. It is engraved with a harp player and a flute player flanking a sacred tree with deity symbols above.

(Baghdad, National Museum of Antiquities ND 785.)
Mallowan, *op. cit.* 1 (1966) 114, pl. 58.

86. Marbly limestone macehead inscribed for King Ashurnasirpal II (883–859 B.C.) as a dedication to the goddess Ishtar.

(British Museum WA 104411. Height *c.* 11.5 cm.)
British Museum: A Guide to the Babylonian and Assyrian Antiquities (London, 1922) 224.

87. Bronze mould designed to produce simultaneously three trefoil barbed and socketed bronze arrowheads; seventh century B.C.; acquired at Mosul.

(British Museum WA 124624.)
H. H. Coghlan, *Man* 52 (1952) 162–4, no. 245.

87

88

88. A model sword and a model adze-axehead in bronze; eighth or seventh century B.C. from Ashur (Ass. 6392a).

(British Museum WA 1922.8–12.130. Lengths *c.* 16 cm.)

    W. Andrae, *Der Anu-Adad-Tempel in Assur.* (Leipzig, 1909) 53, fig. 47.

89. Reconstruction of a house interior in Neo-Assyrian Ashur.

(After W. Andrae, *Das Wiedererstandene Assur* (Leipzig, 1938) fig. 6.)

4. URARTU

P. R. S. MOOREY

Uncontrolled excavations in the nineteenth century at Toprak Kale, near Van in eastern Turkey, revealed a collection of cast metal objects, largely from the furnishing of the shrine of the god Khaldi, that have long dominated discussions of Urartian culture. It is only in the last thirty years that renewed study of them in the light of a steady flow of more varied fresh information from controlled excavations in Turkey (Altintepe, Çavuştepe, Kayalidere), the U.S.S.R. (Arin-berd, Karmir-Blur) and north-west Iran (Bastam) has restored the balance. Although the published evidence for Urartian art tends still to be dominated by metalwork, Urartian architecture, with a little relief sculpture and wall-painting, pottery and non-metallic small objects, are now well enough known for their distinctive characteristics to be defined. At the same time it has become clear that certain types of artefact, notably the large sheet-metal cauldrons with cast bronze fittings, long termed 'Urartian', may well have been produced in workshops located in north Syria or eastern Turkey, not necessarily under Urartian influence or control.

The impact of Assyrian crafts and craftsmen on the one hand, Syro-Phoenician on the other, was considerable in Urartu from the ninth to the sixth centuries B.C. But the result was a far more homogeneous 'Court Style' in Urartian workshops, with a clear character of its own, than was once supposed. Its origins before the ninth century, like those of the Urartian state, remain obscure. There is no clear sign of a legacy from such earlier cultures of Turkey as that of the Hittites. Possible Hurrian precursors are as elusive in art as they are in the evolution of the Urartian language. Van Loon has defined the main characteristics of the Urartian 'Court Style' as: architectonic forms in sculpture, even in minor works; an emphasis on horizontal and vertical lines in both flat and three-dimensional compositions; elegant and highly decorative effects in design; and a taste for fantastic composite creatures. There was no great variety over time or space in the 'Court Style'; but it has a derivative 'Popular Style' more subject to local variation. Characteristic examples of Urartian work disappear after the early sixth century B.C., with the collapse of her political system; but not before exercising some influence on the art of the Scythians of south Russia, notably the fine metalwork from the Kelermes and Melgunov barrow burials, and possibly also on the Medes of Iran.

GENERAL BIBLIOGRAPHY

G. Azarpay, *Urartian Art and Artifacts: a chronological study* (University of California Press, 1968)
B. B. Piotrovskii, *Urartu: The Kingdom of Van and its Art* (London, 1967); and *Urartu* (London, 1969)
M. N. van Loon, *Urartian Art: its distinctive traits in the light of new excavations* (Istanbul, 1966)

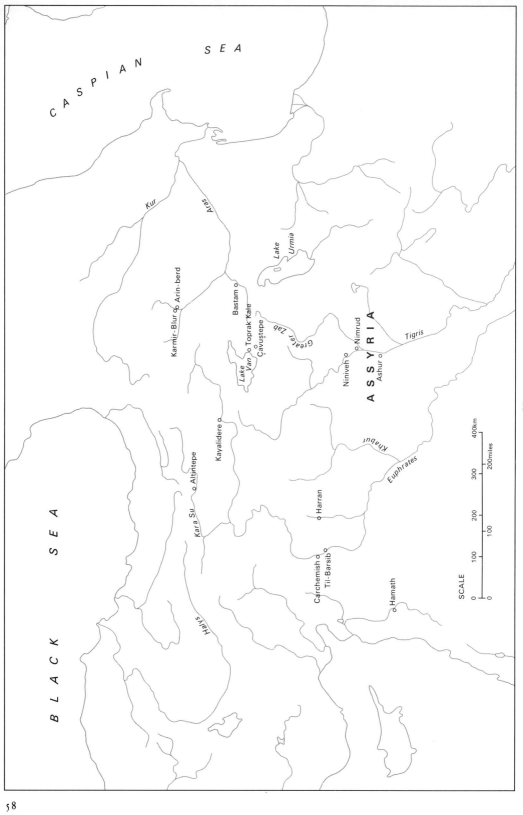

3. Urartu

91

90. Drawing of a relief in the Palace of the Assyrian King Sargon II at Khorsabad showing the Urartian Temple of Khaldi at Ardini-Muṣaṣir. Notice the shields held by the defenders on the roof, especially that to the left, with the lion-head boss.

(After P. E. Botta, *Monument de Ninive* II (Paris, 1849–50) pl. 141.)

91. Part of a seventh-century B.C. bronze model city such as those shown on Assyrian reliefs carried as tribute to the Assyrian king. Illustrations of buildings in elevation are not always explicit on Assyrian reliefs, so this model adds much to understanding architectural details. It probably represents the type of stone-building common in the Urartian citadel of Toprak Kale, near Lake Van, where it was found.

(British Museum WA 91177. 28 cm × 36 cm.)
R. D. Barnett, *Iraq* 12 (1950) 5, pl. 1.2.

92. Bronze model turret, possibly from the city model shown in **91**. The projecting turret rests on horizontally laid tree trunks.

(British Museum WA 91250. Height 16 cm.)
Barnett, *op. cit.* 6, pl. 1.1.

93. Bronze statuette of a god said to have been found at Van. This is one of the very rare surviving examples of Urartian religious statuary. The god's identity is unknown; but the very vertical position of the body and strictly horizontal arms distinguish it from similar Assyrian statuettes; seventh century B.C.

(British Museum WA 91147. Height 19.7 cm.)
Barnett, *op. cit.* 2, pl. 18.2; M. van Loon, *Urartian Art* (1966) 87, pl. 10a.

94. Fragments of a wig and lead garments, originally inlaid with coloured faiences and ivory from a deity statuette; once fitted over a body of ivory. From Toprak Kale, seventh century B.C.

(British Museum WA 123870.)
Barnett, *op. cit.* pl. 13.3.

91250

94

95. Gilt bronze statuette of an attendant, the face inlaid in white stone; from Toprak Kale, seventh century B.C. He wears a long robe with a fleece over the upper part as do Urartians on the reliefs of Sargon at Khorsabad in Assyria. He holds a feather fan and a long cloth like Assyrian palace servants. It may originally have been a furniture support.

(Berlin, Staatliche Museen (East) VA 774. Height 37.5 cm.)

Barnett, *op. cit.* 20, pl. 20; G. R. Meyer, *Altorientalische Denkmäler im Vorderasiatischen Museum zu Berlin* (Leipzig, 1965) pl. 13.

(British Museum WA 91247. Height 23 cm.)
Barnett, *op. cit.* 6–7, pl. 7.2.

97. Gilded bronze griffin, probably a furniture support like the bull sphinx in **96**; Toprak Kale; seventh century B.C.

(Berlin, Staatliche Museen (East) VA 775. Height 21.7 cm.)
Barnett, *op. cit.* 20, n. 2, pl. 18; Meyer, *op. cit.* pl. 132.

98. Gilded bronze fragment from the arm of a piece of furniture; a snarling lion is set on a vertical beam modelled as if laid logs set crosswide. This piece has been twisted so that the lion is now 90° to its original position. Toprak Kale; seventh century B.C.

(British Museum WA 91253.)
Barnett, *op. cit.* 15, pl. 11.1–3.

96. Winged human-headed bronze bull wearing a horned crown; wing and face originally inlaid; Toprak Kale; seventh century B.C. On the top are three hieroglyphs; possibly a fitter's marks for assembling this as part of the supporting frame of a bed or couch, perhaps for a god in a shrine. A deity, for instance, appears on such a throne carved on the Assyrian rock relief at Maltai (W. Bachmann, *Felsreliefs in Assyrien* (Leipzig, 1927) pls. 26, 28, 29).

99. Bronze candelabrum from Toprak Kale inscribed for one of the Urartian kings called Rusa, probably the second *c.* 685–639 B.C. The style of the decoration on this stand is exactly that of the furniture fittings shown in **96–8**.

(Hamburg, Museum für Kunst und Gewerbe 1960.61. Height 1.18 m.)
van Loon, *op. cit.* 98–9, pls. 18, 19; G. Azarpay, *Urartian Art and Artifacts* (1968) 62ff.

97

98

99

100. Bronze shield inscribed by King Rusa III(?), *c*. 629–615 B.C., for the chief Urartian god Khaldi in whose temple at Toprak Kale it was deposited. An Assyrian representation on a stone relief of the Urartian Temple at Muṣaṣir (**90**) shows shields hung on the outer walls. This shield is incised with a frieze of lions *passant* in the style of the later seventh century B.C.

(British Museum WA 22482. Diameter 77 cm.)
  Barnett, *op. cit.* 13–14, pl. 9.

101. Part of a fragmentary bronze belt incised with lions, bulls and floral ornaments; from Gusci, near Lake Urmia. Such belts were commonly worn by soldiers and decorated in this manner, often with fantastic creatures as well as real ones; seventh century B.C.

(Oxford, Ashmolean Museum (de Walden loan). Width 9.5 cm.)
  R. W. Hamilton, *AS* 15 (1965) 41–51.

102. Gold pendant incised with a seated goddess receiving homage from a female suppliant, possibly the Urartian queen; from Toprak Kale; seventh century B.C.

(Berlin, Staatliche Museen (East) VA 4634. Diameter 4.6 cm.)

Meyer, *op. cit*. pl. 137 left; van Loon, *op. cit*. 129.

103. Silver pendant found in a silver cylindrical box at Toprak Kale. It shows a seated goddess approached by a suppliant bringing a kid for sacrifice. Two trees, stylized like spearheads in a distinctively Urartian way, flank the scene; seventh century B.C.

(Berlin, Staatliche Museen (East) VA 46356. Width 6.5 cm.)

Meyer, *op. cit*. pl. 137 right, and *Das Altertum* 1 (1955) 209.

5. THE SYRO-HITTITE STATES

J. D. HAWKINS
(127a, 128 *by P. R. S. Moorey*)

The Hittite Empire, under which the kings of Khatti had conquered and governed Syria from their Anatolian capital Khattusha, foundered in a welter of population movements across the Mediterranean and Fertile Crescent, about 1200 B.C. The Hittites themselves disappeared from their homeland Khatti in central Anatolia along with their language, and their use of cuneiform clay tablets borrowed from Mesopotamia. In their erstwhile south-eastern provinces, however, the south-east Anatolian plateau, the Taurus mountains, Cilicia and northern Syria up to the Euphrates, people of kindred stock held their own and indeed expanded in a political landscape of city states lacking the control of a paramount capital. From the earlier Hittite culture these states inherited and developed a tradition of monumental sculpture and of writing in the indigenous Hieroglyphic script. The language of their inscriptions, however, and presumably also of the population, was not Hittite but the closely related Luwian. Nevertheless the nation continued to be known to its neighbours of the south and east by the term 'Khatti', which our designation 'Late (or Neo-) Hittite' follows.

The Hittite dominion of Syria had not remained immune to the population movements of the period. A new wave of Semitic people, the Aramaeans, seized the opportunity of the relaxation of political control to expand westwards into Syria, as also northwards into upper Mesopotamia and south east into Babylonia, from about 1000 B.C. onwards. Here they founded their tribal states, typically termed 'House' (*Bīt*) of an eponymous ancestor. They borrowed the alphabetic script of their kinsmen the Phoenicians, probably about the mid-ninth century B.C., and the practice of monumental stone sculpture from their neighbours the Hittites, perhaps a little earlier. The nations of 'Khatti and Aram' coexisted in Syria, and though we may infer that it was a world of warring cities and shifting alliances, there is no evidence that the divisions ever followed the racial rift of Hittites and Aramaeans.

For the most part these Iron Age states seem to have been new foundations, even if on ancient sites. Only Carchemish on the west bank of the Euphrates at an important crossing may have preserved a degree of continuity from the imperial past. It must however be admitted that the Iron Age cities of Anatolia, Cilicia and the Taurus, and their Late Bronze Age antecedents, are not on the whole well known. On the Anatolian plateau, designated by the Assyrians as Tabal, while some sites have yielded sculpture and inscriptions of the period (**123, 124**), none has been subjected to large scale excavation over a substantial area. Similarly Maraş, ancient Marqasi, capital of the state of Gurgum, has produced a notable series of sculpture and inscriptions (**106, 107, 108**), purely by chance finds, without ever having been systematically excavated at all. The Cilician plain, site of many ancient cities of the period, including the capital Adana, has not yet yielded any notable contemporary monuments and is represented only by the peripheral, though important, site of Karatepe (**125, 126**). The kingdom of Kummukh, later Commagene, on the west bank of the upper Euphrates has to date produced only isolated sculptures and inscriptions, though it may be hoped that present intensive investigation of its riverine area, especially the ancient capital Samsat, prior to inundation by a barrage now under construction (1982), may change the picture. To the north of Gurgum and Kummukh lay the ancient Melid, modern Malatya, where a series of excavations at the ancient capital, the site of Arslantepe, uncovered the city gate with sculpture and inscriptions *in situ* (**114, 120a**).

In north Syria the sites are comparatively better known. At Carchemish excavations

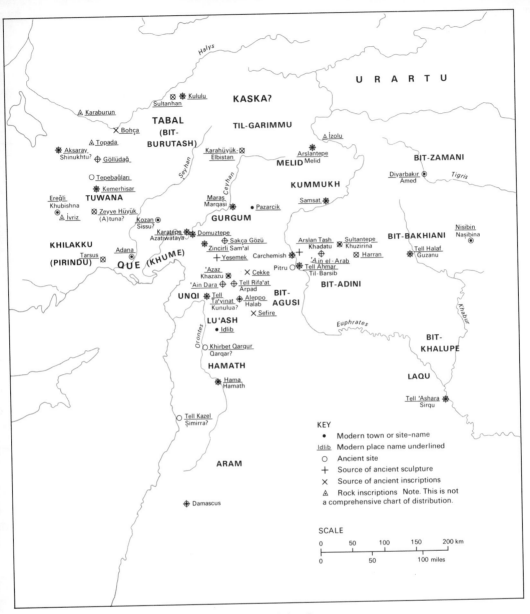

4. The Syro-Hittite States

interrupted by the First World War produced a notable series of monuments (104, 109a, 111b, 112, 116, 118). The citadel of Zincirli, ancient Sam'al, was more intensively investigated and revealed a remarkable Aramaean state in some detail (105, 110, 111a, 113, 115, 121, 122a–b). Palaces have been uncovered in the Plain of Antioch (ancient Unqi), at Sakça Gözü (119), and at Hama (ancient Hamath), a state where control seems to have passed from Hittites to Aramaeans about 800 B.C. Preliminary excavations at Tell Rifa'at, ancient Arpad, capital of Bit-Agusi, revealed little of this important Aramaean state, while east of the Euphrates, excavations at Tell Ahmar and Arslan Tash, cities of the Aramaean Bit-Adini, found few identifiable Aramaean remains but rather earlier Hittite and later Assyrian monuments. The leading Aramaean power of all, Damascus, whose ancient site presumably lies under the modern city, is archaeologically virtually unknown.

The most notable remains of the period are the walled cities, whose elaborate gates may be decorated with stone orthostats sculptured in relief and inscribed. Palace buildings, often incorporating the architectural form the *bīt-ḫilāni* (a columned portico), and temples may have the same decoration. Other forms of sculpture include statues in the round, often colossal, of rulers and gods, free-standing stelae and rock reliefs. The inscriptions accompanying such monumental works, both in Hieroglyphic Luwian and alphabetic Aramaic, are, as might be expected, mostly of a commemorative character, rulers' 'autobiographies' and dedications to gods. It is clear that writing was also used during this period both by Hittites and Aramaeans for more practical purposes, such as letters and contracts, but these must have been on perishable materials, wood, parchment or the like, which have not survived. Only a few lead strips inscribed in Hieroglyphic, and the occasional Aramaic ostracon, attest to this vanished branch of literacy (**127b, c**).

Other material remains of the period either have not yet been assembled by regular excavation or await specialized studies. Syro-Hittite styles of ivory-carving are in process of being identified (**128a–e**), and the important contribution of these peoples to contemporary metal-working is suspected but little known (**127a**). Full scale studies on the seals and the pottery have yet to be undertaken and might still be premature in default of significant accessions of properly excavated material.

Note. In the observations on the illustrations which follow, Hittite personal names are quoted in their Hittite forms, where known, otherwise in their Assyrian forms (italicized); Aramaean names may appear in their Assyrian forms, where known (italicized), or in their purely consonantal Aramaic writings (capitals). Individual inscriptions are referred to after their place of provenance printed in capitals.

GENERAL BIBLIOGRAPHY

E. Akurgal, *The Art of the Hittites* (London, 1962)

K. Bittel, *Die Hethiter.* Die Kunst Anatoliens vom Ende des 3. bis zum Anfang des 1. Jahrtausends vor Christus (Munich, 1976)

P. H. J. Houwink ten Cate, 'Kleinasien zwischen Hethitern und Persern' in E. Cassin (ed.), *Die altorientalischen Reiche* III (Fischer Weltgeschichte, Band 4; Frankfurt am Main, 1967)

W. Orthmann, *Untersuchungen zur späthethitischen Kunst* (Bonn, 1971)

Seton Lloyd, *Early Highland Peoples of Anatolia* (London, 1967)

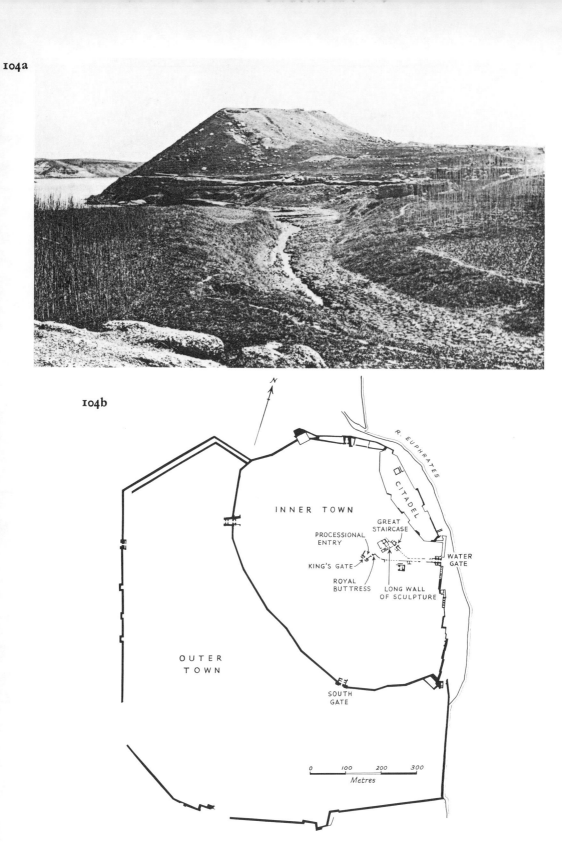

104a

104b

N

R. EUPHRATES

CITADEL

INNER TOWN

GREAT
STAIRCASE

PROCESSIONAL
ENTRY

KING'S GATE

WATER
GATE

ROYAL
BUTTRESS

LONG WALL
OF SCULPTURE

OUTER
TOWN

SOUTH
GATE

0   100   200   300
Metres

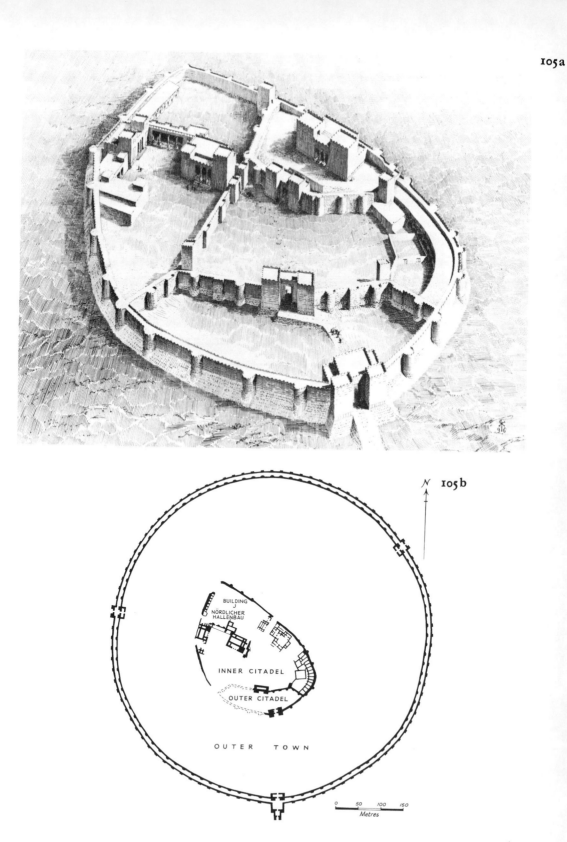

105b

BUILDING
J
NÖRDLICHER
HALLENBAU

INNER CITADEL

OUTER CITADEL

O U T E R   T O W N

N

0   50   100   150
Metres

104. Site of Carchemish. This city, the former capital of the Hittite Empire in Syria, seems to have retained a position of a leading Neo-Hittite state, and in spite of having lost its political dominion remained for its Assyrian neighbours almost synonymous with 'Khatti'. By this, the latest period of major occupation, the city had expanded to an enormous size, stretching from the original tell on the river Euphrates, now the citadel mound, through the inner town protected by earth ramparts to the outer town with its own enceinte. Excavations begun here under the auspices of the British Museum in 1911 continued until their interruption by the First World War in 1914, and after a brief resumption in 1920 were discontinued. It has never been feasible to reopen them.

In the course of the excavations, the circuit of the fortifications was traced, the surface of the tell investigated and some houses of the outer town cleared. But the main work was the excavation of a public quarter of the city stretching from the water-gate on the Euphrates around the foot of the citadel mound. Earlier trials had already recovered sculpture and inscriptions from this area, and the excavations revealed the wall façades and monumental entries of a series of public buildings including a temple of the Storm God of Carchemish. The orthostats of the façades were decorated with relief sculpture and inscriptions, mostly of about 920–880 B.C. (work of the rulers Suhis (II) and Katuwas), with some eighth-century additions; see **109a, 111b, 112, 116, 118**. Should it ever be possible to reopen the excavation of Carchemish, it might be hoped to find much more substantial remains of this period, as well as the remains of the important settlements of the second and third millennia B.C.

((**a**) After D. G. Hogarth *et al.*, *Carchemish* I (London, 1914) Frontispiece (a). (**b**) After C. L. Woolley, *Carchemish* III (London, 1952) pl. 41a, with II (London, 1921) pl. 3.)

105. Site of Zincirli. This site lies at the foot of the Amanus mountains on the east side immediately opposite the exit of one of the west–east passes of the range. From the summit of the Amanus, the town plan is still clearly visible. It consists of an inner citadel ('Burg') standing on the old tell, and an outer town surrounded by a circular double wall punctuated by three gates. The site was excavated by von Luschan and others in five seasons between 1888 and 1902. Apart from tracing the circular city wall, work was concentrated on the citadel itself, where a series of kiosk-like constructions were unearthed, mostly with columned porticoes of the *bīt-ḫilāni* type. These buildings and the gates of the town and citadel had the lower parts of their walls faced with stone orthostats in the Hittite style, and many of these orthostats bore relief sculpture. The sculptural styles identified may be dated to the earlier ninth century B.C. (South City Gate, Outer Citadel Gate – see **110, 113**); the later ninth century (stela of Kilamuwa – see **115**); earlier eighth century (Hadad statue of *Panammu* I – see **122a**); later eighth century (statue of *Panammu* II and the work of Bar-Rakib – see **122b, 121**). The associated Aramaic inscriptions of Kilamuwa, *Panammu* I, *Panammu* II and Bar-Rakib provide an outline history of the dynasty.

(After F. von Luschan, *Sendschirli* II (Berlin, 1898) pls. 29, 30.)

106. Small basalt portal lion, from the tell of Maraş. About 800 B.C. The lion bears across its body and legs a Hieroglyphic inscription, MARAŞ I, which is introduced by a badly damaged portrait figure of the author, Halparuntiyas (III), himself standing on a lion; this can be seen in the recessed panel on the shoulder. Halparuntiyas is almost certainly to be identified with the *Qalparunda*, son of *Palalam*, king of Gurgum (ancient Maraş), mentioned on an Assyrian stele of Adad-nirari III set up in 805 B.C. at Pazarcık and now in the Maraş Museum; this dates him to the end of the ninth century B.C. In his own inscription, Halparuntiyas names in ascending order his progenitors for six generations, which identifies for us the seven-generation dynasty of Gurgum: *Palalam* (I) – Muwanzas – Halparuntiyas (I) – Muwatalis – Halparuntiyas (II) – *Palalam* (II) – Halparuntiyas (III). Two of these rulers can be identified as the authors of other pieces of inscribed sculpture from Maraş (see **107** and **108**). In the rest of his inscription which breaks off abruptly and was clearly continued elsewhere, Halparuntiyas speaks of the events of his reign and his relationship with various gods.

(Istanbul, Ancient Oriental Museum 7698. 90 cm × 62 cm.)

CAH III².1, 382–3, 401; Orthmann, *USK* 524, Maraş B/1. For the inscription Meriggi, *Manuale* II.1, 129–31, no. 33, pl. 15.

107. Fragment of colossal basalt figure, preserved from the waist to the knees, from the tell of Maraş. The front of the fragment shows traces of a tassel hanging from the belt and a staff held in the right hand, and a sword hangs from the belt on the left hip. All these are typical accoutrements of rulers of the period: cf. **109–11.** The light-coloured parts including the feet are modern restorations. Beginning on the right hip and running round the back to the left hip six lines of a Hieroglyphic inscription, MARAŞ 4, are preserved, and this identifies as its author Halparuntiyas, king of Gurgum, son of Muwatalis, great-grandson of Muwanzas. This man is clearly Halparuntiyas II, grandfather of Halparuntiyas III. Shalmaneser III names as kings of Gurgum a *Mutallu* in 858 B.C. and a *Qalparunda* in 853 B.C., clearly Halparuntiyas II and his father, which dates the beginning of the former's reign to the mid-

ninth century B.C. The inscription is introduced by a typical portrait figure ('I am . . .') of the ruler in relief occupying the height of four lines and dressed in the ruler's traditional style: this can be seen in the photograph on the right hip (detail). The inscription, as far as preserved, contains an account of the deeds of Halparuntiyas.

(Istanbul, Ancient Oriental Museum 7772. 98 cm × 60 cm.)

CAH III².1, 382–3, 395–6; Orthmann, *USK* 524, Maraş B/3; Genge, *NSR* 83–4. For the inscription Meriggi, *Manuale* II.1, 127–9, no. 32, pl. 14.

108. Ruler Stela of basalt, from the tell of Maraş. Early tenth century B.C. The stela shows the ruler in an early form of the traditional style, with beard and long hair falling in a bunch on the neck, wearing a long fringed robe and carrying a staff of office (not shown are the usual tasselled belt and the sword hanging from it). A seven-line Hieroglyphic inscription, MARAŞ 8, is written over the background and the robe, but the incised signs are faint and difficult to read. It can however be seen that the

of a whole style of representation of Hittite rulers, and provide a convenient chronological bracket for that style, *c.* 975–850 B.C. Median representations of that style are **109**, **111**; and compare also the crude Aramaean version, **110**.

(New York, Metropolitan Museum of Art 90.21. 1.10 m × 0.56 m.)

CAH III².1, 382–3; Orthmann, *USK* 526, Maraş B/16; Genge, *NSR* 230 and n. 118. For the inscription Meriggi, *Manuale* II.2, 89–91, no. 139, pl. 15.

109. (a) Carchemish, Katuwas Inscription. Basalt orthostat with portrait figure introducing a nine-line Hieroglyphic inscription, excavated out of position in the Processional Entry, Carchemish. Beginning of ninth century B.C. This portrait figure representing 'I am . . .' occupies, unusually, the entire height of the inscription. It is one of this period's best examples of ruler representations, which are found, both in relief, as here, and in the round, as (**b**) and **111**: note

ruler identifies himself by the name which appears in its Assyrian form as *Palalam* (Hittite phonetic rendering uncertain), and names his grandfather as Astu . . . and father as Muwatalis (?). It is probable that he is to be identified with *Palalam* I, the ancestor to whom Halparuntiyas III traced back his genealogy. The seven generations of this dynasty would stretch back from about 800 B.C. at least to about 975 B.C. This would place this stela as the earliest piece of Neo-Hittite sculpture of relatively fixed date and would accord well with its archaic appearance. The figures of *Palalam* I and Halparuntiyas II are respectively early and late examples

the hair bunched on the neck and square cut beard, both composed of 'pot-hook' curls; the brow-band; the long, fringed, belted robe (on this example the usual frontal belt-tassel is not seen); the sword in the belt; and the staff of office. Such portraits of rulers seem to have been common at this period, and offer stereotyped ideals rather than personal likenesses. This ruler gives his name as Katuwas, and at Carchemish his and his father's monuments

74

form a prominent and homogeneous group dating *c.* 920–880 B.C. and typically their sculpture and inscriptions are found together on wall façades decorated with basalt and limestone orthostats, and on basalt door jambs and lions flanking major entrances. Subjects of sculpture include processions of gods (see **112**) and chariots, soldiers and offering bearers, and scenes with gods and fabulous creatures. The inscriptions parallel these with narratives of victories and dedications of buildings and sculpture.

(Ankara, Museum of Anatolian Civilizations 89. 1.28 m × 0.85 m.)
CAH III².1, 383–4; C. L. Woolley, *Carchemish* II (London, 1921) pl. A 13d, and III (London, 1952) 203, 261, 273; Orthmann, *USK* 516, Karkemis K/28; Genge, *NSR* ch. 4. For the inscription J. D. Hawkins, *AS* 31 (1981) 154.

(b) Ain el-Arab Ruler. Basalt statue, found at Ain el-Arab (Arab Pınar), near Arslan Tash. Late tenth to early ninth century B.C. This statue, showing the typical hair-style and accoutrements of the ruler (note also the bracelets, necklace and sandals), was found in unrecorded circumstances in the neighbourhood of Ain el-Arab. It presumably represents a Hittite ruler of Til-Barsib, perhaps one of those named on the Til-Barsib stelae, to the period of which it belongs.

(Aleppo Museum 5914. 1.94 m × 0.47 m.)
CAH III².1, 385; Orthmann, *USK* 476, Ain-el-Arab 1; cf. J. D. Hawkins, *AS* 30 (1980) 155–6.

110. Basalt orthostat showing figure of ruler, excavated *in situ* in the Outer Citadel Gate, Zincirli. Beginning of ninth century B.C. The dynastic sequence of early Zincirli (ancient Sam'al of the state *Bit-Gabbar*) is summarized in the inscription of a later king Kilamuwa (see **115**): *Gabbar* – BMH – *Khayanu* – Š'L (son of *Khayanu*) – Kilamuwa (son of *Khayanu*). Kilamuwa reigned *c.* 840–830 B.C. and his father *Khayanu* is mentioned by Shalmaneser III in the years 858, 857 and 853 B.C. An estimate of the first two reigns (generations?) puts the foundation of this largely Aramaean state by *Gabbar* at the end of the tenth century B.C. The earliest phase of sculpture from Zincirli, probably to be attributed to *Gabbar* himself although it is without inscription, shows a

clumsy Aramaean dependence on the more sophisticated Hittite style of Carchemish. This is well exemplified by the present figure, which, while showing the typical attributes of the Hittite ruler, is rendered in a notably crude style. It presumably represents *Gabbar* or possibly BMH.

(Istanbul, Ancient Oriental Museum 7717. 1.17 m × 0.71 m. Photograph, after Pritchard.)
CAH III².1, 386; F. von Luschan, *Sendschirli* III (Berlin, 1902) 215, fig. 108, pl. 37c; Orthmann, *USK* 539, Zincirli B/5; Genge, *NSR* ch. 2; J. B. Pritchard, *Ancient Near East in Pictures* (ed. 3, Princeton, 1970) fig. 40.

111. (a) Colossal basalt figure mounted on double-lion podium, from near the south-east wall of Building J, Zincirli. Ninth century B.C. This colossus is the best preserved example of a type known also from fragments from Carchemish and Maraş (**107**). Comparison with later similar monuments suggests that it was erected as a funerary memorial to a king, and the lion podium, as well as later textual references, implies some degree of deification. In this piece, in contrast to **110**, not only the ruler's attributes (hair and beard styles, fringed robe, tasselled belt, sword and staff) but also the style of rendering point strongly to its Hittite origins, specifically Carchemish, to an extent which actually suggests the employment of Carchemish craftsmen.

(Istanbul, Ancient Oriental Museum 7768. Height of statue *c.* 3.0 m, of base 0.72 m.)
CAH III².1, 385–6; F. von Luschan, *Sendschirli* IV (Berlin, 1911) 273, 288–9, figs. 261–8, pl. 64; Orthmann, *USK* 545, Zincirli E/1; Genge, *NSR* 83–4, 87.

(b) Only surviving fragment of a colossal statue similar to that of Zincirli, excavated in fragments in front of its *in situ* base, in the Processional Entry, King's Gate, Carchemish. Late tenth to early ninth centuries B.C. The Carchemish colossus, fragmentary but closely similar to that of Zincirli, originally stood on a double-lion base almost identical to the Zincirli base. The Carchemish statue presumably represented either Suhis or Katuwas, to one of whose reigns it must be attributed, while the Zincirli figure must represent *Gabbar* or BMH who are likely to have been the contemporaries of the Carchemish rulers.

(Paris, Louvre Museum AO 10828. Preserved height 42 cm, width 41 cm.)
Woolley, *Carchemish* III 192, pl. B 54a; Orthmann, *USK* 509, Karkemis F/17.

112. Reconstruction of the procession of the gods on basalt and limestone orthostats at the head of the 'Long Wall of Sculpture' at Carchemish (first slab restored from an old drawing; cf. **113**). Reign of Suhis, end of tenth century B.C. The 'Long Wall of Sculpture' shows a victory procession of chariots and infantry headed by this divine procession marching towards a monumental staircase, which ascended to the citadel. A large but incompletely recovered inscription of Suhis was incorporated into the monument and describes the military victories under the gods represented and the setting up of the sculptures and Suhis' own image. The only god individually named is the leader, the 'mighty Tarkhunzas', who is shown in the style traditional in this period, bearded with long curled pigtail, wearing a horned helmet and short, belted, fringed tunic with sword at the waist, carrying an axe raised behind him in his right hand, and a trident representing a thunderbolt in his outstretched left hand. The following goddess may be identified as Kubaba, frequently referred to elsewhere as 'Queen of Carchemish', and the god with the spear as Karhuhas: the triad Tarkhunzas, Kubaba, and Karhuhas are the main group of gods invoked in the Carchemish inscriptions. The following two goddesses, of whom the first is not certainly to be restored in

this position, have not been identified in the inscriptions, though the frontal nude goddess is clearly of the Ishtar type. The presence of the seated queen at the end of this divine file is not explained by the accompanying inscription, but would seem to imply that she was dead and in the company of the gods, thus to some extent deified.

(Ankara, Museum of Anatolian Civilizations 104, 147, 103, 10075. Total length *c.* 7 m; height (restored) *c.* 2 m. Drawing, Hawkins.)
Woolley, *Carchemish* III 164–7; for the reconstruction, J. D. Hawkins, *AS* 22 (1972) 106–7 and the inscriptions, *ibid.* 88–96; Orthmann, *USK* 501–2, Karkemis C/1–4; Genge, *NSR* 72ff.

113. Divine Procession on basalt orthostats excavated *in situ* at the head of the east side of the Outer Citadel Gate, Zincirli. Date, as for **110**, beginning of ninth century B.C. Just as the ruler figure from the Outer Citadel Gate at Zincirli (**110**) showed a clear dependence on Carchemish prototypes, so also does this procession of the gods from the same structure. Indeed it probably shows some misunderstanding of the Hittite iconography occasioned by the transference to an alien, Aramaean context, for the Hittite and Aramaean pantheons were radically different. The gods invoked in the Zincirli inscriptions are Ba'al-Hadad, El, Rešeph, Rakib-El and the Sun, while goddesses are notably absent. The Carchemish triad Karhuhas, Kubaba and Tarkhunzas shown here in this iconographically wrong order, would not appear to have any roots in the local religion. Also the fourth figure, a seated female, seems to have been taken directly from the

deified Carchemish queen of the Long Wall of Sculpture, without any understanding of her position and function. The group, it would seem, was borrowed in its entirety without any regard to the organic unity of the original, and used merely as an element of decoration.

(Berlin, Staatliche Museen (East) VA 2647, 2648, 2649. Total length *c.* 4 m; average height *c.* 1.3 m. Photograph, other than right-hand figure, after von Luschan.)

von Luschan, *Sendschirli* III 213–14, fig. 103, pl. 40; 218–19, figs. 113–15, pls. 41, 38a; Orthmann, *USK* 541, Zincirli B/13–5; Genge, *NSR* 53–4.

114. Divine Procession on orthostat block of white limestone, excavated *in situ* as part of a series forming a dado around the two inner buttresses of the gate-chamber of the Lion Gate, Malatya-Arslantepe. Early ninth century B.C. The Malatya sculpture forms a somewhat anomalous group within the Neo-Hittite

assemblage. Stylistically it has closer affinities to the art of the Hittite Empire than with the rest of the Neo-Hittite group. The accompanying inscriptions are also extremely brief and uninformative. It seems however that its archaic appearance is due to the continuation of a conservative tradition, and not to any markedly greater antiquity. The dado reliefs of the Lion Gate show principally the offering by the king, whose name is written FIST-mili (reading of FIST unknown: the name has often been read as Sulumili on inadequate grounds), of libations to various gods. The gods identified by epigraphs include the Storm God, the Storm God of Melid (ancient Malatya) and another city, the Moon, the Sun, Sauska, the Stag God and Sarrumas. In the present relief the members of the divine procession are not individually identified: the leader may be presumed to be the Storm God; the following goddess iconographically resembles the goddess identified as Sauska, and occupies the place which in Carchemish would be taken by Kubaba; the god with the spear would be Karhuhas in the Carchemish inscriptions but probably Runtiyas/Runzas (the Stag God) elsewhere; the fourth figure, a goddess, remains of uncertain identity, as at Carchemish.

(Ankara, Museum of Anatolian Civilizations 12253. Height 47 cm; width 1.26 m.)
 CAH III².1, 385; L. Delaporte, *Malatya, Arslantepe* I, *La Porte des Lions* (Paris, 1940) 30–1, pl. 20. 1; Orthmann, *USK* 520, Malatya A/5a; Genge, *NSR* 172–7.

115. Kilamuwa Stela, bearing Phoenician inscription, excavated partially *in situ*, north-west side of the entrance to Building J, Zincirli. About 830 B.C. In the first part of this inscription the author Kilamuwa (KLMW) son of *Khayanu* (ḤY') boasts greater success than all his predecessors at maintaining his kingdom against its hostile neighbours, particularly the king of the Danuna (DNNYM) against whom he 'hired' the Assyrian king. In the second part he describes the domestic scenes of concord and prosperity which characterized his reign. His father ḤY' has been identified with *Khayanu*, contemporary with the young Shalmaneser III. The reference to 'hiring' the Assyrian king against the Danuna can only refer to the campaigns of Shalmaneser III against Que in 839, 834 and 833 B.C., which places Kilamuwa in the later ninth century B.C. The inscription and sculpture show a number of remarkable features. The language is Phoenician although the dynasty was largely Aramaic, with some members including Kilamuwa himself bearing Hittite names. Unusually for a Semitic alphabetic inscription, the letters are in relief, rather than incised, and the lines are separated by relief rulings, characteristics shared only with later Zincirli inscriptions, as are also the introductory portrait figure representing 'I am ...' and the divine symbols. The epigraphic features are clearly following the model of the Hittite Hieroglyphic inscriptions of the preceding century, but the portrait figure itself and the divine symbols show not Hittite but Assyrian influence. It has been plausibly suggested that the direct model for this would have been the Assyrian stela set up by Shalmaneser near Sam'al after his defeat of Khayanu in 858 B.C. Thus we have the first securely dated

Aramaean inscription written in Phoenician following a Hittite model and showing the earliest onset of strong Assyrian influence on the local sculpture.

(Berlin, Staatliche Museen (East) VA 56579. Height 1.56 m; width *c.* 1.3 m.)
 CAH III².1, 397–8; von Luschan, *Sendschirli* IV 374ff., fig. 273; G. Meyer, *Altorientalische Denkmäler im vorderas. Museum zu Berlin* (Leipzig, 1965) figs. 78–9; Orthmann, *USK* 545, Zincirli E/2; Genge, *NSR* 41–2. For the inscription Rosenthal in *ANET* 654–5.

116. Basalt orthostats with Hieroglyphic inscription and sculpture, excavated *in situ* at the 'Royal Buttress', King's Gate, Carchemish. Early eighth century B.C. The scene and accompanying inscriptions announce the advancement of the young Kamanis (left-hand figure)

by the ruler Yariris (formerly read Araras: right-hand figure). Contrary to what has been usually supposed, Yariris does not name Kamanis as his own son but as the son of his lord Astiruwas. He must therefore have been active as regent and guardian. The iconography supports this: it is Kamanis who holds the staff of office and wears the characteristic dress of the ruler, long fringed robe, tasselled belt and sword. The representation of Yariris is more enigmatic. Very unusually for a Hittite ruler he is shown beardless and his hair-style is also distinctive. The overgarment of a shawl with a triangular tasselled end hanging forward over the right shoulder is a new feature, and it covers his own sword of which only the pommel and end of the scabbard are visible. In the small portrait figure introducing his inscription, however, he is shown in the normal robe and tasselled belt. His sceptre carried upside down doubtless has a symbolic significance: cf. attendant with sceptre (**119**). In this and his other inscriptions Yariris claims not only that he was known abroad but also that he could read and speak foreign languages, claims which exhibit a remarkably cosmopolitan attitude for a Hittite ruler. The regency of

Yariris can be dated to the second generation before *Pisiri* who reigned *c.* 740–717 B.C. (see **118**), i.e. to the early eighth century.

(Ankara, Museum of Anatolian Civilizations 90–1. Height *c.* 1.1 m; total width 1.56 m. After Hogarth.)
  CAH III².1, 406–7; Hogarth *et al.*, *Carchemish* I pls. B6–7a; Woolley, *Carchemish* III 193ff.; Orthmann, *USK* 510, Karkemis G/5; Genge, *NSR* ch. 7.3. For the evidence of the inscriptions, Hawkins, *AS* 29 (1979) 157–60.

117. Well preserved basalt stela with flat obverse, apsidal reverse, from Cekke, Syria (north of Aleppo near the Syrian-Turkish frontier). About 760 B.C. On the obverse is seen the bearded pigtailed Storm God wearing a horned helmet, long, fringed robe and upward-pointing shoes, holding the traditional thunderbolt in his left hand and an uncertain object in his right, standing on a bull which he leads with reins. The inscription on the obverse, bottom and top refers to the setting up of the stela by a vassal of Sasturas, and the establishment of offerings to the Storm God ('Celestial Tarkhunzas'). The reverse bears a long, twelve-line Hieroglyphic inscription, of which

reappears as father of *Pisiri*, last king of Carchemish (see **118**) which dates this stela to the preceding generation, about 730 B.C.

The stela was found in no very clear context at Cekke, about 50 km north-north-east of Aleppo and 70 km west-south-west of Carchemish. It is not certain whether it can be taken as evidence of the extension of Carchemish territory to this point, which is so close to Arpad.

(Aleppo Museum 2459. Height 1.62 m; width 38 cm.)

CAH III².1, 406–7; R. D. Barnett, *Iraq* 10 (1948) 124–36, pls. 19–22; Orthmann, *USK* 482, Djekke 1; Genge, *NSR* 157ff. For the evidence of the inscription J. D. Hawkins, *AS* 29 (1979) 160–2 and in greater detail, J. D. Hawkins and A. Morpurgo-Davies, *Festschrift G. Neumann* (ed. J. Tischler; Innsbruck, 1982) 91ff., 96ff.

118. Ruler Orthostats: damaged basalt orthostats with sculpture and inscription, excavated *in situ* on the south-east side of the entrance of the Gatehouse on the Great Staircase, Carchemish. Reign of *Pisiri*, which began before 738 B.C. and ended in 717 B.C. In spite of the damage to this piece, probably inflicted deliberately in antiquity, it remains highly significant. Enough remains of the details of the sculpture to identify the style with that found in the later phase of Sakça Gözü (see **119**) and at Sam'al under Bar-Rakib (see **121**), and thus to date it to the period extending from the later reign of Tiglath-pileser III into the early reign of Sargon, a period when *Pisiri* is known to have been on the throne of Carchemish. So the author's name, missing from the inscription, may be restored with some confidence. In the inscription he names his father as Sasturas, doubtless the same man as the vizier of Kamanis on CEKKE (see **117**). The dynastic sequence drawn from the Carchemish inscriptions, Astiruwas – Yariris – Kamanis – Sasturas – *Pisiri*, cannot be less than three generations, probably at least a century, which provides the approximate chronological framework for the sculptures and inscriptions of Yariris, Kamanis and *Pisiri* together with related styles. It is interesting to note that this work attributed to *Pisiri* combines sculpture of the most developed style with a curiously archaizing inscription. This was to be the last

lines 4–7 are extended round onto the obverse. This records the purchase by Kamanis king of Carchemish and his vizier ('first servant') Sasturas of a city (re)named Kamana, and the settlement in it of fifteen pairs of fathers and sons individually named. This is a particularly fine example of a type of document little known in this period of a land donation or charter. Kamanis is clearly the now reigning successor of Yariris. Sasturas has been identified as Sarduri king of Urartu, but now that it is clear that he is called 'servant' of the king of Carchemish, this is clearly out of the question. He

in the Carchemish series of sculpture since *Pisiri* was carried off to Assyria in 717 B.C. and Carchemish reduced to an Assyrian province.

(London, British Museum WA 125003, 125009. Height 1.17 m; total original width 1.46 m.)

CAH III².1, 412, 418, 423; Woolley, *Carchemish* III pls. 21–22a, b and p. 161; Orthmann, *USK* 499, Karkemis Ba/1–2; Genge, *NSR* 160–7. For the inscription J. D. Hawkins, *AS* 31 (1981) 157–60.

119. Basalt orthostats from the north-west side of the Palace Entrance, Sakça Gözü. Later reign of Tiglath-Pileser III or reign of Sargon, later eighth century B.C. In spite of their well-preserved state the sculptures of Sakça Gözü remain somewhat enigmatic since no explanatory inscription was found with them. Thus it is not clear to which ancient state the site belonged: it lies almost equidistant from Zincirli

118

119

a

b

120a

120

and Maraş but could also have belonged to the borders of Kummukh (Commagene). Of particular interest is the figure of the ruler, which shows details of rendering comparable with those visible on the fragmentary *Pisiri* figure from Carchemish (**118**), particularly the beard, posture, and folds of the garments. On the other hand the figure differs rather markedly from that of Bar-Rakib of Sam'al (**121**) especially in the face, hair and beard style, and head gear. This speaks against the attribution of these sculptures to the Zincirli group, although they share many common features and are likely to be contemporary. The presentation of the ruler is, however, significantly repeated in the following example, **120a**. Compare also the four-winged griffin with cone and situla with the fragmentary figure supporting the ruler on **118**; the latter is undoubtedly to be restored as a similar being. Compare also the

ivory caryatid griffin, **128e**. The attendant holds the sceptre reversed, perhaps to show that he carries it on behalf of the ruler and does not wield it himself.

(Ankara, Museum of Anatolian Civilizations 10112, 10113, 18051, 10117, 1808. Height 90 cm; total length (**a**) 99 cm, (**b**) 1.31 m. Drawing, J. D. Hawkins.)

CAH III².1, 423; J. Garstang, *Liverpool Annals* I (1908) 108–9, pl. 40.1–2; E. Akurgal, *Art of the Hittites* (London, 1962) pl. 134; Orthmann, *USK* 530–1, Sakcagözü A/1–2 and A/5–7; Genge, *NSR* 150–3.

120. (a) Colossal limestone figure excavated in the Lion Gate, Malatya. Later eighth century B.C. This statue was found without qualifying inscription and in curious circumstances, in that after being dislodged from its podium in one of the chambers of the gatehouse, it had

121

been formally buried in a 'grave' in the ruins of the gate. A comparison with the relief figure of the Sakça Gözü ruler (**119**) shows that this is essentially the same figure in the round and much enlarged. The wide distribution of the early Neo-Hittite ruler figure (cf. **107–11**) cautions us against identifying the Sakça Gözü and Malatya figures as representations of the same individual solely on the grounds of this resemblance. Yet it has been pointed out that there was one known ruler who could have reigned in Malatya and Sakça Gözü at the same time, namely *Mutallu* of Kummukh, to whom Sargon II presented Melid (the ancient Malatya) in 712 B.C. before he deposed him for disloyalty in 708 B.C. That both these anonymous figures represent him remains possible.

(Ankara, Museum of Anatolian Civilizations 56. Height 3.8 m.)
  CAH III².1, 423; L. Delaporte, *Malatya* (Paris, 1940) 35ff., pls. 26–31; Orthmann, *USK* 522, Malatya A/12; Genge, *NSR* 152.

(**b**) Fragments of head and shoulders of white limestone statue and its inscribed base,

excavated in the gate-chamber of the South Gate, Carchemish. Mid-eighth century B.C. The statue originally sat on its base on a further podium in the north recess of the east side of the South Gate. It appears to have been deliberately destroyed in antiquity, perhaps by Sargon's army at the capture of the city in 717 B.C. Similarities between this fragment and the *Pisiri* figure (**118**), as well as its apparent lateness of style suggest an attribution to *Pisiri* himself. But an uncertain reading on the fragmentary base suggests on the contrary the possibility of an attribution to *Pisiri*'s predecessor Kamanis.

(Ankara, Museum of Anatolian Civilizations. Height of statue fragment 85 cm.)
  CAH III².1, 412; Woolley, *Carchemish* II pl. B27a, A13a; Orthmann, *USK* 512, Karkemis J/1; Genge, *NSR* 167.

121. Basalt portal orthostat, excavated *in situ* on the east side of the entrance of the *Nördlicher Hallenbau*, Zincirli, 730–720 B.C. The relief shows Bar-Rakib son of *Panammu*, identified by the Aramaic inscription, seated on his throne facing a standing scribe. The dedication is to Ba'al-Harran, the Moon God Sin, whose symbol appears between the two figures. The later dynasty of Sam'al, successors of Kilamuwa (**115**), have left a number of Aramaic inscriptions on sculpture, which give an interesting history of the state over five generations: QRL – *Panammu* (I) – Bar-Ṣur – *Panammu* (II) – Bar-Rakib, the last of whom succeeded his father *Panammu* when he died fighting for the Assyrians at the siege of Damascus in 733–732 B.C. Bar-Rakib himself, in a reign of indeterminate length, carried out a substantial programme of construction, adorning the buildings with a series of sculptured orthostats in the latest Zincirli style. In his depictions of himself, he showed a figure quite distinct in appearance and clothing from the typical late Neo-Hittite ruler figures, as seen in **118–20**, who were clearly his contemporaries. These differences mark a continued distinction between Hittite and Aramaean styles, although by this date the two originally distinct sculptural traditions had more or less fused into a single style.

(Berlin, Staatliche Museen (East) VA 2817. Height 1.12 m; width 1.16 m.)

CAH III².1, 416; von Luschan, *Sendschirli* IV 345ff., fig. 255, pl. 40; Orthmann, *USK* 545, Zincirli F/1; Genge, *NSR* 145–50. For the inscription most recently J. C. L. Gibson, *Textbook of Syrian Semitic Inscriptions* II, *Aramaic Inscriptions* (Oxford, 1975) 93, no. 17.

122. (**a**) Colossal basalt figure bearing a 34-line Aramaic inscription on the skirt, found at Gerçin, near Zincirli. Early eighth century B.C. The author of the inscription is *Panammu* son of QRL, who was probably the great-grandfather of Bar-Rakib (**121**). His father QRL

122a

(vocalization of this apparently non-Aramaic name is unknown) also seems to have reigned in Sam'al, and the four-generation dynasty preceding Bar-Rakib must ascend about a century from 730 B.C., which means that QRL must have succeeded Kilamuwa (**115**) fairly closely. The inscription dedicating the statue to the Storm God Hadad describes the reign of *Panammu* as a time of peace and prosperity, but also contains hints of a darker past and future.

(Berlin, Staatliche Museen (East) VA 2882. Height 2.85 m; width at belt 1.2 m. Photograph, after von Luschan.)

CAH III².1, 408; von Luschan, *Sendschirli* I 49ff., fig. 19, pl. 6; Orthmann, *USK* 484, Gerçin 1; Genge, *NSR* 143–5. For the inscription most recently Gibson, *op. cit.* 121, 60–76, no. 13.

(**b**) *Panammu* II Statue. Lower part of colossal basalt statue bearing 23-line Aramaic inscription, found by the excavators of Zincirli in 1888 at Tahtalı Pınar, originally from Gerçin(?), 732 B.C. The period of dynastic history between *Panammu* I and Bar-Rakib is found on this inscribed funerary statue set up by Bar-Rakib for his father *Panammu* (II) son of Bar-Ṣur in 732 B.C. Here it is related how Bar-Ṣur was killed in a bloody dynastic struggle and *Panammu* fled to the protection of Tiglath-pileser III, who reinstated him in Sam'al. *Panammu* II as a loyal vassal 'ran at the wheel of his lord Tiglath-pileser', and died fighting for him at Damascus, whereupon 'the whole army of his lord, the king of Assyria, wept for him'.

The colossal Hadad statue with its apparently funerary inscription of *Panammu* I and the inscribed memorial colossus of *Panammu* II appear to be part of a tradition which can be traced back to the colossal deified ruler, perhaps Gabbar (above, **111a**).

(Berlin, Staatliche Museen (East) VA 3012. Preserved height 1.93 m. Photograph, after von Luschan.)

CAH III².1, 412, 414–15; von Luschan, *Senschirli* I 48, 53ff., figs. 16, 17, pl. 8; Orthmann, *USK* 534, Tahtalı Pınar 1; for the inscription, Gibson, *op. cit.* 76–86, no. 14.

123. Rock relief *in situ* on cliff near abundant spring at Ivriz in the north foothills of the Taurus range, near modern Ereğli. Later eighth century B.C. Excavated sites of the Neo-Hittite period on the Anatolian plateau are rare, and surviving monuments scarce except for a group dating from the second half of the eighth century B.C. Among these the sculptures associated with Warpalawas of Tuwana (= classical Tyana, the modern province of Niğde) are outstanding. This rock relief, deservedly one of the best known monuments of its age, shows on the right the small figure of the king Warpalawas in an attitude of adoration; and on the left the massive figure of the god, 'Tarkhunzas of the Vineyard' as he is named on another Warpalawas inscription, from whose feet grain and vines spring up. The god is shown in traditional gear rendered in modernized style, his axe and thunderbolt replaced by symbols of generous fertility. The king is richly dressed and the carefully rendered details of his fibula and the embroidery of his clothing are striking. Warpalawas is attested as tributary to Tiglath-pileser III in 738 and 732 B.C. and was still on the throne in about 710 B.C., doubtless one of the most prominent of the surviving Neo-Hittite kings of the Anatolian plateau, caught between the pressures of Phrygia and Assyria.

(Height of god *c.* 6 m.)

CAH III².1, 413, 421; Orthmann, *USK* 487, Ivriz 1. For the inscriptions Meriggi, *Manuale* II.1, 15–16, no. 7.

124. Storm God Stela, of black basalt, recently discovered lying face down at the threshold of the Akmedrese (Dışarı Camii). End of eighth century B.C. This stela, a well executed example of a type traditional since the tenth century B.C., is of particular interest since on its side it bears an inscription of Warpalawas' son, who styles himself king. Since Warpalawas can be shown to have still been on the throne in 710/09 B.C., the stela must date later than that, which makes it the latest piece of Neo-Hittite sculpture and Hieroglyphic inscription with a relatively assured date, with the doubtful exception of Karatepe. The Hieroglyphic tradition, terminated in Syria by the destruction of the Hittite states by the Assyrians, seems to have lingered somewhat longer on the Anatolian plateau, but even so, it hardly seems to have survived to about 700 B.C., unless this piece could be a few years later. Standing below the winged disk and rendered with his traditional attributes of axe and thunderbolt in an

Assyrianizing style, this Storm God, like his fellow from Ivriz, has grain and vines springing from his feet, which characterizes him too as 'Tarkhunzas of the Vineyard'. This type of theophany seems to be referred to in an inscription from Tabal, where it is said of this god: 'He came with all goodness, and the corn(?) flourished forth at (his) foot, and the vine was good here' (SULTANHAN stela, with the new fragment, ll. 2–3, §§5–7).

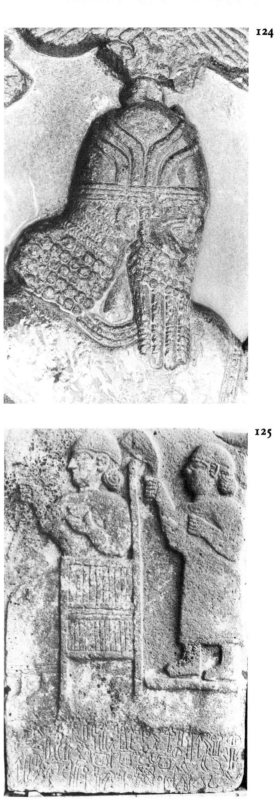

(Niğde Museum. Height 2.18 m; width 1 m.)
  CAH III².1, 423, 429; M. Kalaç, *VIII Türk Tarih Kongresi* 239–43, pls. 135–44.

125. Basalt Ruler orthostat with sculpture and inscription, excavated fallen in the South (Upper) Gate at Karatepe and restored to approximate position on the south-east side, now *in situ*. Beginning of seventh century B.C.(?) The decipherment of the (Hittite) Hieroglyphic Luwian script was confirmed and extended by the discovery, in 1946 at Karatepe in the hills of north-east Cilicia, of a long Hieroglyphic Luwian–(Alphabetic) Phoenician bilingual inscription. This is written on the sculptured gate orthostats of the small hill-top fortress, where the nearly complete bilingual pair from the North (Lower) Gate is duplicated by a somewhat damaged pair from the South

Gate. The inscription is that of a certain Azatiwatas, vassal of the king of Adana, who built the fortress and named it Azatiwataya after himself, and in it he boasts at length of the benefits of peace and security which he bestowed upon Adana. The dating of the inscription and sculpture has been debated ever since their discovery, and alternatives ranging from the early ninth to the early seventh centuries B.C. have been suggested and defended both by historical and stylistic arguments. This relief shows a seated ruler, presumably Azatiwatas himself, with an attendant. A section of the Hieroglyphic inscription (Ho. XXX, 149–XXXII, 161) runs across the bottom of this slab.

(Height 1.25 m; width 88 cm.)
  CAH III².1, 430–1; H. Cambel, *Oriens* 1 (1948) pl. 6b; U. B. Alkım, *Revue Hittite et Asianique* 9/50 (1948–9) fig. 11; Orthmann, *USK* 496, Karatepe B/19. For the Hieroglyphic inscription most recently Hawkins and Morpurgo-Davies, *AS* 28 (1978) 114–18; the Phoenician, F. Bron, *Karatepe* (Geneva–Paris, 1979).

126. Basalt orthostats with Banquet Scene, excavated in the South Gate at Karatepe, fallen from plinths and restored to their approximate positions, now *in situ*. (a) beginning of seventh century B.C.(?), (b) early ninth century B.C., reused (?). The sculptures of Karatepe fall into two markedly separate styles: style 2, represen-

ted by **125** and the left-hand slab here; and style 1 by the right-hand slab here. Characteristic of style 1 are the extraordinary facial features seen here and motifs and details of style, all of which seem to have close links with the early Aramaean art of the earlier ninth century B.C., especially that of Zincirli (cf. **113**). Style 2 on the other hand looks more like crude provincial renderings of the assimilated Hittite–Aramaean style of the later eighth century B.C. Recent studies favour the view that Azatiwatas himself belongs to the beginning of the seventh century B.C. and that sculptures of style 2 are his work; while sculptures of style 1, with their strong ninth-century links, are best regarded as reused work, perhaps brought from the neighbouring site of Domuztepe. The feasting ruler on the right-hand slab would not represent Azatiwatas, who is perhaps shown on **125**, but instead an earlier ninth-century ruler on the throne of Adana.

CAH III².1, 430–1; Cambel, *loc. cit.* pl. 3a, b; Alkım, *loc. cit.* fig. 7b, c; Orthmann, *USK* 494, Karatepe B/1–2. For a recent elucidation of the sculpture I. Winter, *AS* 29 (1979) 115–51 and J. Deshayes, *RA* 75 (1981) 32–46. For the history, Hawkins, *AS* 29 (1979) 153–7; P. Garelli, *RA* 75 (1981) 54–60. General: Hawkins and Orthmann, 'Karatepe' (*Reallexikon der Assyriologie* V/5–6 (1980) s.v., 409–14.

127. (a) Bronze statuette of a rider and camel found at Camirus on Rhodes in 1864. This is a fine example of a whole series of bronze objects found in western contexts that have been attributed by style or subject, or both as here, to Syrian metal workshops; later eighth or early seventh century B.C.

(London, British Museum WA 135845. Height 8 cm.)

H. B. Walters, *Catalogue of Bronzes . . . British Museum* (1899) no. 222.

(b) Assur lead strip *a*, bearing Hieroglyphic text, excavated by the Deutsche Orient-Gesellschaft expedition to Assur 1903–1913. Late eighth century or early seventh century B.C. Seven lead strips were found, all rolled up, including two rolled together, inscribed in two registers on either side with the texts of six letters: four short (strips *a–d*), one long (strip *e*); and one extra-long (strips *f+g*). They are all with the possible exception of strip *e*, written by a certain Taksalas to various people, and consist principally of demands that certain goods and commodities should be sent. The presence of the letters in Assur and a reference to Carchemish in strip *a* suggest that the correspondence might have passed between these two cities. These letters are the sole survivors of what we must assume to have been a common type of document, the Hieroglyphic Luwian letter, and they offer a range of vocabulary and even grammatical forms not attested in other kinds of Hieroglyphic inscription. They are now paralleled by the recent discovery at Kululu near Kayseri of other Hieroglyphic lead strips, which consist of economic documents, issues of commodities to named recipients.

(Original perished. 9.9 cm × 3.6 cm. Photograph, after Andrae.)

W. Andrae, *Hettitische Inschriften auf Bleistreifen aus Assur* (WVDOG no. 46; Leipzig, 1924); for the text, Meriggi, *Manuale* II.1, 135–6, no. 37.

(c) Assur ostracon, bearing Aramaic text,

also excavated at Assur by the Deutsche Orient-Gesellschaft expedition. Mid-seventh century B.C. The text consists of a letter from Bel-eṭir to Pir'i-Amurri, both of whom seem to have been high officials of Ashurbanipal, king of Assyria, and the contents appear to relate to

the revolt of Ashurbanipal's brother, Shamash-shuma-ukin, king of Babylon. The letter is one of the earliest examples of cursive Aramaic written with pen and ink.

(Berlin, Staatliche Museen (East) VA. 42 cm × 60 cm. Photograph, after Lidzbarski.)

(British Museum WA (ND 7907). 84 cm × 56 cm.)
M. E. L. Mallowan, *Nimrud and its Remains* II (London, 1966) 485–6, pl. 381; I. Winter, *Metr. Mus. Journal* 11 (1976) 52.

(b) Carved ivory pyxis from the 'Burnt Palace' at Nimrud, showing a lion-hunt in a landscape of olive trees. It is carved in the North Syrian style of the second half of the eighth century B.C.

(London, British Museum WA 118173. Height 8.5 cm.)
R. D. Barnett, *The Nimrud Ivories* (London, 1975) 190, pl. 18; Winter, *loc. cit.* fig. 13.

(c) Carved ivory pyxis, discoloured by fire, from the 'Burnt Palace' at Nimrud. Procession of musicians with double pipes, timbrel and psaltery approaching an enthroned goddess through a grove of palms and lotus trees. Traces of a Phoenician or Aramaic inscription on the base; second half of the eighth century B.C.

(London, British Museum WA 118179. Height 6.7 cm.)
Barnett, *op. cit.* 191, pls. 16, 17, 132.18, 20.

(d) Carved ivory top of a flywhisk handle from the 'Burnt Palace' at Nimrud. The posture

M. Lidzbarski. *Altaramäische Urkunden aus Assur* (WVDOG no. 35; Leipzig, 1921) 5–15; for the text, most recently, Gibson, *op. cit.* 98–110, no. 20.

128. (a) Carved ivory bed or couch end from Room SW7 in Fort Shalmaneser at Nimrud. The human figures, each with a pail and cone (symbols of fertility) may be wearing garments fortified with scale armour; the inner pair are bearded, the outer clean-shaven. Winter has suggested that carved ivories in this style were produced in the same cultural context as the Zincirli and Sakça Gözü reliefs in the third quarter of the eighth century B.C.

of the young men, with Egyptian-style head-dresses, suggests that they may be dancing round the 'sacred tree' behind them. In their left hands they hold tendrils from the tree; second half of the eighth century B.C. Compare the flywhisk shown in **119**.

(London, British Museum WA 118196. Height 13.2 cm.)

Barnett, *op. cit.* 213, pl. 88.1.

(**e**) Openwork carved ivory winged genius with a griffin's head raising his arms as a 'supporter', perhaps on a piece of temple furniture; from Toprak Kale, near Van, in eastern Anatolia. This motif originated centuries earlier in Syria and the style of the figure suggests it was made in a North Syrian workshop of the eighth century B.C. Compare **118, 119**.

(London, British Museum WA 118953. Height 11 cm.)

Barnett, *op. cit.* 229, pl. 131; M. N. van Loon, *Urartian Art* (Istanbul, 1966) 134–5.

6. PHOENICIA AND THE PUNIC WORLD

DOMINIQUE COLLON

The Phoenicians were a branch of the Semitic Canaanites, settled along the narrow, fertile coastal strip of what is present-day Lebanon and southern Syria, and on the offshore islands. The Lebanon, Nosairi and Ansariye mountains form a natural barrier separating this coastal belt from the Syrian hinterland and there are only a few roads through these mountains linking the two areas. As a result, the Phoenicians turned their attention to maritime trade and their name was given to them by the Greeks with whom they came into contact, probably in the second half of the second millennium B.C.; it is first found in Homer and seems to have denoted a dark red, purple or brown colour (see also below, **134**).

The Phoenician coast has many natural harbours, four of which were particularly important. To the north lay the island city of Arvad which extended onto the mainland opposite and thus controlled one of the passes across the mountains and the road through the Homs Gap between the Lebanon and Nosairi mountains (**129**). Byblos (Gebeil) was a fine natural harbour used for trade with Egypt from about 3000 B.C. onwards. Sidon, another fine harbour, and Tyre (**130**), which was also an island foundation, stood north and south of the Leontes (Litani) River which marks the southern limits of the Lebanon range and the gateway to the Bekaa.

In this section the culture of the Phoenicians in the first millennium B.C., down to about 525 B.C., will be illustrated. During this period they established an overseas trading empire and founded a number of maritime colonies on Cyprus and along the Mediterranean and Atlantic coasts. These western extensions of Phoenician culture are known as Punic and the most famous was Carthage which will be discussed at greater length below (**138–141**).

The map shows the location of the main Phoenician cities and other sites along the Levant coast and further inland. The coastal strip is never more than 20 km wide and the part of it known as Phoenicia is only some 300 km long. Seasonal water-courses flowing down to the sea from the mountains can hamper north–south communications and the routes inland across the mountains are few, with the Homs Gap providing the easiest access to the interior.

GENERAL BIBLIOGRAPHY

D. Harden, *The Phoenicians* (London, 1962)
D. Baramki, *Phoenicia and the Phoenicians* (Beirut, 1961)
S. Moscati, *The World of the Phoenicians* (London, 1968)
A. Parrot, M. H. Chéhab and S. Moscati, *Les Phéniciens* (Paris, 1975).

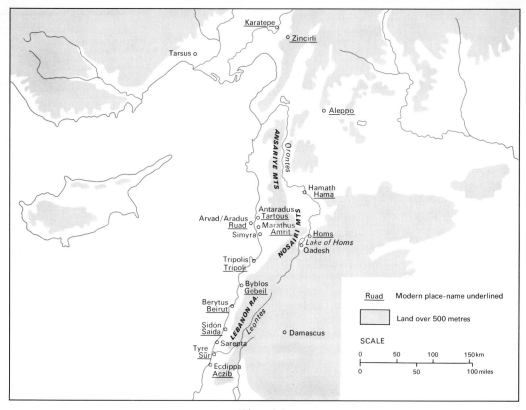

Karatepe
Zincirli
Tarsus o

Aleppo

ANSARIYE MTS

Orontes

Hamath
Hama

Antaradus
Arvad/Aradus Tartous
Ruad Marathus
Simyra Amrit Homs
Lake of Homs
Qadesh

NOSAIRI MTS

Tripolis
Tripoli

Byblos
Gebeil

Berytus
Beirut

LEBANON RA.

Leontes

Sidón
Saida

Damascus

Tyre Sarepta
Sür

Ecdippa
Aczib

Ruad   Modern place-name underlined

Land over 500 metres

SCALE

0   50   100   150 km

0   50   100 miles

5. Phoenicia

129. View of the harbour walls of Arvad, one of the most important Phoenician cities. It was situated on an island about 3 km offshore. Its modern name is Ruad and the Greeks called it Aradus. The island was only about 1,500 m in circumference and the city was densely populated. Its suburbs extended onto the mainland (Antaradus, present-day Tartous); it founded cities along the coast and controlled others. The inhabitants of Arvad were intrepid warriors and are recorded as having sent a contingent to the Battle of Qadesh in 1300 B.C. The huge blocks of the wall which originally surrounded the city (see also **131a**) and protected its harbours are still to be seen. The strategic importance of the island is well attested by the fact that it was the last Levantine stronghold of the Crusaders.

H. Frost, *Annales archéologiques arabes syriennes* 14 (1964) 67–74 and 16 (1966) 13–28.

130. (a) Tyre, as it appeared in 1938. It was one of the greatest of the Phoenician cities, and, like Arvad, located on an island. It is now linked to the mainland by a narrow strip of land: this represents the silt which has built up on either side of the mole constructed by Alexander the Great when he besieged the city in 332 B.C. The island had harbours to north and south and it was from these that the Tyrians set out to establish colonies overseas, the most famous of which was Carthage (**138–141**). A great source of wealth was Tyrian purple (**134**).

Harden, *Phoenicians* pl. 3; see also N. Jidejian, *Tyre through the Ages* (Beirut, 1969), for further information.

(**b**) Tyre, as it was depicted in the ninth century B.C. on one of the bronze strips which decorated the gates set up by the Assyrian king Shalmaneser III (859–824 B.C.) in his residence at Imgur-Bel (Balawat) in northern Iraq. The strip shows the fortified island city, Tyrian ships sailing across to the mainland (see also **131**), and Tyrians bearing tribute before the Assyrian king, preceded by Assyrian officials. The stela showing the subjugation of a Tyrian king in the reign of Esarhaddon of Assyria in the seventh century B.C. is illustrated in **51**.

(London, British Museum WA 124661. Height of frieze 8.5 cm.)

L. W. King, *Bronze Reliefs from the Gates of Shalmaneser* (London, 1915) pls. 13–14; Harden, *Phoenicians* pl. 47.

131. (a) A series of limestone reliefs, which decorated the palace of the Assyrian king Sargon II (722–705 B.C.) at Khorsabad in northern Iraq, shows Phoenician ships carrying huge logs of wood and towing others. There were ample supplies of suitable timber in the mountains of Phoenicia, coveted by the Assyrians and used by the Phoenicians to build the ships for their trading ventures. In the reliefs, the ships are being rowed towards the mouth of the Orontes, up the coast (indicated at the top of the relief), past the islands of Tyre (to the right – see **130**) and Arvad (to the left), whose massive walls are depicted (**129**). The ships are of the type known as *hippoi* (see also **130b**), with horse-headed prows, and the oarsmen face the direction in which they are rowing; one example is masted. The shipping lanes are guarded by a winged human-headed bull or *lamassu* – better known as the guardian of Assyrian palace entrances – and by a winged bull, probably a symbol of the weather-god Adad. Fish and marine creatures are depicted in the waves.

(Paris, Louvre AO 19889. Height 2.83 m.)

P. E. Botta, *Monument de Ninive* 1 (Paris, 1849) pls. 32–3; Harden, *Phoenicians* pl. 48; P. Albenda, *A Mediterranean Seascape from Khorsabad* (Assur 3/3, 1983).

(**b**) Other types of vessels are depicted on Assyrian reliefs from the palace of Sennacherib at Nineveh, illustrating the flight from Tyre of Luli, king of Tyre and Sidon, in 701 B.C. Both types of ship have an upper deck and two banks of oars (the oarsmen face the stern with its double steering-oars). One type of ship has a sharp prow for ramming.

(Reproduced from Layard, *Monuments* 1 71, courtesy of the Trustees of the British Museum. The scene is completed, on the right, by a drawing showing the city of Tyre but the actual reliefs are no longer extant.)

R. D. Barnett, *Antiquity* 32 (1958) 226, pl. 22b; Harden, *Phoenicians* pl. 50.

132a

132b

132c

132d

132. The Assyrians not only carried off wood from the Levant. In the store-rooms of their palaces at Arslan Tash, Khorsabad and especially Nimrud large quantities of ivories were found, often elements of furniture, which were mostly manufactured in the workshops of Syria and Phoenicia. The styles of the different workshops are distinctive but there are many cases where attribution is difficult. The selection presented here probably came from Phoenician workshops and dates to the eighth century B.C.

(a) One of a number of similar plaques, found at various sites, fitted with dowels. A woman, wearing an Egyptian type of wig, is shown at a balustraded window. Found in the North-West Palace at Nimrud.

(London, British Museum WA 118159. Height 9 cm.)

(b) Plaque showing a winged sphinx surrounded by ornamental palmettes. This is a Phoenician adaptation of an Egyptian theme: note particularly the way the double Egyptian crown has been distorted so as to be barely recognizable. This plaque illustrates the *ajouré* technique of ivory carving. Found in Fort Shalmaneser at Nimrud.

(London, British Museum WA 134322. Height 7 cm.)

(c) Two seated figures, holding *was* sceptres, face each other on either side of a cartouche. At first sight this plaque seems to have close affinities with Egypt; however the elements are used in a way no Egyptian would have dreamt of using them (e.g., the *ankh* beneath the thrones), and the inscription within the cartouche is made up of pseudo-hieroglyphs. The cut-out areas held coloured glass inlays, and this and similar ivories must have come from a workshop where craftsmen in glass and ivory worked side by side. Found in the North-West Palace at Nimrud. A very similar relief was found on Samos.

(London, British Museum WA 118120. Height 7.3 cm.)

(d) Two winged griffins are carved in high relief within an ornamental palmette. The ivory was partly gilt and inlaid with lapis lazuli and other semi-precious stones and coloured glass. Found in the North-West Palace at Nimrud.

(London, British Museum WA 118157. Height 14 cm.)
R. D. Barnett, *A Catalogue of the Nimrud Ivories in the British Museum* (London, 1975) (a) C.12, pl. 4; (b) Suppl. 33, pl. 134; (c) C.48, pl. 8; (d) D.9, pl. 9.

133. Metalwork was also carried off as booty by the Assyrians and many decorated bronze bowls of eighth-century B.C. Phoenician workmanship were found in the Nimrud store-rooms (a and b). Phoenician bowls were also items of trade and have been found as far afield as Crete (see under b), Cyprus (see **210**) and Italy (c) in tombs of the eighth and seventh centuries.

(a) A central star pattern, ornamented with silver studs, is surrounded by bands depicting rows of animals.

(London, British Museum WA N.1. Diam. 22.7 cm.)

(b) A central rosette is surrounded by concentric bands of 'marsh pattern' which form a base for confronted winged sphinxes and standards, some of which are topped by winged scarabs. A bowl with closely related design was found in the Idaean cave in Crete and was probably an import from Phoenicia.

(London, British Museum WA 115505 (=N.9). Diam. 21 cm.)

(c) This silver bowl depicts the victorious Pharaoh in the centre, surrounded by two concentric bands of pseudo-hieroglyphs. Between them is a frieze of four boats containing deities, alternating with four papyrus clumps in which Isis suckles Horus. The original owner's name, Eshmanazar, has been inscribed in Phoenician. Found in the Bernardini tomb in Praeneste in Italy, together with other imported objects including a silver gilt Phoenician bowl; the tomb has been dated *c.* 680–660 B.C.

(Rome, Museo Preistorico. Diam. 19.5 cm. After Harden.)
O. Montelius, *La civilisation primitive en Italie* II (Stockholm, 1904) pl. 369. 7a and b; Harden, *Phoenicians* 189, fig. 54.
For these bowls see: Harden, *Phoenicians* 186–90, pl. 46; M. Cristofani, *L'arte degli Etruschi – produzione e consumo* (Turin, 1978) 39ff. with copious references.

134. Yet another product of Phoenicia was the purple dye which was extracted from the murex. Huge heaps of shells, for instance near Tyre and Sidon and at various Punic sites, testify to the importance of the industry which was a Phoenician monopoly. The shell illustrated here is not a murex, but a tridacna, from the Red Sea. Decorated examples have been found at many Phoenician and Punic sites and were carried off as booty to Assyria. The present example comes from Rhodes.

133c

(Karlsruhe, Badisches Landesmuseum 68/38a. Width 21.5 cm.)

R. A. Stucky, *The Engraved Tridacna Shells* (*Dedalo* 19, 1974; Sao Paulo) no. 68; Boardman, *GO* 72, fig. 58 and 271, n. 139.

135. (a) A limestone stela depicting, in relief, a lion standing on mountains and supporting a god who brandishes a weapon and grasps a small lion by the hind legs; above is a winged sun disk and a crescent and disk. The lion is inscribed with a dedication to the god Shadrapha. The stela should probably be dated to the sixth century B.C. but earlier dates have also been suggested. Found at Marathus (Amrit).

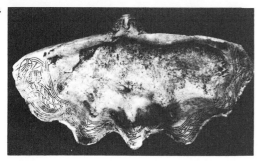

34a

34b

135a

(Paris, Louvre AO 22247. Height 1.7 m.)
Collection De Clercq: Catalogue des antiquités assyriennes II (Paris, 1903) pl. 36.

(**b**) An alabaster relief with a design of typically Phoenician palmettes between bands of guilloche above a panel depicting a couchant sphinx. Although an eighth- to seventh-century date has been proposed for this relief, the curved ends of the sphinx's wings probably indicate Persian influence and a sixth- to fifth-century date. It was found at Aradus (Ruad – see **129**).

(Paris, Louvre AO 4836. Height 99 cm.)
G. Contenau, *Les antiquités orientales* (Paris, 1930) pl. 35.

These two examples of relief sculpture show that the Phoenicians were accomplished craftsmen in this medium also. The earlier Ahiram sarcophagus (**136b**) and the later Sidonian sarcophagi of the fifth century onwards, indicate that the Phoenicians were not daunted by scale.

136. (a) The same type of palmette as on **135b** appears in a composite form beneath a winged disk on an earlier cylinder seal, here illustrated in its modern impression. Such seals were impressed on clay tablets inscribed in cuneiform, and a seal on a tablet found at Nimrud in Assyria, and dating to about 650 B.C., also depicts a palmette tree and a monkey and may have come from the same workshop. The present seal is inscribed in Aramaic with the name of its owner (Shadah or Sharah), and monkeys are shown playing the flute on either side of a figure in Assyrian dress who grasps the fore-paws of two griffins.

(Private collection. Height 2.55 cm.)

Cf. M. E. L. Mallowan, *Nimrud and its Remains* (London, 1966) fig. 134:8.

136

136

The seal's alphabetic inscription brings us to the greatest contribution of the Phoenicians to civilization: the diffusion of the alphabet. This is discussed in greater detail elsewhere. The famous bi-lingual Karatepe reliefs helped in the decipherment of hieroglyphic Hittite (see **125**). Another long Phoenician inscription is that of Kilamuwa at Zincirli (**115**).

(**b**) The Ahiram sarcophagus, traditionally dated to the thirteenth century B.C., was inscribed on one side of the lid about 1000 B.C. with one of the earliest inscriptions in the Phoenician alphabetic script (**376a**). Recently Edith Porada has demonstrated that there are good grounds for dating the sarcophagus itself to about 1000 B.C. The lid is decorated with two lions and two figures, perhaps the king and his son. The sarcophagus rests on four lions and the reliefs which decorate it show the king seated on a sphinx throne (see also **141c, d** and **144**); attendants and mourning women make up the remainder of the scenes which were originally painted. Found at Byblos (Gebeil).

(Beirut, National Museum. Length (without lion projections) 2.30 m. After Jidejian.)
Harden, *Phoenicians* 118–19, fig. 34 and pl. 15; N. Jidejian, *Byblos through the Ages* (Beirut, 1968) pls. 92–7; E. Porada, *Journal of Ancient Near Eastern Society of Columbia University* 5 (1973) 354–72.

137. A growing population and increasing Assyrian cupidity were two of the reasons which led the Phoenicians to establish trading colonies overseas. They already had close ties with Cyprus and probably had a colony at Citium called Qartikhadast, while Utica, in present-day Tunisia, was traditionally founded as early as 1100 B.C. The Phoenicians chose good harbours which could easily be defended on the landward side, and established their Punic colonies along the North African coast, in Sicily, Malta, Sardinia, Spain, and on the Atlantic coast on either side of the Straits of Gibraltar, at Gades (Cadiz), and Lixus and Mogador. Although their earliest settlements had probably been seasonal anchorages with few structures ashore, their later colonies were protected by strong walls which have survived at a number of sites. The examples illustrated here come from the island of Motya off the west coast of Sicily. Fine ashlar masonry, often with drafted edges, was used for the town wall (**a**).

A coarser type, which came to be known as *opus punicum*, consisted of large stone uprights with rubble fill between (**b**) and was often used for houses, as here where slots for doorframes can be seen in the uprights.

Cf. Harden, *Phoenicians* 37, pls. 13–14; N. Sandars, *The Sea Peoples* (London, 1978) 146–7, 151ff.

138. Carthage, the most famous Punic city, was traditionally founded in 814 B.C. by Elissa (Dido), a refugee from Tyre. The Carthage promontory is a rocky headland with two large natural harbours on either side, the lakes of Ariana (Sebkhet er Riana) and Tunis, both now largely land-locked. Traces of the earliest occupation have to a great extent disappeared under later building but as Carthage grew, so it extended along the coast. Shipping between the east and west Mediterranean basins had to pass through Carthaginian waters and Carthage became powerful because of her control of this trade route. Eventually this brought her into conflict with the Etruscans and, later, with the Romans: hence the Punic Wars culminating in the fall of Carthage and its destruction in 146 B.C.

(**a**) Map of the Tunis and Carthage area. The original settlement occupied only a small area of the peninsula, probably at the foot of Cape Carthage (Sidi Bou Said) which provided a good look-out point in all directions.

(**b**) Map of Carthage. The high ground of Cape Carthage is to the north (see **a**). The original settlement probably extended as far as a point south east of Byrsa hill: sixth- and fifth-century sherds have been found in excavations on the coast in this area and wall alignments already seem to have been those of later Punic, Roman and present-day Carthage. There is as yet no evidence of early Punic settlement on the hill of Byrsa but there was a necropolis surrounding it down to the sixth century B.C., which then seems to have been abandoned for three centuries. There is no evidence for a Punic 'lower city'. Recent excavations have established that the city harbours and the eastern part of the Tophet were not in use before the fourth century B.C.

137a

137b

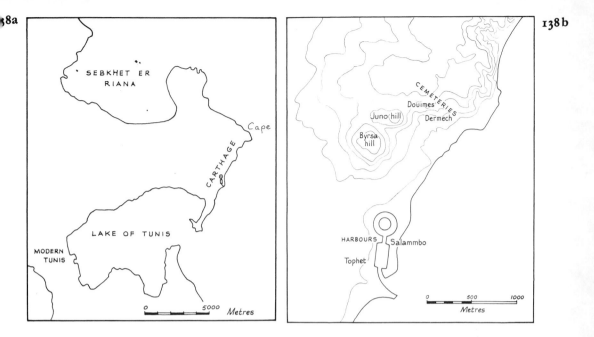

SEBKHET ER RIANA

Cape

CARTHAGE

LAKE OF TUNIS

MODERN TUNIS

0   5000
Metres

CEMETERIES

Doüimes

Juno hill   Dermech

Byrsa hill

HARBOURS   Salammbo

Tophet

0   500   1000
Metres

139a

139b

139. The Tophet or Tanit Precinct at Carthage is one of the few places where early Punic levels have been reached. Here, at Salammbo, a small shrine on bedrock, known as the 'Chapelle Cintas', was associated with cremation burials in urns, and other pottery datable to the eighth century B.C. Later cremation burials were marked by limestone stelae, some of which bore crude designs while others were more elaborate and sometimes inscribed. The burials are all of children and continued until the destruction of the city in 146 B.C. Recent excavations have shown that child sacrifice was common at all periods, and not only at times of national emergency, although sometimes animals were substituted.

(a) A selection of pottery from the Tanit Precinct, Levels I–III. The wares are buff and wheel-made, with occasional simple painted decoration in black, brown or red paint. Eighth to fourth centuries B.C.

(London, British Museum WA 118333–8.)
D. B. Harden, *Iraq* 4 (1937) 59ff.; P. Cintas, *Céramique punique* (Paris, 1950).

(b) A sandstone stela, set in a limestone base and with a limestone plaque let into one face. This plaque bears an eleven-line inscription in Punic script recording seventeen generations of priests of Tanit. The stela is dated to the early fourth century B.C. when limestone was replacing sandstone as a material for the stelae in the Tophet; the inscription, however, records the names of priests who must have lived in the early days of Carthage.

(Height 95 cm. After P. Bartoloni.)
C. G. Picard, *Catalogue du Musée Alaoui*, N.S. 1: *Collections puniques* (Tunis, n.d.) Cb 366; P. Bartoloni, *Le stele archaiche del Tofet di Cartagine* (Rome, 1976) no. 29; *Corpus Ins. Sem.* 1.3, fasc. 1 (1926) no. 3778; Harden, *Phoenicians* pl. 31.
J. G. Février, 'Les sacrifices d'enfants' in *Arch. viv.* 115ff.; Harden, *Phoenicians* 94ff.; L. E. Stager, *The Oriental Institute Annual Report 1977–78* (Chicago) 27–36; *id.* in *Phönizier im Westen* (Madrider Beiträge 8, H. G. Niemeyer, ed.; Mainz, 1982) 155–66.

(c) Aerial photograph of the harbour area, from the north.

(a) after Harden, *Phoenicians* fig. 3; (b) after J. C. Pedley (ed.), *New Light on Ancient Carthage* (Ann Arbor 1980) 134; (c) after *Antiquaries Journal* 55 (1975) pl. 1.)
Harden, *Phoenicians*; B. H. Warmington, *Carthage* (Harmondsworth 1960); G. C. and C. Picard, *The Life and Death of Carthage* (London 1968); summary reports and a bibliography of recent excavations are published by the Institut National d'Archéologie de Tunisie in *CEDAC Carthage Bulletin* annually.

140. Male and female clay masks, dating to the seventh and sixth centuries B.C., have been found at Carthage, in Sardinia and Ibiza. Some are crude but others are extremely sophisticated.

(a) Clay mask from Grave 7 at Tharros in Sardinia. The mask has cut-out eyes and mouth, and suspension holes above the ears. There is a small plaque with a lion's head in relief on the forehead.

(London, British Museum WA 133128. Height 17 cm.)
H. B. Walters, *Catalogue of the Terracottas in the British Museum* (London, 1903) 138, B 393.

(b) Clay female mask in Graeco-Phoenician style; the nose and ears were perforated to receive jewellery. Found in the Dermech cemetery in Carthage.

(Tunis, Bardo Museum. Height 32 cm. After *Arch. viv.* no. 78.)
G. C. Picard, *Sacra Punica* (=*Karthago* 13 (1965/6)).

141. The Punic world used the Phoenician alphabet, and scarab stamp seals were adopted for sealing documents and goods.

(a) An imitation of an Egyptian Ramesside scarab, from Carthage. Scarab-seals of this type have been found on both east and west Mediterranean sites. Seventh century B.C.

(Tunis, Bardo Museum.)
J. Vercoutter, *Les objets égyptiens et égyptisants du mobilier funéraire carthaginois* (Paris, 1945) no. 239.

(b) Green jasper scarab from Tharros in Sardinia. It shows monkeys associated with a distinctive palmette; compare **136a**, but here the tall palmette is of Greek type. Fifth century B.C.

(London, British Museum WA 133322. Length 17 mm.)
H. B. Walters, *Catalogue of Engraved Gems and Cameos in the British Museum* (London, 1929) no. 387, pl. 7.

(c) Green jasper scarab from Ibiza. It depicts a figure seated on a sphinx throne (see also **144**) holding a plant standard before an incense-burner; above are a crescent and disk.

140a

140b

141a

141d

141b

141c

(Barcelona, Archaeological Museum 9346. Length 17 mm.)

J. Boardman, *Escarabeos de piedra procedentes de Ibiza* (Madrid, 1984) no. 67.

(d) The same motif is found on a gold ring from a fifth-century tomb at Utica. It was worn on the deceased's right hand and was probably an heirloom of the sixth century. The seated figure has been interpreted as the god Baal Hammon.

(Utica Museum. Length 19 mm.)

L. Foucher, in *Arch. viv.* 130 (XLIV), 133, 135; and cf. J. Leclant, *ibid.* 95ff.

142. There were several Punic settlements on Sardinia and a large necropolis was excavated at Tharros. In addition to many scarabs (as 141b) much fine jewellery has been found in the tombs, together with many other objects.

(a) The palmette motif already seen on 135b, 136a, 141b, reappears in granulated and repoussé decoration on hinged gold plates with silver bands linking them into a bracelet or head-band. The Tharros cemetery was in use over a long period of time and objects from it are often difficult to date. This piece of jewellery has been dated to the seventh or sixth century. Tharros Grave 8.

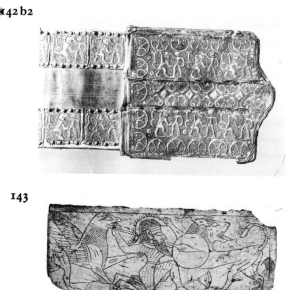

143

(Madrid, Museo Arqueologico Nacional 28562. Length of belt 68.3 cm; width 6.6–7.1 cm.)

A. Blanco Freijeiro, *Archivo Español de Arqueologia* 29 (1956) 3ff.; Harden, *Phoenicians* pl. 96.

143. The style of the lion-combat on the Aliseda belt is derived from the East. That on the ivory plaque illustrated here is more Greek and indicates the variety of styles at the disposal of Punic craftsmen. This, and many other ivories, were found in tumuli in the Carmona district of Spain: some are combs showing gigantic hares being attacked by lions and an identically-shaped comb, but decorated with an Egyptian sphinx, a bull and lotus blossom, was found in Carthage. These ivories have been dated to the sixth century B.C.

(New York, Hispanic Society of America D513. Length 12.7 cm.)

On the Carmona ivories, and on an example from Samos, B. Freyer-Schauenburg, *Madrider Mitteilungen* 7 (1966) 89ff.; Boardman, *GO* 213.

(London, British Museum WA 133392. Length 13.2 cm.)

F. H. Marshall, *Catalogue of the Jewellery, Greek, Etruscan, and Roman in the Departments of Antiquities, British Museum* (London, 1911) nos. 1542 and 1539–40, pls. 24, 25; Harden, *Phoenicians* pl. 104.

(**b**) A gold belt also has the distinctive palmette in granulation at each end, framing heroes in conflict with lions – a motif which is repeated along the full length of the belt. It was part of the Aliseda Treasure, found in Spain in 1920, which can also be dated to the seventh or sixth centuries B.C.

144. (**a**) The alabaster figure from Galera, near Granada, in Spain, shows the mixture of styles we have come to expect from Phoenician and Punic works. The sphinxes which support the throne wear the double crown of Upper and Lower Egypt but the guilloches round their necks are Syrian. Sphinx thrones can be traced back to an ivory from Megiddo of the thirteenth century B.C. and to the Ahiram sarcophagus which may date to about 1000 B.C. (**136b**); we have already seen them on seals **141c, d**.

(Madrid, Museo Arqueologico Nacional 33438. Height 17.8 cm.)

Harden, *Phoenicians* pl. 72.

144b

(**b**) An actual sphinx throne was found in the third-century temple of Eshmun in Sidon. Phoenician and Punic art was not only eclectic, it was also, paradoxically, conservative.

(After Parrot *et al.*)

M. Dunand, *Bulletin du Musée de Beyrouth* 20 (1967) 42f. and pls. 4, 6; A. Parrot, M. Chéhab, S. Moscati, *Les Phéniciens* (Paris, 1975) pl. 116; N. Jidejian, *Sidon through the Ages* (Beirut, 1971) 59ff., pl. 180.

7. ISRAEL AND JUDAH

P. R. S. MOOREY

Whereas the history and culture of other Near Eastern countries in the early Iron Age has been almost entirely reconstructed in modern times from archaeological evidence, that of Israel and Judah survived in the Old Testament narrative. Historically this is a uniquely detailed, if at times very selective, account which archaeological sources have done little to amplify. The Assyrians' royal records and reliefs sculptured on palace walls in Assyria vividly document their campaigns against Israel and Judah, whilst some marked changes in local architecture and minor crafts, like potting, may be attributed to the impact of Assyrian cultural overlords. In the region itself, by contrast, the evidence of monuments is very meagre. Very few rulers of Israel and Judah, and none of the United Monarchy, are yet recorded in contemporary extra-Biblical inscriptions. The historical and cultural value of the 'Moabite Stone' and the 'Siloam Inscription' of Hezekiah's reign is restricted. Clay sealings are all the evidence there is at present for the papyrus rolls which must have been the primary form of record in royal chancelleries and the Temple establishment. More widely relevant, and steadily increasing in number, are simple administrative lists and accounts, letters and legal documents, written in ink on *ostraca* (pottery fragments). The evidence they yield is integrated with information provided by stamped jar handles, notably the royal Judaean series, and inscribed seals, to describe the administrative structures and procedures of the period.

Excavation on sites of this period has steadily intensified, though relatively little of the material produced has yet been fully absorbed into the cultural history of the region, still predominantly studied through the Old Testa-ment. Secular architecture and urban development are relatively well known; but only recently has attention been given to rural settlements and the pattern of land-use throughout the region at this time. Religious installations are not so commonly excavated as might be expected and the precise cult role of those that have been, at sites like Arad, Beersheba, Dan and Jerusalem (outside the Temple area), is often controversial. The persistence of Canaanite custom in popular religious practice is marked. Apart from the reign of Solomon, which is still little known from the archaeological record, this region did not enjoy great material prosperity and was regularly the prey of predatory neighbours. As a consequence luxury industries are rarely evident, and when they are it is commonly in products either of foreign manufacture or foreign inspiration, like the 'Samaria Ivories'. These illustrate the cultural importance of the many Phoenician contacts recorded in the Old Testament. They are also clear in such crafts as stone dressing and seal cutting. Cultural contacts with the Aramaean states of Syria are less obvious and what Egyptian influence there was, by contrast with earlier periods, is likely to have been largely indirect through Phoenicia, save perhaps in the Gaza area.

GENERAL BIBLIOGRAPHY

R. D. Barnett, *Illustrations of Old Testament History* (London, 1977)

H. Th. Bossert, *AltSyrien* (Tübingen, 1951)

H. Gressmann, *Altorientalische Bilder zum Alten Testament* (Berlin and Leipzig, 1927)

J. B. Pritchard, *The Ancient Near East in Pictures relating to the Old Testament* (Princeton, 1954); and *Supplement* (Princeton, 1969)

Y. Yadin, *The Art of Warfare in Biblical Lands* (London, 1963)

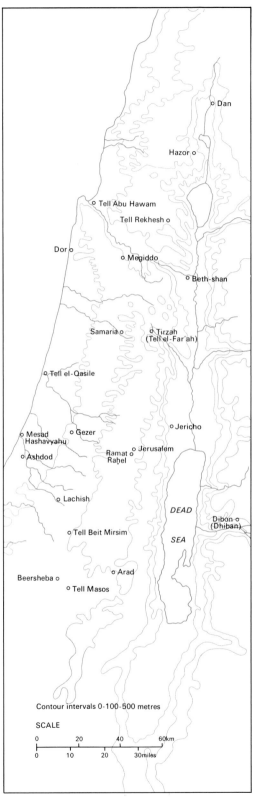

6. Israel and Judah

Contour intervals 0-100-500 metres

SCALE

| Dan |
| Hazor |
| Tell Abu Hawam |
| Tell Rekhesh |
| Dor | Megiddo |
| Beth-shan |
| Samaria | Tirzah (Tell el-Far'ah) |
| Tell el-Qasile |
| Jericho |
| Mesad Hashavyahu | Gezer |
| Ramat Rahel | Jerusalem |
| Ashdod |
| Lachish |
| DEAD | Dibon (Dhiban) |
| Tell Beit Mirsim | SEA |
| Arad |
| Beersheba |
| Tell Masos |

145. A small section of the relief on the 'Black Obelisk' (1.98 m high) of King Shalmaneser III of Assyria (858–824 B.C.) found at Nimrud. It shows a ruler named as 'Jehu, son of Omri' prostrating himself before the Assyrian king. This is a reference to Shalmaneser's campaign of 841 B.C. when he pressed deep into Syria and Phoenicia, taking tribute from Tyre, Sidon and Israel. A suggestion that the king depicted is Jehoram, not Jehu, is not yet established; the titling may mean no more than 'Jehu of Samaria (Beth-Omri: House of Omri)'.

(British Museum WA 118885.)
Layard, *Monuments* 1, pl. 53–6; C. J. Gadd, *The Stones of Assyria* (London, 1936) 147–8; P. K. McCarter, *BASOR* 216 (1976) 5–7; *ANET* 280ff. for textual references.

146. Restored black basalt stela from Dhiban (O. T. Dibon) in Jordan, dating from between 840 and 820 B.C., commemorating the victories of Mesha, King of Moab, over Israel (2 Kings III: 4–27). This is one of the few non-Assyrian monumental historical inscriptions directly relevant to the period of the divided monarchy.

(Paris, Louvre AO 5066. Height 1.00 m.)
ANET 320–1 for text.

147. Modern bronze cast of a jasper seal (now lost) inscribed '(Belonging) to Shema, servant of Jeroboam' i.e. Jeroboam II (782–753 B.C.), excavated at Megiddo in 1904. This very fine seal offers a glimpse of the high level of material culture achieved in Israel under this king.

(Jerusalem, Israel Museum. 3.7 cm × 2.7 cm.)
G. Schumacher, *Tell el-Mutesellim* (Leipzig, 1908) 99, fig. 147.

148. Ivory plaque for inlay into a piece of wooden furniture, originally with inlays of coloured glass or semi-precious stones, from Samaria. It shows the Child Horus, wearing the *atef* crown, seated on a lotus flower. Such Egyptian motifs, and coloured inlays, are thought to have been particularly popular with Phoenician ivory carvers, but may also have been current in south Syrian workshops. The ivory fragments excavated at Samaria were in debris which gave no sound evidence for their date. Their relevance to the decoration of Solomon's Temple in Jerusalem and to Ahab's 'Ivory House' at Samaria has long been recognized; but this piece, and those in **149**, **150**, may be of the eighth rather than the ninth century B.C.

(Jerusalem, Rockefeller Museum. 6.1 cm × 5.3 cm.)
J. W. and G. M. Crowfoot, *Early Ivories from Samaria* (London, 1938) 12, pl. 1.1.

149. Ivory plaque for inlay into a piece of wooden furniture, from Samaria. It shows a winged and skirted sphinx standing in a lotus thicket. Such inlays are the nearest approximation yet available for the appearance of the 'cherubim' of Solomon's Temple.

(Jerusalem, Rockefeller Museum. 8.6 cm × 7.1 cm.)
Crowfoot, *op. cit.* 20, pl. 5.1.

150. Ivory border panel for inlay into a piece of wooden furniture, from Samaria; a letter *tav* is incised on the back to assist in fitting the piece into its correct position. The lion

151

152

grappling with a bull was among the oldest of Near Eastern pictorial designs, originally symbolizing the threat of predatory beasts to domestic flocks.

(Jerusalem, Rockefeller Museum. 11.5 cm × 4.2 cm.)
Crowfoot, *op. cit.* 25, pl. 10.1.

151. The water system at Hazor, like that at Megiddo, epitomizes both the scale and insecurity of urban life in Israel in the ninth century. It was skilfully designed to ensure water supplied to cities exposed to constant threats from Aramaean Syria and Assyria.

Y. Yadin, *Hazor* (Schweich Lectures, London, 1972) 161ff., pl. 29.

152. A 'proto-Aeolic' stone capital from the porch of the citadel building in the ninth-century stratum VIII at Hazor. Such capitals are among the few decorated architectural features found in the primary cities of Israel and Judah.

Y. Yadin, *Hazor* III–IV, pls. 46–8 (buildings and capital *in situ*); P. Betancourt, *The Aeolic Style in Architecture* (Princeton, 1977) 28–9, pl. 6; Y. Shiloh, *The Proto-Aeolic Capital and Israelite Ashlar Masonry* (*Qedem*, 11, 1979), pl. 1).

153. Fragment from a jar incised with the words 'belonging to Makhbiram' from a prosperous eighth-century merchant's house at Hazor (area A: stratum VI).

(Jerusalem, Israel Museum.)
Y. Yadin, *Hazor* II, pls. 169.5, 170.5.

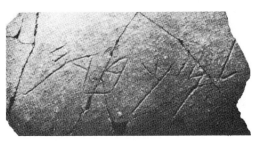

154. Fragment from a jar with a painted inscription reading 'Jeroboam, son of Elm(athan?)' from the same context as the inscription in **153**.

(Jerusalem, Israel Museum. Width 10.5 cm.)
Y. Yadin, *Hazor* II, pls. 169.6, 170.6.

155. An ivory cosmetic spoon from the house of Makhbiram (see **153**) in eighth-century Hazor. The back of the bowl is carved as a

154

156

155

woman's head with a dove on each side. This illustrates the simpler ivory artefacts produced under the inspiration of fine Phoenician and south Syrian ivory carving (cf. 148–50).

(Jerusalem, Israel Museum. Length 13.7 cm.)
Y. Yadin, *Hazor* II, pls. 167–8.

156. Bone mirror handle from a house not far from that of Makhbiram in stratum VI at Hazor. It is carved with a four-winged genius, hands outstretched on each side to grasp the volutes of a squat 'sacred tree'.

(Jerusalem, Israel Museum. Height 18.5 cm.)
Y. Yadin, *Hazor* I, pls. 150–1.

157. The 'Holy of Holies' in the sanctuary built within the fortress at Arad in Judah as in stratum IX, of the earlier eighth century B.C., with two incense altars and a stone stela (*massebah*), with traces of red paint, in place. This is the only shrine with such form and furnishing yet found.

(Photograph, Inst. of Archaeology, Tel-Aviv University.)
R. Amiran and Y. Aharoni, *Ancient Arad* (Israel Museum, 1967) 29.

158. The main courtyard of the sanctuary at Arad in the ninth and eighth centuries B.C. with an 'altar of burnt offering', about 2.5 m × 2.5 m, in the north-west corner, built of earth and undressed stone (cf. Exodus XX: 25).

Amiran and Aharoni, *op. cit.* 28.

159. Restored limestone horned altar discovered dismantled and incorporated into the walls of stratum II storehouses, destroyed by Sennacherib, at Beersheba. A similar altar has been excavated at Tell Dan in Israel, where it formed part of a large sanctuary. The location of the sanctuary at Beersheba is debatable; but finds of this kind are slowly extending understanding of religious practice outside Jerusalem under the divided monarchy.

Z. Herzog *et al.*, *BASOR* 225 (1977) 49ff.

160. A selection of eighth-century pottery from one of the storerooms in the city at Beersheba.

Y. Aharoni (ed.), *Beer-sheba* I (Tel Aviv, 1973).

161. Inscription (whitened for photography) from the rock-cut tomb in Silwan, on the eastern side of the Kedron Valley in Jerusalem, of Sheban-Yahu (Shebna), royal steward of King Hezekiah (715–687/6 B.C.). Isaiah rebuked this high official for the ostentatious tomb he had built in his own life time (Isaiah XXII: 15, 16).

159

160

161

162a

162b

(British Museum WA 125205. Length 1.32 m.)

R. D. Barnett, *Illustrations of Old Testament History* (London, 1977) 72–3.

162. After recent excavations at Lachish (Tell ed-Duweir) it has been shown that both four-winged scarab beetle and winged disk seal impressions on jars, inscribed 'of the King' and bearing the name either of the towns Hebron, Ziph, Socoh or the enigmatic *Mmsht*,

belong to the reign of Hezekiah (715–687/6 B.C.). Precisely what administrative innovation they reflect is not yet fully understood; but it may in part be connected with preparations to resist Assyrian threats (D. Ussishkin, *Tel Aviv* 4 (1977) 54–7). (a) shows a four winged scarab beetle (right) inscribed with the name of Hebron and a winged disk marked Socoh.

(British Museum 132062, 132079 from Tell ed-Duweir (Lachish).)

(b) shows a four winged scarab beetle, inscribed Ziph; a winged disk inscribed Hebron; and a winged disk inscribed *Mmsht*.

(British Museum WA 132065, 130261, 132072, from Tell ed-Duweir (Lachish).)
O. Tufnell, *Lachish* III (London, 1953) 340ff.

163. Six sided baked clay prism (the 'Taylor Prism') inscribed in Akkadian with an account of eight campaigns of King Sennacherib of Assyria (705–681 B.C.). This includes an account of his campaign against King Hezekiah, but does not refer to plague devastating the Assyrian army as in 2 Kings XIX: 35.

(British Museum WA 91032. Height 38.5 cm.)
D. D. Luckenbill, *Ancient Records of Assyria and Babylonia* II (Chicago, 1927) 115ff.

163

164. Fragmentary Mosul-marble relief, part of a great series in room XXXVI of King Sennacherib's palace at Nineveh in Assyria showing his army sacking Lachish (to left), taking away captives and booty. This is one of the early representations of the one humped camel as a pack animal.

(British Museum WA 124907. Height 2.57 m.)
Layard, *Monuments* II, pls. 20–4; Gadd, *op. cit.* 174.

165. Stone bowl with composite feet formed of ducks' heads and bulls' hooves; possibly of Assyrian origin; from Tell el Qitaf in Bethshan valley; seventh century B.C. It is objects of this kind which reflect the Assyrian presence.

(Jerusalem, Israel Museum 49:900. Diameter 17.8 cm.)
R. Amiran, *'Atiqot* 2 (1959) 129ff., pl. 19.

166. A bronze bowl in Assyrian style if not of Assyrian manufacture (cf. the silver bowl from Nimrud **78**), from Samaria region; later eighth or seventh century B.C.

(Jerusalem, Israel Museum 70.96.202. Diameter 18.8 cm.)
R. Hestrin and E. Stern, *IEJ* 23 (1973) 152ff., fig. 1, pl. 46.

167. A baked clay bowl of local manufacture but imitating so called 'palace style' Assyrian pottery, itself ultimately imitating metal bowls, as here: from Tell Rekhesh; seventh century B.C.

(Jerusalem, Israel Museum 69:981. Diameter 15.5 cm.)
Hestrin and Stern, *loc. cit.* 152ff., fig. 2, pls. 4–6.

168. Series of limestone balusters (restored) from the principal building of the citadel at Ramat Raḥel, used as railings for windows, in the eighth century B.C. A fragmentary sculptured relief from the same site seems to show a window balustrade of just this sort. They also appear on ivory inlays in the 'Phoenician style' showing a woman at a window – probably a prostitute attracting custom (R. D. Barnett, *Nimrud Ivories* 145ff.).

165

167

166

169. Potsherd painted in red and black with an outline drawing of a man, possibly a king, from stratum VA, of the seventh century B.C., at Ramat Raḥel in Judah.

(Jerusalem, Israel Museum. 12.5 cm × 7.5 cm.)
P. Matthiae in Y. Aharoni, *Excavations at Ramat Raḥel, Seasons of 1961 and 1962* (Rome, 1964) 54–8, pl. 48.1, fig. 38.1.

(Jerusalem, Israel Museum. Height of capital and shaft 36.5 cm.)
Y. Aharoni, *Excavations at Ramat Raḥel, Seasons of 1971 and 1962* (Rome, 1964) 56–8, pl. 48.1, fig. 38.1; Betancourt, *op. cit.* 42, pls. 26–7.

170. Clay sealing with the impression of a seal inscribed 'Ge'aliahu, son of the King', from Bethzur, late seventh or early sixth century B.C. This sealing is from a role of papyrus, traces of which appear on the back. Officials

with this title clearly ranked very high, but were not necessarily the king's actual offspring.

(Jerusalem, Rockefeller Museum. Width 1.3 cm.)
Inscriptions Reveal (Israel Museum, 1973) no. 21.

171. Letter inscribed on a large potsherd found in the guard room of the gate of a late seventh-century B.C. fort at Meṣad Ḥashabyahu, near Yavneyam in Israel. In this Hebrew letter a reaper complains that an official has unjustly confiscated his garment.

(Jerusalem, Israel Museum 60–7. 21 cm × 16 cm.)
Inscriptions Reveal no. 33.

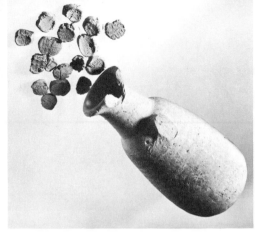

172. Juglet from a small store room at Tell ed-Duweir (Lachish) containing 17 seal impressions from papyrus rolls, a Hebrew *ostracon* listing recipients of goods and a group of weights; early sixth century B.C.

(Jerusalem, Israel Museum 68–25A. Bullae about 1.0 cm × 1.2 cm.)

Inscriptions Reveal nos. 26–31.

173. One of a group of 'letters' on potsherds found in the debris of a gatehouse in the city wall of Lachish (Tell ed-Duweir). They were letters received by Ya'osh, military governor of Lachish, from Hosha 'yahu, a subordinate officer in a small outpost near Lachish at the time of Nebuchadrezzar's invasion in 587 B.C.

(British Museum WA 125702. 9 cm × 10 cm.)

O. Tufnell *et al.*, *Lachish* I, 34–5; III, 332.

8. EGYPT

I. E. S. EDWARDS (174–182)
T. G. H. JAMES (183–195)

Works of high artistic merit and technical skill, which have survived from the time when Egypt was ruled by kings of Libyan stock (the Twenty-second to Twenty-fourth Dynasty, *c.* 945–715 B.C.), are not very numerous, but they include some pieces which find a place in most anthologies of Egyptian art. With very few exceptions, the most notable productions date from the earlier part of the Twenty-second Dynasty, when internal conditions were stable and when, for a short time, it seemed possible that Egypt would again play an important role in the affairs of the Near East.

A remarkable renaissance in the culture of Egypt followed the conquest of the land by the Nubian kings who established the Twenty-fifth Dynasty (*c.* 747–656 B.C.). The effects of this renaissance were to be felt in all branches of the fine arts, in the development and use of the written word, and in religion. It was strongly permeated with an archaizing tendency which evinced itself in the studying, copying, and adaptation of ancient forms. Under the stimulus of this remarkable movement the skills in the ancient crafts, in which the Egyptians of the earlier great periods had excelled, were revived; the techniques of stone-working, in particular, reached notable heights. The artistic advances made during the Nubian dynasty continued to be maintained during the Twenty-sixth Dynasty (664–525 B.C.), but the products of Egyptian artists and craftsmen in this later period lacked some of the freshness and spirit of the preceding dynasty. The spirit was in the end to be almost completely extinguished by the Persian conquest of Egypt in 525 B.C.

GENERAL BIBLIOGRAPHY

C. Aldred, 'Statuaire' in J. Leclant, *Le monde égyptien. L'Egypte du crépuscule* (Paris, 1980) 120–60

B. V. Bothmer, *Egyptian Sculpture of the Late Period* (Brooklyn, 1960) Introduction and 1–66

W. Stevenson Smith, *The Art and Architecture of Ancient Egypt* (Harmondsworth, revised ed. by W. K. Simpson, 1981)

J. Yoyotte, *Treasures of the Pharaohs* (Geneva, 1968) 179–213

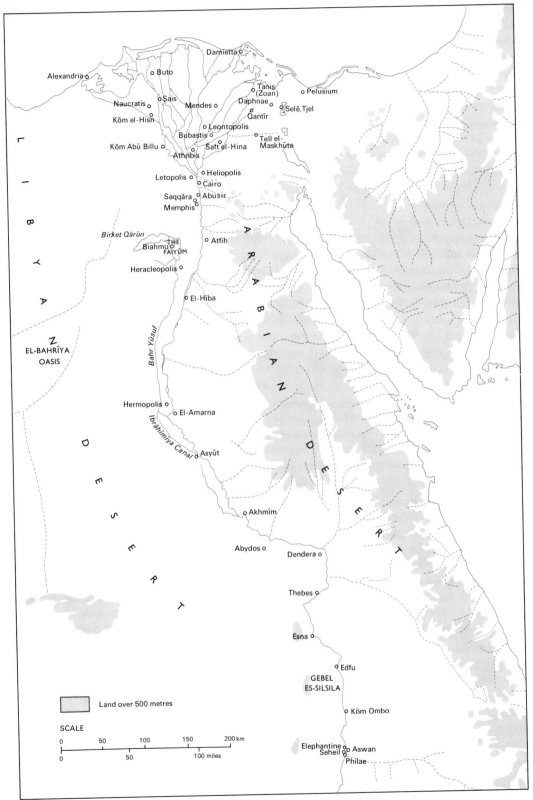

Damietta

Alexandria

Buto

Tanis
(Zoan)

Pelusium

Sais

Naucratis

Mendes

Daphnae

Selē, Tjel

Kōm el-Hisn

Qantīr

Leontopolis

Bubastis

Kōm Abū Billu

Saft el-Hina

Tell el-
Maskhūta

Athribis

Letopolis

Heliopolis

Cairo

Saqqāra

Abūsir

Memphis

Birket Qārūn

Atfih

Biahmu

THE
FAIYŪM

Heracleopolis

L
I
B
Y
A
N

El-Ḥība

Z

EL-BAHRĪYA
OASIS

Bahr Yūsuf

A
R
A
B
I
A
N

Hermopolis

El-Amarna

Ibrāhīmīya Canal

Asyūt

D
E
S
E
R
T

Akhmīm

D
E
S
E
R
T

Abydos

Dendera

Thebes

Esna

Edfu

GEBEL
ES-SILSILA

Kōm Ombo

Elephantine

Aswan

Seheil

Philae

Land over 500 metres

SCALE

0   50   100   150   200 km

0   50   100 miles

7.A Egypt

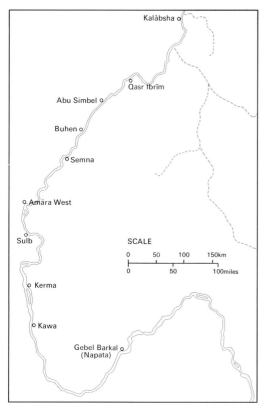

B Nubia

of the king's reign, which would explain why the court was never finished and work on its pylon may not have begun, the existing pylon being almost certainly of later date. Even without the inscriptional evidence, there would be no doubt that the court was constructed of newly-quarried stone, whereas the buildings of Shoshenq I's successors at Karnak, Bubastis and Tanis (*CAH* III².1, 556–7) consisted very largely, if not entirely, of re-used stone from earlier monuments, particularly those of Ramesses II, which had been dismantled (*CAH* III².1, 578). New material, in this instance limestone, also seems to have been used for the temple dedicated to Amun at el-Hība, which Shoshenq I began to build and his son, Osorkon I, completed (*CAH* III².1, 543, 549, 551 and 557). Some fragments of its wall-reliefs showing the king are now in the Heidelberg Museum.

Top. Bibl. II², 34–6; *Chicago Epigraphic Survey, Rel. and Ins. at Karnak* III, *The Bubastite Portal* (OIP 74; Chicago, 1954); D. B. Redford, *JEA* 59 (1973) 16–30; E. Naville, *Bubastis* (London, 1887–9); L. Habachi, *Tell Basta* (Suppl. *Ann. Serv.* Cahier 22; Cairo, 1957); K. Kitchen, *The Third Intermediate Period in Egypt (1100–650 B.C.)* (Warminster, 1973) 318, fig. 3 (Bubastis, Tanis); P. Montet, *La nécropole royale de Tanis* (Paris, 1947–61) I–III; H. Ranke, *Koptische Friedhöfe bei Karâra und der Amontempel Scheschonks I bei el-Hibe* (Berlin and Leipzig, 1926); W. Wolf, *Die Kunst Aegyptens* (Stuttgart, 1957) 638, fig. 679 (El-Hība); E. Feucht, *Studien zur altägyptischen Kultur* 6 (1978) 69–77 (El-Hība).

174. Shosenq I, having conducted a triumphant campaign in Palestine, which is mentioned in the Old Testament (*CAH* III².1, 545–7), proceeded to commemorate his victory by constructing at Thebes a colonnaded court west of the Second Pylon of the temple of Amun at Karnak. By the side of its monumental gateway, the so-called Bubastite Portal, shown here, the king appears in the presence of the god to whom he ascribed his military achievement; the places which he conquered are individually named. The material for the building was obtained from the sandstone quarry at Gebel es-Silsila where an inscription gives the information that the architect of the court was a certain Haremsaf, who visited the king in his Delta residence, named Pi-Ese, and reported to him that work was progressing quickly: 'there is neither sleeping by night nor indeed slumbering by day' (*CAH* III².1, 544). The inscription is dated in Year 21, probably the last year

175. Besides the Bubastite Portal and its adjacent historical record, another gateway of the Twenty-second Dynasty bore pictorial and inscriptional records of the highest importance, though of a different character. This was a gateway built of pink granite re-used blocks in the temple of Osorkon II at Bubastis. Its scenes, carved in relief, depicted episodes in the royal jubilee festival (*ḥeb-sed*). Found as long ago as 1891–2, they are still the most complete – though not the earliest known – record of that ceremony. In the relief shown here Osorkon II and his wife Karoama stand in an attitude of veneration before a deity, whose image is lost. Thus represented, the king is fulfilling a wish, which he expressed in the text of a stela carved in one piece with a kneeling statue of himself, that Karoama might participate in his jubilee

festivals in the life to come (*CAH* III².1, 554). Granite from earlier monuments was freely re-used at this period and the high degree of skill visible in this piece is by no means exceptional among the many sculptures of its kind found at Bubastis.

(London, British Museum 1077. Height 1.75 m.)
Top. Bibl. IV, 29; Kitchen, *op. cit.* 318, fig. 3b; E. Naville, *The Festival Hall of Osorkon II* (London, 1892); E. Uphill, *Journal of Near Eastern Studies* 24 (1965) 365–83; *An Introduction to Ancient Egypt* (British Museum; London, 1979) 72, fig. 23; H. K. Jacquet-Gordon, *JEA* 46 (1960) 12–23.

176. The kneeling figure of Osorkon II holding a stela already mentioned, of which the head is in Philadelphia and the body in Cairo, is believed to be the earliest statue of the Twenty-second Dynasty which was specially carved for the king whose name it bears. Sometimes royal statues underwent a change in their identity more than once and the names of all their previous owners were by no means invariably erased. A fine grey granite head (**a**) belonged to a colossal seated statue which was usurped by at least three kings in the course of its long history. It was one of a pair of similar statues which stood at the entrance to the first hall of Osorkon II's temple at Bubastis. If the inscriptional evidence of the two statues is combined it can be shown that they were adopted in turn by the Hyksos king, Seuserenre Khyan (*c.* 1620 B.C.), Ramesses II (*c.* 1250 B.C.) and finally Osorkon II (*c.* 860 B.C.). Very probably they were brought to Bubastis from Avaris (Qantir), the Hyksos capital and Ramesside place of residence, like many other pieces of sculpture, but their style suggests a pre-Hyksos origin. Colossal statues, although dating back to the Old Kingdom, were not common until the reign of Amenophis III in the Eighteenth Dynasty (*c.* 1400 B.C.) and no complete example from the Middle Kingdom is known. The remains, however, of two sandstone seated colossi, with parts of an inscription of Ammenemes III (*c.* 1820 B.C.), were found in 1888 by

175

176a

176b

Sir Flinders Petrie at Biahmu in the Faiyūm. It has been conjectured that these were the two colossi described by Herodotus (II.149), but, whether this surmise is right or not, they show that colossal statues were made in the Twelfth Dynasty. Perhaps the two seated colossi at Bubastis were also made for Ammenemes III and his names were erased on this statue by either Khyan or one of the subsequent usurpers.

A small group of royal sculpture is characterized by the representation of the king in a semi-prone position pushing some object forward to be accepted by a god. In (b) Osorkon III of the Twenty-third Dynasty (c. 775 B.C.) is portrayed in such a manner, with his right knee bent and his left leg, which is broken at the thigh, outstretched backwards. The object which he is presenting is a model of the sun's bark, of which only the stern part is preserved (*CAH* III².1, 578). It was the hope of every Egyptian king that after death he would traverse the sky daily in the boat of the sun god and sail with him at night through the underworld. The two journeys were accomplished in different barks, which, however, were identical in form, one regular feature being an out-board curving stern-post such as can be seen, as well as a steering oar, in the surviving part of the bark in this model. Both the day- and the night-barks are named in the pedestal inscription and it would seem that the king intended the sun god to use the boat for whichever journey he wished.

((a) London, British Museum 1063. Height 76 cm. (b) Cairo Museum JE 37427 (42197). Height 18 cm.)

Top. Bibl. IV, 28 (a) and II² 143 (b); Naville, *op. cit.* 26–8, pls. 1, 10, 12 (a); E. A. W. Budge, *Egyptian Sculptures in the British Museum* (London, 1914) 10, pl. 12 (a); G. Legrain, *Statues et statuettes de rois et de particuliers* (Cairo Mus. Cat. gén. 42197) III pl. 5 (b).

177–81. In no branch of art were the Egyptians of the Libyan Period more successful than in the production of bronze figures. Four of the best known examples are **177–80**. The earliest in date (**177**) represents Osorkon I (c. 900 B.C.) holding a vase (*CAH* III².1, 579). Hollow cast, it shows in its most simple form a characteristic feature of this period: the incrustation of the surface with another metal, in this instance

gold. The same technique, but more elaborately executed, can be seen in the gold and copper inlay of the belt and apron of a bronze torso of Pedubast I (**178**), the first king of the Twenty-third Dynasty (c. 800 B.C.). In this piece the thickness of the bronze varies from three to fifteen millimetres. Beyond doubt the *chef d'oeuvre* of the period in bronze is a figure, now in the Louvre (**179**), which Jean François Champollion acquired in Alexandria and brought to France in 1829 (*CAH* III².1, 578–9). Its original provenance was Karnak. Damascened in gold, silver and electrum, it represents the God's Adoratrice Karomama Merytmut,

grand-daughter of Osorkon I (*c.* 850 B.C.), performing a ritual ceremony. In her hands she probably held a pair of gold sistra. She is clothed in a close-fitting gown with short, pleated sleeves flared at the elbows, over which she wears a broad bead-collar and a skirt in the form of a pair of wings folded across the front. Gold leaf once covered the parts of the figure which are now bare. An inscription on the base states that the figure was made at the command of Karomama's treasurer and overseer of the household, Iahentefnakht. It has been conjectured that it was placed in the bark of Amun when the god's statue was carried in procession on ceremonial occasions.

An innovation of the Libyan Period, which was to increase in popularity in the two following dynasties, was the introduction of an archaistic style in art, and particularly the portrayal of the human figure in the mode and costume of the Old and Middle Kingdoms (*CAH* III².1, 579). An early and outstanding example is a bronze figure of a son of a Libyan

chieftain whose name may be read either Bepeshes or Pashasu (180). In his right hand he held a long staff and in his left probably a sceptre. Both in the style of the wig and in dress the figure is reminiscent of wooden figures made in the Fifth and the Sixth Dynasties – a date to which it was once wrongly ascribed.

Of special interest, both historically and

artistically, is a small figure in solid gold representing the ram-headed god Arsaphes (**181**). It was found in 1904 by Sir Flinders Petrie when excavating the floor of the hypostyle hall of the temple of Arsaphes at Heracleopolis. The horned god wears the so-called *atef*-crown, a royal headdress and kilt. At the back of his head is an eyelet for suspending the figure as an amulet on a necklace which may have been placed on a statue of the god in his temple. An inscription engraved on the under-side of the base records that the figure was dedicated to the god by Neferkare Peftjauawybast, the local kinglet of Heracleopolis, who resisted the Delta coalition of Tefnakhte and is shown on the stela of Py kissing the ground in the presence of the Nubian king (*CAH* III².1, 568, 573 and 574).

(**177** Brooklyn Museum 57.92, Charles Edwin Wilbour Fund. Height 14 cm. **178** Lisbon, Gulbenkian Foundation. Height 73 cm. **179** Paris, Louvre N 500. Height 59 cm. **180** Paris, Louvre E 7693. Height 48 cm. **181** Boston, Museum of Fine Arts 06.2408. Height 6 cm.)

Top. Bibl. IV, 58 (**177**) and IV, 119 (**181**); *Ancient Egyptian Sculpture lent by C. S. Gulbenkian Esq.* (British Museum; London, 1937) pls. 22–3 (**178**); C. Aldred in J. Leclant, *L'Égypte du crépuscule* (Paris, 1980) 126, pls. 105, 108 (**178**); J. Vandier, *Les antiquités égyptiennes au Musée du Louvre. Guide Sommaire* (Paris, 1973) 121, pl. 10.2 (**179**), (**180**); H. Jacquet-Gordon, *Zeitschrift für äg. Sprache* 94 (1967) 86–93 (**179**); J. Yoyotte, *Bull. Soc. fr. d'ég.* 64 (1972) 31–52 (**179**); id. *Bull. Inst. fr. Caire* 57 (1958) 81–9 (**180**); W. M. F. Petrie, *Ehnasya 1904* I (London, 1905) 18–19, pl. 1 (**181**); W. S. Smith, *Ancient Egypt as represented in the Museum of Fine Arts, Boston* (Boston, 1952) 165, fig. 99 (**181**); E. R. Russmann, in *Essays in honor of Dows Dunham* (Boston, 1981) 154, figs. 8, 9 (**181**).

182. The usurpation by provincial Libyan rulers of customs which had previously been royal prerogatives became common as the authority of the kings became weaker and more restricted (*CAH* III².1, 571–2). As an example, the green glassy faience headless figure (**a**) represents the Libyan chief and priest of Amon-Re, Smendes, kneeling and offering two vases, perhaps containing wine, to his god, Amon-Re. In earlier times this posture would have been adopted by the king alone in performing this rite. The inscription reproduces

the words of Smendes. It is addressed to priests and scribes, assuring them that the great god will be pleased with them if they recite a magical invocation for funerary offerings on behalf of the chief. The figure seems to have been dedicated by a person named Iahnufe.

The faience plaque (**b**) with traces of green glaze shows the Twenty-third Dynasty king, Iuput II, king of Leontopolis, who is represented on the stela of Py with his fellow-kings Osorkon IV and Peftjauawybast (see on **181**) kissing the ground in submission to the Nubian king (*CAH* III².1, 573–4). While the general appearance of the king is suggestive of the archaizing art of the Libyan Period (see **180**), the helmet with its ring-decoration, the thick lips and neck, the pronounced navel and the low hips are all features which are common in sculptures of the Nubian Twenty-fifth Dynasty. If the plaque were not inscribed with the king's names, it would probably be dated to the Nubian Period.

((**a**) Brooklyn Museum 37.344E, Abbott Collection. Height 14 cm. (**b**) Brooklyn Museum 59.17, Hood Collection. Height 29 cm.)

E. Riefstahl, *Ancient Egyptian Glass and Glazes in the Brooklyn Museum* (New York, 1968) 106, pl. 59 (57) (**a**), pl. 61 (59) (**b**); J. Yoyotte, *Mém. Inst. fr. Caire* 66 (1961) 127, no. 30, pl. 3 (**a**); R. Fazzini, in *Miscellanea Wilbouriana* (New York, 1972) 63–70, fig. 39 (**a**, **b**); G. A. D. Tait, *JEA* 49 (1963) 93–139 (**b**); Russmann, *op. cit.* 155, fig. 10 (**b**).

183. The great necropolis of Thebes, lying on the west bank of the Nile opposite the city, fell into disuse, it would seem, after the Twenty-first Dynasty, at least as a place in which the great Theban officials and priestly dignitaries were buried in large tombs. The outstanding exception is the High Priest of Amun, Harsiese (*CAH* III².1, 556). In the course of the Twenty-fifth Dynasty, however, the grand tradition of tomb-construction was revived in the area of the necropolis known today as the Asasif. The new tombs, the first of which seems to have been prepared for Harwa, major-domo of Amenirdis, the God's Wife of Amun, and virtual ruler of the Theban region, were constructed, generally speaking, on a plan very different from that employed for the tombs of important Theban officials during the New Kingdom. The Asasif tombs were distinctly more 'architectural', provided with imposing

brick pylons and enclosure walls, sunken open courts and subterranean suites of rooms. The model is probably to be found in the New-Kingdom tombs of the Saqqara necropolis which were similarly copied for some great Memphite burials of the Saïte Period, such as that of Bakenrenef. The decoration of these tombs was substantially based on the scenes found in Old-Kingdom private burials at Saqqara and elsewhere, and on the royal rituals and religious texts of earlier periods, including the Pyramid Texts, the Book of the Dead, and those compositions found in the tombs of the Valley of the Kings at Thebes. The finest decoration, in terms of interest, execution and colour, is to be found in the Tomb of Mentu-emhat, Fourth Prophet of Amun and principal officer of state in the Theban Principality from the reign of Taharqa of the Twenty-fifth Dynasty (690–664 B.C.) to at least Year 14 of Psammetichus I of the Twenty-sixth Dynasty (650 B.C.). The great brick pylon of his tomb lies on the left of the view of the Asasif shown here.

Top. Bibl. I².1, 56 (Mentuemhat), 68 (Harwa); III², 588 (Bakenrenef); M. Bietak, *Das Grab des 'Anch-Hor* I (Vienna, 1978) 19ff.; II (1982) *passim*; J. Leclant, *Montouemhat* (Cairo, 1961) 171ff., pls. 55–65; Smith, *Art and Architecture of Ancient Egypt* 409.

184. During the Twenty-fifth and Twenty-sixth Dynasties the Theban Principality was ruled on behalf of the absent king by the God's Wife of Amun, supported by her steward or major-domo and the priesthood of Amun. The succession of the God's Wives was by the legal process of adoption, and the office was used throughout the period for clearly political purposes. At the outset of the Nubian intervention in Egyptian affairs, Py arranged for his sister Amenirdis to be adopted by the incumbent Shepenupet; when Amenirdis succeeded Shepenupet in about 700 B.C., she in turn adopted her niece Shepenupet II, a daughter of Py. The exceptional status acquired by these ladies required exceptional burials for them. The open court in front of the great mortuary temple of Ramesses III at Medinet Habu was chosen as a suitable site, and two of the tomb-chapels, shown here, remain in a good state of preservation. Of these the one on the left was constructed for Amenirdis by Shepenupet II.

Behind the pylon which forms its façade is a small court, and beyond that is the chapel proper, in the form of a cella with a barrel-vaulted roof and surrounded by a roofed passage or ambulatory. The burial was placed in a chamber beneath the chapel, just about big enough to receive the large stone coffin of Amenirdis, which was probably removed for re-use in antiquity. The structure on the right contains the chapels of Shepenupet II and her successor Nitocris, and also, as an addition, one for Mehytemuskhet, the true mother of Nitocris. These surviving chapels were originally flanked by two more, built chiefly of mud-brick, for Shepenupet I and for Ankhnesneferibre who succeeded Nitocris in 584 B.C. The sarcophagi of Nitocris and Ankhnesneferibre were removed in antiquity and have been found elsewhere. Originally all four chapels were linked by internal doors.

Top. Bibl. II², 476ff.; U. Hölscher, *The Excavation of Medinet Habu*, V: *Post-Ramessid Remains* (Chicago, 1954) 17ff.; J. Leclant, *Recherches sur les monuments thébains* (Cairo, 1965) 354ff.; C. E. Sander-Hansen, *Das Gottesweib des Amun* (Copenhagen, 1940) *passim*; W. J. Murnane, *United with Eternity. A concise Guide to the Monuments of Medinet Habu* (Chicago, 1980) 82ff.

185. The cult of the Apis Bull, which flourished in Memphis from at least the time of the First Dynasty (*c.* 3100 B.C.), was closely associated with that of the living king. As a divine symbol of strength and fertility, the Apis Bull was also linked with the cults of the sun god Re, and the great creator god Ptah. The association with Ptah was particularly close, and the quarters provided for the living Apis were, certainly from the time of the New Kingdom, placed near the great temple of Ptah in Memphis. The cult achieved increased importance during the Late New Kingdom and the Libyan Period, and the ritual embalming and burial of the dead Apis in the so-called Serapeum at Saqqara were given special emphasis and invested with great ceremony. In 1941 an area near the temple of Ptah was excavated, and structures connected with the care of the Apis in life and in death were exposed. The buildings go back in date probably to the reign of Shoshenq I of the Twenty-second Dynasty (*c.* 945–924 B.C.), but the northern part of the site was apparently developed during the Twenty-sixth Dynasty.

Among the altars and other objects discovered during the excavations was this huge alabaster table on a base 5.40 m long and 3.07 m wide, the whole estimated to weigh almost 50 tons. It was carefully designed to receive the body of the dead Apis Bull for treatment in the course of mummification. Externally it is decorated to appear as if it were a great bed: in high relief on both of the long sides are elongated lion-figures, one of the conventional forms in which beds were made. The upper surface is shaped into a shallow basin gradually deepening towards one end where a hole pierces the end wall. This outlet leads to an alabaster basin, placed beneath to catch whatever liquids flowed from the table. At the opposite end, the table is approached by shallow steps cut into the base. It is reasonable to suppose that this great table was used for the washing of the body, perhaps after the long process of dehydration during mummification had been completed.

Top. Bibl. III².2, 841; Mustafa el-Amir, *JEA* 34 (1948) 51–6; J. Dimick in R. Anthes, *Mit Rahineh 1955* (Philadelphia, 1959) 75f.; J. Vercoutter in *Lexikon der Ägyptologie* I (Wiesbaden, 1975) 338ff.

186. The temple built by King Taharqa at Kawa in Nubia was essentially Egyptian in architecture and decoration. It was conceived in the king's sixth regnal year (684 B.C.), and he sent workmen from Memphis to execute his plan. When it was complete it would emphasize the identification which Taharqa sought to make between his rule in Egypt and the best royal and religious traditions of the past. Of the reliefs on the temple walls, based on Egyptian originals in the Memphite region, the most striking are those found on the east face of the entrance pylon. At Kawa the building stone is a greyish yellow sandstone, a far less sympathetic material for fine relief-work than the hard limestone employed for the best Old-Kingdom structures in the Memphite necropolis. The scene reproduced here is located on the south wing of the pylon; it shows the king, represented as a sphinx, trampling on three foreign foes, an Asiatic, a Libyan, and an inhabitant of the land of Punt, a still unlocated foreign emporium from which exotic products were acquired by the Egyptians from the time of the Old Kingdom. The hieroglyphic legend in front of the royal head reads 'trampling all foreign lands'. On the part of the wall to the right of the scene, but not shown here, is a figure of the goddess of

the West, and below, three smaller figures of Libyans named Wesa, Weni and Khu-ites, two males and a female. Not only is the whole scene distinctly Memphite in style and execution, but it can closely be compared generally and in detail with scenes found in the mortuary-temples of Kings Sahure and Nyuserre of the Fifth Dynasty at Abusir, and of Phiops II of the Sixth Dynasty at Saqqara. The actual source of the Kawa scene is most probably that of Sahure. The subject of the king as a sphinx trampling on his enemies is one found frequently on royal monuments, but the clinching coincidence between the Kawa and Memphite scenes is to be found in the three Libyans, whose Kawa names are found equally on Sahure's monuments, although, interestingly, written with some small variants in the hieroglyphs. The Kawa scenes, therefore, were not copied slavishly from the Memphite originals, but reproduced from memory and, perhaps, from rough notes taken by the Egyptian craftsmen before they left Memphis for Nubia.

(Height *c.* 2.10 m. Photograph, after Macadam.)

M. F. L. Macadam, *The Temples of Kawa* II (Oxford, 1955) 63ff., pls. 9, 49; Smith, *Art and Architecture of Ancient Egypt* 400; *id. Africa in Antiquity: The Arts of Ancient Nubia and the Sudan* I (Brooklyn, 1978) 88, fig. 58; A. Spalinger, *SSEAJ* 9 (1979) 125ff.

187. A devotion to the Theban cult of the god Amun, and the belief that this cult had fallen

187

into neglect in its Egyptian centre, were among the reasons, particularly the expressed reasons, for the invasion and conquest of Egypt by the Nubian kings. But subsequent to the conquest these kings, and particularly Shabako (*c.* 716–702 B.C.), extended their solicitude to other ancient cults and cult-centres in Egypt. Of these one of the most important was that of Ptah in the northern capital of Memphis. The most significant testimony of Shabako's attention is the so-called Shabako Stone, a rectangular slab of basalt carved with a text which declares itself to be a copy of an Old-Kingdom original, rescued from its worm-eaten state by order of the king. The text is laid out in the form of an Old-Kingdom document, and the language is distinctly archaic. Two principal views of the nature of the text have been put forward: that it is a dramatic composition expounding the theological system embodied in the cult of Ptah, with sections of commentary; and that it is a religious treatise enlivened by sections of dialogue delivered ostensibly by the gods, and thought to be derived from separate 'mystery' plays or compositions. The common belief until recent years has been that this 'Memphite Theology', as the text is usually called, truly represents a copy of a very early composition. Recently, however, this view has been challenged, and good reasons have been given for considering the whole to be a kind of archaizing 'forgery' perpetrated under Shabako. The extent to which the surviving text – sadly mutilated by the later use of the slab as a nether mill-stone – is based on ancient originals may never be established. But there is no reason to doubt that Shabako's intention in having this monument carved and set up was inspired by reasons similar to those which were adduced formerly when the inscription was thought to represent a rescued ancient document.

(London, British Museum 498. 93 cm × 138 cm.)
Top. Bibl. III².2, 873 (very full bibliography); M. Lichtheim, *Ancient Egyptian Literature* I (Berkeley, 1973) 51ff. and III (1980) 5; F. Junge, *Mitt. deutsch. Inst. Kairo* 29 (1973) 195–204.

188. The God's Wife of Amun, Ankhnesneferibre, was the last to hold this important office. The daughter of King Psammetichus II (595–589 B.C.), she was adopted as God's Adoratrice of Amun by Nitocris in 593 B.C., succeeding to the superior position in 584 B.C. on the death of Nitocris. Her incumbency lasted until Egypt was invaded by the Persians in 525 B.C. A tomb-chapel with burial vault was prepared for Ankhnesneferibre at Medinet Habu, beside those of her predecessors (**184**), but it cannot be established that her burial actually took place there. Her great schist(?) sarcophagus was ultimately found in the early nineteenth century at the bottom of a deep shaft at Deir el-Medina, a good half-mile distant from Medinet Habu. Changes made to the inscriptions on the coffin, and an added text show that it had been usurped by a priest of Monthu, Pimonth, in the early Roman Period. To add to the confusion, the sarcophagus of Nitocris was recovered from an adjacent shaft at Deir el-Medina. Some scholars claim that these shafts were the original burial places of these God's Wives, but the weight of evidence still falls to the advantage of Medinet Habu. The sarcophagus of Ankhnesneferibre is precisely rectangular and chest-shaped, with a slightly vaulted lid; it is 2.60 m long and weighs about 4 tons. The coffer and lid are covered, inside and out, with immaculately carved hieroglyphic texts representing late versions of the Pyramid Texts of the Old Kingdom. There are also three figures: on the outside of the lid a fine low relief carving of Ankhnesneferibre; on the inside of the lid, the goddess Nut with outstretched arms spanning the vault of heaven, in this case, the coffin-lid itself; and on the floor of the coffer the goddess of the West, a form of Hathor. The styles of these three figures are different, the most refined and conventional being that of the owner of the coffin on the lid. She is shown wearing the characteristic headdress of the God's Wife of Amun and holding the usual symbols of royal power, the crook and flail. The subtlety of the carving is outstanding, particularly the way in which the form of the body is suggested beneath the loosely flowing robe. In the detail shown here, the head of Ankhnesneferibre is seen to be rendered with great sensitivity. It is scarcely a true portrait, but it yet incorporates a degree of brutal realism rarely found in Egyptian royal portraiture before the Twenty-fifth Dynasty. The subject was very old at the time of her death; she is not shown as a very old woman, but still in a state of advanced maturity not commonly adopted for funerary representations.

(London, British Museum 32.)

Top. Bibl. 1².2, 685f.; E. A. W. Budge, The Sarcophagus of Ānkhnesrāneferāb (London, 1885); C. E. Sander-Hansen, Die religiösen Texte auf dem Sarg der Anchnesneferibre (Copenhagen, 1940); G. Nagel, Rapport sur les fouilles de Deir el Médineh (Nord), 1928 (Cairo, 1929) 15ff.; U. Hölscher, op. cit. 28f.

190

189

189. Sculptures of the Nubian kings of the Twenty-fifth Dynasty are not rare, although they have survived in patchy sequence, and many are not attributed with certainty to their particular subjects. The greatest number of sure identity belong to Taharqa (690–664 B.C.), who is known specifically to have made use of Egyptian craftsmen in the Kawa temple (see on **186**). The reliefs in this Nubian temple were executed, it would seem, by these Egyptian craftsmen after true Egyptian prototypes; the sculptures placed in the temple, on the other hand, were apparently carved after Egyptian originals by craftsmen who were not wholly accomplished in the Egyptian style. This small grey granite sphinx with a head incorporating, possibly with true realism, the features of Taharqa, provides a fine example of such sculpture. The form of the sphinx has rightly been compared with Middle-Kingdom originals, but its execution is altogether more heavy and 'lumpy' than those of the earlier period. It is, however, most striking in the head which shows the king wearing the double uraeus (royal serpent) on his brow, a characteristic peculiarity of royal representations of this time, which has been thought to indicate sovereignty over Egypt and Nubia. It has been commonplace to draw attention to the brutal quality of the face, here surrounded by an exaggerated lion's ruff which sets off the rounded features in a dramatic manner. By Egyptian standards the face is indeed coarse and brutal, and it may rightly be supposed that it presents the Nubian's features only slightly modified in the Egyptian-inspired form of the sphinx. But 'brutal' is perhaps too emotional an adjective, implying an excessively subjective response to the contemplation of the face of a king known to be active and ruthless. The face is undoubtedly strong, and it is certainly unrefined; but it also possesses qualities which suggest a subject of thoughtful and steady character. All such interpretations, however, are speculative, and it is surely sufficient to appreciate the piece as a fine, confident, sculpture.

(London, British Museum 1770. Height 41 cm.)
Top. Bibl. VII, 190; A. Russman, *The Representation of the King in the XXVth Dynasty* (Brussels, 1974) 11ff., 50, fig. 12; S. Wenig, *Africa in Antiquity* II (1978) 168; C. Aldred, 'Statuaire' in J. Leclant, *L'Égypte du Crépuscule* (Paris, 1980) 132, fig. 135.

190. Problems of identification also beset the study of most of the surviving sculptural representations of kings dated with a fair degree of certainty to the Twenty-sixth Dynasty. The few firmly assigned royal heads barely provide a minimal framework within which other heads can be satisfactorily accommodated. The fine light-coloured quartzite head taken as an example here presents the student with the problem in a tantalizing manner. Superficially the face appears conventional – it is somewhat larger than life-size – but when subjected to close analysis it cannot be identified from any of those heads the subjects of which are known. By negative as much as positive argument the choice has been reduced, for most students, to Amasis, the penultimate monarch of the dynasty (570–526 B.C.), who usurped the throne from Apries. If the question of identification is placed in suspense, the head may be evaluated as a striking example of the highly accomplished sculptor's craft of the Twenty-sixth Dynasty. The stone, which is extremely hard, has been carved and modelled with exactness and subtlety, some of the detail, such as the eyebrows, being indicated delicately without being rendered precisely in a plastic manner. In spite of the fullness of the face and apparent blandness of expression, both of which characteristics are common to much ordinary, run-of-the-mill, Saïte sculpture, this head presents an individual character of firmness and strength. The king is shown wearing a helmet-shaped crown known as the blue crown, usually associated with the king in a warlike role; it carries the royal serpent, the uraeus, here depicted with an elaborate double figure-of-eight arrangement of coils.

(Philadelphia, Univ. Mus. E.14303. Height 43 cm.)
H. W. Müller, *Studi Rosellini* 2 (1955) 181–221; *id. Zeitschrift für äg. Sprache* 80 (1955) 46–68; Bothmer 57f.; E. Brunner-Traut, *Zeitschrift für äg. Sprache* 97 (1971) 18–30, pl. 3d.

191. In the execution of private sculpture during the artistic renaissance of the Twenty-fifth and Twenty-sixth Dynasties, the Egyptian craftsmen achieved a level of precise workmanship scarcely equalled in the earlier great periods. The working of hard stones, in particular, was mastered as never before: granite, basalt, schist, quartzite and diorite were carved seemingly as easily as limestone in the Old Kingdom. In matters of style inspiration was regularly drawn from the past. This archaizing tendency in its application demonstrated no planned consistency; all good periods were available to draw on. In the multiplication of sculptures made for some of the most important officials a variety of ancient sources can often be distinguished. Some of the finest pieces, including some based on ancient models, appear to be attempts at true portraiture, but claims in particular cases must always be accompanied by reservations. As contrasting examples of sculptures of the same person, two illustrated here represent Harwa, the major-domo of Amenirdis, who held his office during the reigns of Shabako to Taharqa (*c.* 716–664 B.C.). He seems to have been the first to have a large tomb made for himself in the Asasif at Western Thebes (**183** and comment), and he also may have set the fashion for having a multiplicity of votive statues carved on his behalf. The first **(a)** is of the type known as 'block statue', in which the subject is shown seated on the ground with his knees drawn closely to his body, the whole form being enveloped in a tightly fitting

garment. The type, first developed during the Middle Kingdom, became exceptionally popular during the Twenty-fifth Dynasty, and remained so until Ptolemaic times. Its particular attraction as a votive form was that it provided useful broad, flat, surfaces for the reception of inscriptions. Harwa's block statue, which is made of schist, is covered with texts, mostly of conventional character, including standard offering formulae, common statements of his virtues, and addresses to deities. The head is the most striking feature: the face is full and almost square, and expresses a bland calmness which suits the votive nature of the sculpture. He is shown in a very different manner in the second piece (**b**), which is also made of schist. Here Harwa is depicted squatting on the ground, his knees away from his body, and supporting in front of himself figures of two goddesses which have been identified as Hathor (on his right)

and Tefnut. It has been suggested that these figures both show Amenirdis in the guise of the goddesses. Her name is inscribed on the flat surface between the two small figures. In this unusual small sculpture Harwa is again represented with a full, squarish, face, but here without a wig. His body is corpulent, as it appears in others of his sculptures; it has even been questioned, on the basis of this corpulence and on the nature of his subsidiary title 'overseer of the harem', whether he might have been an eunuch. Other evidence is lacking, and Egyptian records do not in general support the use of eunuchs even in sensitive areas of administration like royal harems. The further suggestion that Harwa was Nubian, on the basis of his sculptural physiognomy, is likewise unsupported by other evidence.

((**a**) London, British Museum 53306. Height 38.5 cm. (**b**) London, British Museum 32555. Height 18.5 cm.)
  B. Gunn and R. Engelbach, *Bull. inst. fr. d'arch. or.* 30 (1930) 791–815; K. Bosse, *Die menschliche Figur der Rundplastik der ägyptischen Spätzeit* (Glückstadt, 1936) 51; Bothmer xxxvi, 6; H. De Meulenaere, *Lexicon der Ägyptologie* II (1977) 1021 f.

to Eighteenth Dynasty originals. In the proper tradition of such statues, Pesishuper is depicted holding a papyrus roll in his left hand, with its opening page lying on his lap; on it he has written out his name and titles. By the side of his left hand lies a palette with two ink-cakes representing the usual black and red colours employed in most writing. Another, superfluous, palette hangs over his left shoulder, often so shown in earlier scribal statues. There is a certain lack of symmetry both generally in the body, and particularly in the head, which, whether by design or accident, imparts an element of additional interest to the effect produced by the sculpture. Here is an individual full of lively attention – an admirable representative of the artistic renaissance of the Twenty-fifth Dynasty.

(London, British Museum 1514. Height 53 cm.)

Top. Bibl. II², 278; J. Leclant, Enquêtes sur les sacerdoces et les sanctuaires égyptiens à l'époque dite 'éthiopienne' (Cairo, 1954) 78ff.; Bothmer 12; T. G. H. James, Bull. soc. fr. d'ég. 75 (1976) 7ff.

192. The scribal statue, deriving from Old-Kingdom prototypes, remained popular throughout the Pharaonic Period. Over the centuries its essential pose – the man as a scribe squatting with a papyrus open on his tightly-drawn skirt – was simplified and rendered less naturalistically. To be a scribe was honourable, and to be shown as a scribe in no way demeaning even for the highest officials in the land. The red quartzite scribal statue of Pesishuper, which comes from Karnak, eliminates the detailed representation of the subject's legs. The lower part of the body is converted into a convenient 'pad' for the reception of finely carved hieroglyphic texts. Sculpturally, attention is drawn to the head and torso of Pesishuper, who was chamberlain of Amenirdis, and content to describe himself as 'scribe'. The double wig he is shown wearing represents a rare Twenty-fifth-Dynasty revival of a type of wig worn by important officials during the Eighteenth Dynasty; the folds of flesh on the body, which indicate the prosperous circumstances of Pesishuper's life, are also to be traced

193. During the Twenty-sixth Dynasty large numbers of private votive sculptures were made for placing in temple courts, so that their subjects could, through their sculptural forms, participate in the offerings made to the temple deities, and derive other benefits from association with the sacred places. One of the most common types of these sculptures shows the subject holding a divine figure or a shrine containing a divine figure; the subject may be standing or kneeling. The example shown here has been reassembled from fragments retrieved from a deposit of rejected temple-furniture and sculpture near the temple of the Apis and the Mother of Apis at North Saqqara. In spite of its damaged condition, it can still be appreciated as an unusually fine statue. It was made for the official Bakennanefu, also called Menkhibpsamtik, but was at a later date usurped by someone named Horpaese, son of Horemheb; Horpaese's dedication is added in the demotic script. Bakennanefu is shown kneeling and holding a shrine containing a figure of Ptah, the principal deity of Memphis. It is probable that the statue was first placed in the temple of Ptah in Memphis, subsequently taken to Saqqara and placed in the temple of Apis, and then thrown out, broken up and deposited. The body is amply rendered and given the attributes of great muscular strength; but the focus of attention is the head, superbly carved with much subtle modelling of the features. In the face the cheek bones are pronounced and the mouth full and naturalistic. These features are set off, but in no way diminished in their effect by the precise, almost mechanical carving of the eyes, eyebrows and ears. The full bag-wig is commonly found in sculptures of private persons during the Twenty-sixth Dynasty, to the later part of which this piece should be assigned.

(Toronto, Royal Ontario Museum 969.137.1. Height 59 cm.)

W. B. Emery, *JEA* 53 (1967) 143, pl. 23.1, 2; W. Needler, *Rotunda* 2.4 (Fall, 1969) 31; H. S. Smith, *A Visit to Ancient Egypt* (Warminster, 1974) 53, pl. 6D; G. T. Martin, *The Tomb of Ḥetepka* (London, 1979) 58f., pl. 51 (texts only).

194. The exceptional achievement of bronze-casters during the otherwise artistically undistinguished dynasties which immediately preceded the renaissance of the Nubian and Saïte Dynasties, has already been noted (comment on **177–81**). During these later dynasties the activities of craftsmen in bronze were greatly expanded, and very large quantities of bronze figures were produced. The vast majority of these figures, however, are of ritual and votive character – statuettes of deities inscribed briefly with inscriptions seeking benefits for specified individuals. Workmanship is generally good, but artistic quality rarely exceeds a moderate level. The reason for this decline in quality, it has been suggested, was the revival of stone-carving. Judgement in this matter, however, has undoubtedly been influenced by the mass of indifferent bronzes of the later period set against a handful of outstanding bronzes which have survived from the earlier period. Some large, fine bronzes are, unfortunately, of uncertain date, and may well be assigned to the Twenty-fifth or Twenty-sixth Dynasty. Further, of the many surviving divine bronzes, many are not to be dismissed as mass-produced. One of the Memphite god Nefertum, shown here (**a**) is a splendid representative of the genre, not previously published. It shows the god in conventional attitude, wearing his usual lotus headdress with tall feathers, and holding a curved sword or falchion. Details are embellished with gold inlay: the eyes, the sacred

Horus-eyes on the base of the headdress and on the shoulders, and the criss-cross markings on the beard. The lotus-flower was originally inlaid with coloured opaque glass. The votive text on the base, addressed to Nefertum, is mostly obscured, and the dedicator's name cannot be read with certainty.

More individual, but equally fine, is the

193

figure of Khonsirdis (b) who is represented in a standing posture, holding in front of his body a divine effigy, now lost apart from its base, most probably of the god Osiris. This small effigy was cast separately and fitted to the principal

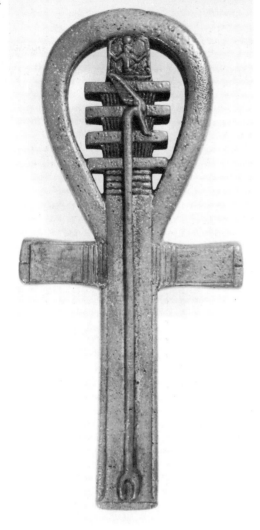

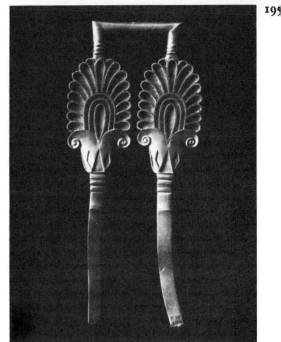

figure by means of a tenon and a retaining pin. Khonsirdis is depicted wearing a tightly fitting long skirt with projecting 'apron', and a priestly leopard-skin. Inscriptions on the apron, the edge of the leopard-skin, and elsewhere name him as the Governor of Upper Egypt, and a royal titulary places him in the reign of Psammetichus I (654–610 B.C.). The eyes are inlaid with silver, a figure of Osiris is engraved on the right shoulder, and a small scene on the apron shows Khonsirdis making offering to Osiris. The figure, which has lost its base, is particularly well moulded. The detail of the dress is precise and crisp, and the indication of the limbs through the clinging folds of the garment is masterly and in the best tradition of

New-Kingdom sculpture from which this piece derives its inspiration. Small imperfections in the casting were repaired very neatly in antiquity by small inserts of bronze.

((**a**) London, British Museum 64480. Height 37 cm. (**b**) London, British Museum 14466. Height 35.5 cm.)
  H. R. Hall, *JEA* 16 (1930) 1f.; Bothmer 3, 16; J. Leclant, *Montouemhat* (Cairo, 1961) 270; T. G. H. James, *Egyptian Sculptures* (London, 1966) pl. 31; *id.* (ed.), *An Introduction to Ancient Egypt* (London, 1979) 226f.

195. The paucity of surviving material in the category of the minor arts from the Twenty-fifth and Twenty-sixth Dynasties is due surely to the wholesale plundering of Egypt after the Persian invasion in 525 B.C. Jewellery, fine vessels of precious metals and glazed composition (faience), and the small items of personal property which provide such a striking and informative legacy of earlier periods, are almost wholly lacking, except for the contents of the Nubian royal tombs which are, for the most part, undistinguished. From the evidence of less precious objects, particularly amulets, divine figures, and *ushabtis* (funerary deputies), the craft of faience-making was brought to a high degree of excellence: the core material was fine and hard, capable of being modelled and moulded with the preservation of sharp detail. The glazes used were limited in their range of colours, compared with those found during the New Kingdom, and they show a slightly matt, but very attractive texture and surface. The composite amulet of pale green faience (**a**) was supposedly found in an unspecified temple of Taharqa at Gebel Barkal in the Sudan, but confirmation of this provenance is lacking. From the colour of its glaze, and from its style, it is probably of Egyptian origin, but could have been an import into Nubia. The primary shape is that of the Egyptian *ankh*-symbol, the 'life'-sign (here the two side-arms are restored), in to which is incorporated the *djed*-pillar, an emblem of endurance associated with the cult of Osiris, and along which is superimposed the *was*-sceptre of power. At the top of the *djed*-pillar a small plaque bears a figure in relief of Heh, a god of infinite space, holding palm-fronds notched with the years of infinity. Of a quite different tradition is a gold vessel-handle in which both Egyptian and Greek elements may be distinguished (**b**). The two bars of the handle are made in the form of palmettes rising out of formalized papyrus-umbels; the flowers were originally inlaid with coloured opaque glass or semi-precious stones, more probably the former. This remnant of what must have been a splendid dish or tray was found buried with silver scrap in the ruins of the camp set up by Psammetichus I at Daphnae for the quartering of foreign mercenaries. The hybrid nature of the decoration well suits the provenance, but it would be idle to speculate on the nationality of its maker.

Among the few impressive objects of small scale which have survived from antiquity, and can with certainty be dated to the Twenty-sixth Dynasty, are gold signets, the marks of office belonging to important officials. The example illustrated here (**c**) is of special interest because the legend contains the title and name of a well-known high official, the major-domo of the God's Adoratrice of Amun, Shoshenq. Two major-domos of this name are known to have served Ankhnesneferibre, daughter of Psammetichus II (595–589 B.C.), who held office until 525 B.C.: Shoshenq, son of Harsiese, early in her reign, and Shoshenq, son of Pedineith, at the end. As the Shoshenq of the ring is described as major-domo of the God's Adoratrice, not of the God's Wife, it is possible that Shoshenq, son of Harsiese, is to be preferred, for Ankhnesneferibre was the God's Adoratrice before she became God's Wife. Although Shoshenq's signet is shaped like a ring, it was not to be worn as a ring, and indeed it would have been very uncomfortable to wear; it weighs 81 grammes. The depressions on the back of the inscribed plate were designed to receive the tips of the thumb and forefinger when the instrument was used for sealing.

((**a**) London, British Museum 54412. Height 23.5 cm. (**b**) Boston, Museum of Fine Arts 87.763. Length 12.5 cm. (**c**) London, British Museum 68868. Width 3.5 cm.)
  J. Leclant, *L'Égypte du Crépuscule* (Paris, 1980) 236, fig. 230; W. M. F. Petrie, *Nebesheh (AM) and Defenneh (Tahpanhes)* (London, 1888) 75, pl. 41.10; Smith, *Art and Architecture of Ancient Egypt* 406, fig. 402; J. Bourriau, *JEA* 65 (1979) 153, pl. 26.3; L.-A. Christophe, *Ann. Serv. Ant. Eg.* 54 (1956) 83–100.

9. CYPRUS

V. KARAGEORGHIS
(224 *by* T. B. *Mitford*)

The successive and rapid political changes in the eastern Mediterranean during the first half of the first millennium B.C. had their impact on the island of Cyprus, whose position made her an easy prey for all those who wanted to dominate that crucial area of the ancient world. After close relations with the Aegean world during the closing years of the second millennium B.C., which resulted in the gradual hellenization of her population, the island found herself in close contact with the Near East at the beginning of the first millennium and particularly with the Phoenicians from the ninth century B.C. These Near Eastern mariners, who established themselves in the south coastal city of Citium and dominated a wide area, exploited her copper mines and her forests for timber, siding always with those who were in power against the local population.

The Assyrians, who ruled Cyprus from the end of the eighth century B.C., granted some autonomy to the island's kingdoms for as long as the local kings paid their tribute. For more than a century, under the benevolent rule of the Assyrians, the Cypriots developed their own culture, centred on the courts of the various kings. The exuberant character of this culture, which was partly based on old Cypriot tradi-

tions and on elements which were imported from both the Near East and the Aegean, is best represented by the Royal Tombs of Salamis, where wealth and pomp rivalled that of the Assyrian kings, but burial customs recalled elements of Greek, 'Homeric' traditions.

The Egyptians conquered Cyprus about 560 B.C. but before the end of the century the Persians dominated the island and ruled her ruthlessly for more than two hundred years. In the meantime connexions with the Near East and the Aegean continued, according to the political allegiances of the divided kingdoms of the island. But whereas in the major urban centres political events and expediences influenced the development of the arts, especially in sculpture, in the countryside the rural population remained faithful to age-long traditions, based on the old, prehistoric fertility cults. The island's rural sanctuaries of this period, with their numerous terracotta votive offerings, reflect a truly Cypriot character, which is fresh, lively and unique.

GENERAL BIBLIOGRAPHY

CAH III.1, ch. 12; III.3, ch. 36c
V. Karageorghis, *Kition* (London, 1976); *Salamis in Cyprus* (London, 1969)

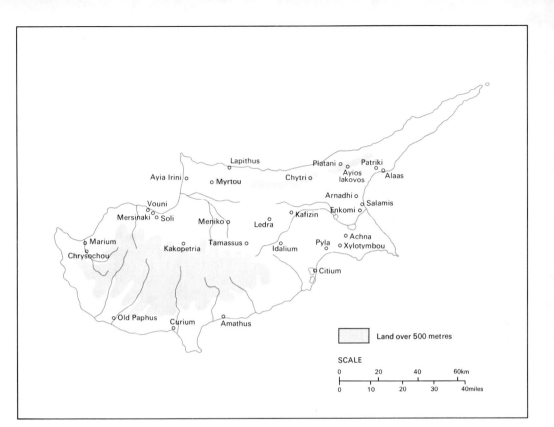

Land over 500 metres

SCALE

0	20	40	60km

0	10	20	30	40miles

Map labels: Lapithus, Platani, Patriki, Ayia Irini, Myrtou, Chytri, Ayios Iakovos, Alaas, Arnadhi, Vouni, Salamis, Mersinaki, Soli, Meniko, Ledra, Kafizin, Enkomi, Marium, Tamassus, Pyla, Achna, Chrysochou, Kakopetria, Idalium, Xylotymbou, Citium, Old Paphus, Curium, Amathus

8. Cyprus

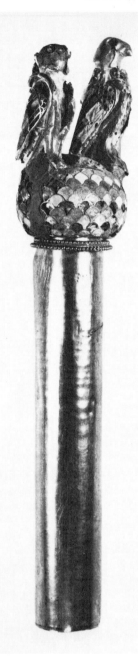

two falcons with cloison-decorated wing feathers and inlaid eyes. It was found in a shaft
196. Gold sceptre from Curium-Kaloriziki. grave and was probably a royal symbol of
Eleventh century B.C. It consists of a tubular authority (as for Homer's σκηπτοῦχοι βασιλεῖς).
rod of thin gold sheet, fixed to a longer shaft.
It is surmounted by a sphere decorated with a (Cyprus Museum J 99. Height 16.5 cm.)
scale pattern of cloisons containing paste in   G. H. McFadden, *AJA* 58 (1954) 131–42; *CAH*
white, green and mauve, with two hoops of Plates to Vols. I and II pl. 151c; H. G. Buchholz
granulation below. On the sphere are perched and V. Karageorghis, *Prehistoric Greece and Cyprus*
(London, 1973) no. 1788.

197. Terracotta figurines representing the goddess with upraised arms: (a) from the sacred area of Citium; eleventh century B.C.; (b) from Morphou; eighth century B.C. The type was introduced to Cyprus from Crete at a time when there were close relations between the two islands, in the eleventh century. The Cretan goddess was identified with the Cypriot goddess of fertility, who was widely worshipped in Cyprus, particularly in the Late Bronze Age temples of Paphus and Citium. The type survived in Cyprus down to the Classical period, having retained its original Cretan characteris-

tics, such as the cylindrical or bell-shaped body, accentuated facial features (swollen eyes, large pointed nose, large ears and often with spots painted in red on the cheeks).

((a) Cyprus Museum, Kition 381. Height 14.5 cm. (b) Cyprus Museum 1958/v–7/3. Height 16.3 cm.)
 J. Karageorghis, *La Grande Déesse de Chypre et son Culte* (Paris, 1977) pls. 21a, 23a.

198. Pyxis of Proto-Bichrome ware from Alaas, tomb 16/16. First half of the eleventh century B.C. The form imitates sub-Minoan prototypes, but the decoration in two colours and the lotus flower attest Near Eastern influences.

(Cyprus Museum. Height 23 cm.)
 V. Karageorghis, *Alaas* (Nicosia, 1975) pls. 12, 56.

199. Kalathos of White Painted I ware, from Salamis, tomb 1, no. 137. Middle of the eleventh century B.C. Decorated on the outside with triangles and a goat, recalling the *agrimi* of sub-Minoan pottery. The tomb in which this was found is the earliest so far identified at Salamis and its discovery helped to date the origin of the city to the eleventh century.

(Cyprus Museum. Diameter 19.5 cm.)
 M. Yon, 'La Tombe T.I du XIe siècle av. J.-C.', *Salamine de Chypre* II (Paris, 1971) 58–9, no. 137.

200. 'Samaria ware' double bowl from the temple of Astarte at Citium. End of the ninth century B.C. It is one of the largest of its kind and was no doubt used for ritual purposes.

(Larnaka District Museum, Kition 927. Height 21 cm, diameter 34 cm.)
 V. Karageorghis, *Kition* 102, pl. 78; id. *Excavations at Kition* IV (Nicosia, 1981) 25, no. 53, pls. 21.19–20; 25, 29.

as incense-burners. They are mainly of clay but some specimens in bronze are also known.

(Famagusta, Chr. Hadjiprodromou Coll. Height 70 cm.)

V. Karageorghis, *Rivista di Studi Fenici* 3 (1975) 161–7.

202. Amphora of Bichrome III ware, the 'Hubbard Amphora', from Platani, Famagusta District. Late ninth century B.C. The main zone between the handles is decorated on one side with a pictorial composition representing funerary ritual of oriental character (*CAH* III².1, 528, fig. 51); the other side, illustrated here, is decorated with dancing women and a lyre player, in the fashion of Greek Late Geometric compositions. It is one of the most ambitious compositions of the Iron Age pictorial style and does not follow the normal stylistic rules of this class.

(Cyprus Museum 1938/XI–2/3. Height 68 cm.)
P. Dikaios, *BSA* 37 (1936–7) 56–72.

201. Wall-bracket (or lamp-holder) of Bichrome III ware. It is decorated at the top with two bucrania, and with a figure of the naked Astarte in relief, her arms bent forwards. Her cult became the official cult of the Phoenician world from about the middle of the ninth century B.C. Such wall-brackets, used in Cyprus and other Near Eastern sites since the Late Bronze Age, were usually hung on walls of sanctuaries and were used as lamp-holders or

203. Bronze cauldron on an iron tripod stand, from Salamis, Tomb 79, no. 202. About 700 B.C. The cauldron is decorated with eight

griffin protomes and four janus-headed sirens around the rim. The type is known in Etruria, Delphi, Olympia and other Greek sites (see **292**) but this is the first to have been found in the east, and it is unusual in many ways, not least that the sirens are hammered, not cast, and the griffins cast, not hammered like most early examples (see on **293**). It may have been made in Cyprus, where copper was plentiful, by an artist who was familiar with the stylistic trends of the eastern Mediterranean at the end of the eighth century. Though it is probably safer not to give this work a distinct artistic label it is clear that Phoenician elements are prevalent in its style.

(Cyprus Museum. Height of cauldron 55 cm, of tripod stand 70 cm.)

V. Karageorghis, *Excavations in the Necropolis of Salamis* III (Nicosia, 1973) 25–7, 97–108, pls. H, 129, 130, 243, 245.

204. Chair from the 'Royal' Tomb 79 at Salamis. About 700 B.C. It was made of wood and covered all over with ivory plaques (see **205**). The back-rest is decorated with guilloche, anthemia and a thin sheet of gold. It recalls the throne of Penelope (*Od.* XIX.55–6). The chair has been restored, the wooden part having completely disintegrated.

(Cyprus Museum. Total height 90 cm.)

Karageorghis, *Salamis* III 87–8, pls. A, B, 61–3, 240–1.

205. Ivory open-work plaque, from the same tomb (no. 258). It is carved in relief on both sides in the shape of a sphinx wearing the double crown of Upper and Lower Egypt. It is decorated with cloisons of thin sheet gold filled with paste of blue and red-brown. The eyes were inlaid. The technique is that of similar ivories from eastern sites, notably Nimrud (see **148–50**). The style is Phoenician Egyptianizing. It was fixed to the side of the throne, **204**.

(Cyprus Museum. Height 16 cm.)

Karageorghis, *Salamis* III 37, 87–97, pls. B.1–2, 62, 241.

206. The dromos of 'Royal' Tomb 79 at Salamis. Horses had been sacrificed in honour of the dead in the dromos, where chariots and hearses were also found. Large numbers of vases, mainly amphorae, are seen on either side of the dromos. Such burials recall 'Homeric' funeral customs. Horse sacrifices are known during the Late Bronze Age in the Near East and Asia Minor as well as in Mycenaean Greece and other areas (e.g. Scythia, China). They were

208

209

offered as tomb gifts to warriors and nobles as a mark of distinction. The horses sacrificed in the dromoi of the Salamis tombs were of the species *equus egyptiacus*, much shorter than the modern Arab horse.

Karageorghis, *Salamis* III ch. 2.

207. Skeletons of horses and the impressions of a chariot found in the dromos of Tomb 79 at Salamis. See **206**.

208. The façade of 'Royal' Tomb 3 at Salamis and part of its dromos. Seventh century B.C. The drafted edges of the stones recall Anatolian prototypes. The built tomb had a long, narrow dromos and was covered by a tumulus of earth. Such built tombs were known in Cyprus during the Late Bronze Age, at Enkomi, but their reappearance in the Iron Age may be due to influence from Anatolia, and there are many other Anatolian characteristics in the tomb architecture of Cyprus in the seventh and sixth centuries. These may be attributed to itinerant architects or builders, who also taught the Cypriots to pile tumuli over the tombs.

V. Karageorghis, *Excavations in the Necropolis of Salamis* I (Nicosia, 1967) 25–53.

209. Iron sword from Salamis, Tomb 3 (no. 95). Seventh century B.C. The pommel was of perishable material and was fixed with rivets, the heads of which were covered with a thin sheet of silver. This recalls the silver-studded (ἀργυρόηλος) swords of Homer.

(Cyprus Museum. Length 92 cm.)
Karageorghis, *Salamis* I 43.

210. Interior decoration of a silver bowl from Salamis, Tomb 2 (no. 71). Seventh century B.C. The bowl had been reworked after its original decoration had been worn away. These 'Cypro-Phoenician' bowls have been found in Cyprus and elsewhere in the Mediterranean and were probably made on the island by Phoenician artists.

(Cyprus Museum. Diameter 14.5 cm.)
Karageorghis, *Salamis* I 19–20; for bowls of this type, E. Gjerstad, *Opusc. Arch.* 4 (1946) 1–18.

211. Pair of iron fire-dogs and bundle of twelve spits found in the dromos of Salamis, Tomb 79. About 700 B.C. Such objects were found in other tombs of the Archaic period in Cyprus and in eighth–seventh-century tombs at Argos (*CAH* III².1, 781, fig. 86) and in Crete. They were possibly intended to be used for the preparation of a meal after the burial, such as Homer describes in detail. The fire-dogs are in the shape of Greek warships.

210

(Cyprus Museum. Length of fire-dogs 1.10 m, of spits 1.53 m.)

Karageorghis, *Salamis* III 118; on such finds, J. Boardman, *Kretika Chronika* 1971, 5–8.

212. Jug of Bichrome IV ware, decorated in the 'free-field' style. Seventh century B.C. The scene depicts a large bird and an homunculus, and may well show a Pygmy and Crane, from the myth which was known to Homer (*Il.* III.3–6) and depicted on later Greek vases.

(Cyprus Museum 1938/IX–8/1. Height 35 cm.)

V. Karageorghis, *Rev. Arch.* 1972, 47–52; *id.* and J. des Gagniers, *La céramique chypriote de style figuré* (Rome, 1974–5) 35, IX.10.

213. Jug of Bichrome IV ware of the same style and date as the last. From Arnadhi (Famagusta District). It shows a bull smelling a lotus flower. This style flourished mainly in the eastern part of the island and is one of the finest expressions of Cypriot vase-painting from any period.

(Cyprus Museum 1951/I–2/9. Height 28 cm.)

Karageorghis and des Gagniers, *op. cit.* 48, XVI.b.14.

211

215

213

214. Skyphos of Bichrome ware, from Salamis, Tomb 23 (no. 28). Early seventh century B.C. The shape and decoration imitate East Greek subgeometric cups.

(Cyprus Museum. Height 11 cm.)
 V. Karageorghis, *Excavations in the Necropolis of Salamis* II (Nicosia, 1970) 51, pl. 102.

215. Faience flask in the form of a kneeling woman in an Egyptian style. Found on an eighth–seventh-century floor in the temple of

Astarte at Citium. Such flasks may have contained water of the Nile which was thought to have rejuvenating qualities. They were widely exported in the Mediterranean.

(Cyprus Museum, Kition 1747. Height 7 cm.)
    G. Clerc *et al.*, *Kition* II, *Objets Égyptiens et Égyptisants* (Nicosia, 1976) 185–8, pl. 20.1–4; V. Webb, *Archaic Greek Faience* (Warminster, 1978) 29.

216. Terracotta votive figures found in the open-air sanctuary of Ayia Irini. The sanctuary was first built in the Late Bronze Age and continued in use down to the end of the Archaic period. The god who was worshipped in it was a god of fertility but he combined other functions. The terracottas, about two thousand of them, are now divided between the Cyprus Museum (as illustrated) and the Medelhavsmuseet, Stockholm.

    E. Sjöqvist, *Archiv für Religionswissenschaft* 30 (1932) 308–59; E. Gjerstad *et al.*, *Swedish Cyprus Expedition* II (Stockholm, 1935) 777–91.

217. Terracotta chariot model from the sanctuary of Ayia Irini. Sixth century B.C. The chariot was used for warfare quite late in Cyprus, as recorded by Herodotus for the early fifth century (v.113), long after it had been abandoned in Greece.

(Cyprus Museum, A.I. 1781 + 798. Length 27.5 cm.)
    Gjerstad, *op. cit.* 740, pl. 235.3.

218. Clay 'Minotaur' with snakes coiling over his head and shoulders. From the sanctuary of Ayia Irini. Sixth century B.C. Snakes had long been represented as familiars of chthonic and fertility deities. This type of monster appears to have had some specific identity in Cyprus.

(Cyprus Museum, A.I. 2101. Height 63.9 cm.)
    Sjöqvist, *op. cit.*; for this type in Cyprus and Greece see R. V. Nicholls, *BSA* 65 (1970) 28.

219. Terracotta figurine of a priest wearing a bull's mask. Sixth century B.C. Actual bulls' masks appear to have been used in sanctuaries of the Late Bronze Age as also at Citium in the ninth-century Phoenician temple. By wearing the mask the priest acquired the qualities of the bull-god.

219

(Cyprus Museum, A.I. 2170. Height 19.5 cm.)
Sjöqvist, *op. cit.*; V. Karageorghis, *Harvard Theological Review* 64 (1971) 262.

220. Façade of a built chamber tomb at Tamassus. Sixth century B.C. On either side of the entrance are pilasters in relief with 'Aeolic' capitals. The interior imitates wooden architecture, probably influenced by Anatolian prototypes.

H. G. Buchholz, *Arch. Anz.* 1973, 322–8.

221. Limestone statuette of a man (once Cesnola Collection). Sixth century B.C. Egyptian domination over Cyprus from about 560 B.C. brought deep changes in the styles of Cypriot sculpture, which now imitates very closely Egyptian sculpture, not only in posture but also in dress. This is an eloquent example of the new Cypro-Egyptian style.

(Paris, Louvre MNB 408. Height 29 cm.)
Perrot-Chipiez, *Histoire de l'Art* III 549, fig. 405; A. Caubet, *Antiquités de Chypre au Musée du Louvre* (Paris, 1976) no. 36.

222. Limestone statue of Zeus Keraunios, from the temple of Melqart, Citium. End of the sixth century B.C. The style is Archaic Cypro-Greek. The god wears a form of aegis, holds a thunderbolt aloft in his right hand and his eagle (the claws only remain) in his left.

(Cyprus Museum, Kition 139. Height 56 cm.)
Gjerstad, *op. cit.* III, 32–3, 57ff., pls. 14, 15.1–2; V. Tatton-Brown, *Cyprus B.C.* (London, 1979) no. 330.

223. Terracotta figurine of the god Baal-Hamman ('god of the incense altar') from the Meniko sanctuary. Mid-sixth century B.C. He is enthroned, horned. Many incense-altars were found in his sanctuary.

(Cyprus Museum. Height 18.5 cm.)
V. Karageorghis, *Two Cypriote Sanctuaries of the*

222

223

224

end of the Cypro-Archaic period (Nicosia, 1977) pls. 6, 29; Tatton-Brown, *op. cit.* no. 291.

224 (by T. B. Mitford). The Bronze Tablet of Idalium, reverse side. This famous document, by far the longest syllabic inscription known, is perfectly preserved and almost completely intelligible. The text in 31 lines is sinistroverse with relatively regular marks of punctuation. It was found on the western acropolis of Idalium shortly before 1850 and in that year acquired by the Duc de Luynes. Hung in the temple of Athena, it is now thought between 478 and 470 B.C., after Idalium had survived a first siege by the 'Medes' and the men of Citium, the Tablet publishes a covenant between King Stasicyprus and the city on the one hand, a doctor Onasilus and his brothers on the other. They were commanded during the siege to tend the wounded without fee, and the reward then promised them is here carefully specified: to the doctor and his brothers jointly *either* one talent of silver *or* lands in perpetuity in the district of Alampria (of which the name is preserved by the modern village of Alambra); to the doctor himself *either* the sum of four 'axes' and two 'double minas' (?) of Idalium *or* in perpetuity lands in the plain of Melania and a garden extending to the river Drymius and the domain of the Priestess of Athena. King and city swear to respect their bond. Notable is the dating of the inscription by eponym – and not by regnal year and the dyarchy of king and city: good evidence for a constitutional monarchy.

(Paris, Cabinet des Médailles inv. br. 2297. 21.4 cm × 14 cm.)

O. Masson, *Inscriptions Syllabiques Chypriotes* (Paris, 1961) no. 217.

10. THE NATIVE KINGDOMS OF ANATOLIA

M. MELLINK (225–240)
O. MASSON (240–243)

The Phrygians of the ninth to seventh centuries B.C. lived on the plateau of Western Anatolia. They controlled the countryside from strongholds. These were either citadels built on Bronze Age mounds, newly fortified with stone and mudbrick defensive walls, such as Gordium on the Sangarius river (**225–6**) and the nearby site of Yenidoğan-Hacıtuğrul, east of Polatlı, or fortresses set on natural rock formations, such as the stronghold nicknamed Midas City in the western Phrygian highlands (**228**). These citadels were raided by Cimmerians and Scythians, repaired by local Phrygian chieftains, vassals of the Lydians, in the seventh and sixth centuries B.C., and ultimately captured by the Persians under Cyrus.

The Lydians, survivors of Bronze Age West Anatolians, controlled the fertile lower Hermus valley and adjoining districts to north and south. Famous horsemen, they gathered strength under the Mermnad dynasty of Gyges which ruled from Sardis. They expanded their territory to the Halys after the fall of the Phrygian king Midas. Their role as transmitters of East Greek culture lasted into the Persian era. Their southern neighbours, the Carians, lived in the coastal districts from Miletus to Caunus; unlike the Lydians and Phrygians, they were sailors and pirates, presumably as heirs to Bronze Age traditions. Their adventures overseas carried them into Egypt as mercenaries of Psammetichus I. Their coastal neighbours were the Lycians, whose fame as seafarers also dates from the Bronze Age. Their harbours were at the mouths of rivers such as the Xanthus river, with citadels inland near the forests and mountains. Proudly independent, they maintained their own traditions in spite of Hellenization.

GENERAL BIBLIOGRAPHY

E. Akurgal, *Phrygische Kunst* (Ankara, 1955)
G. Bean, *Turkey beyond the Maeander* (London, 1971)
G. M. A. Hanfmann, *From Croesus to Constantine* (Ann Arbor, 1975)
C. H. E. Haspels, *The Highlands of Phrygia* (Princeton, 1971)
R. S. Young, *Gordion Excavation Reports* 1, Three Great Early Tumuli (Philadelphia, 1981)

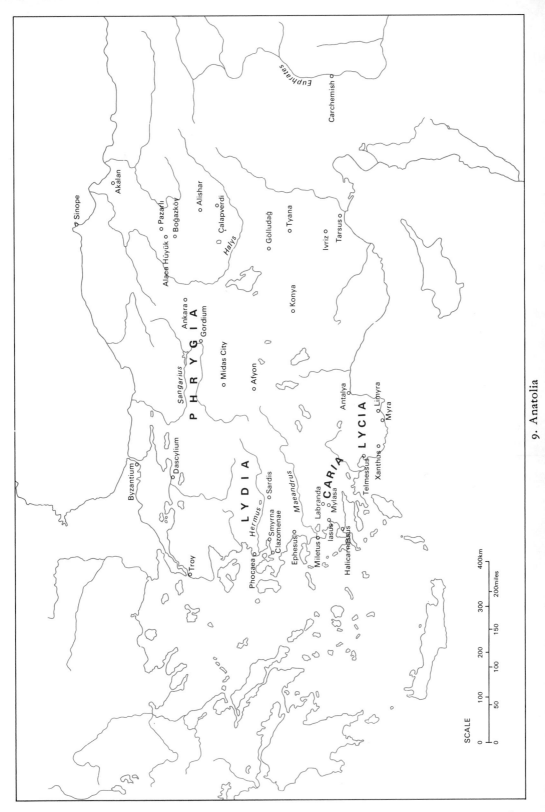

Sinope

Akalan

Alaca Hüyük
Pazarlı
Boğazköy
Alishar
Çalapverdi

Halys

Gölludağ
Tyana

Ivriz
Tarsus

Carchemish

Euphrates

Ankara
Gordium

P H R Y G I A

Midas City

Afyon

Konya

Troy

Dascylium

Byzantium

L Y D I A

Sangarius

Sardis

Smyrna
Clazomenae

Phocaea

Hermus

Maeandrus

Ephesus

Labranda
Iasus
Mylasa

Miletus

Halicarnassus

C A R I A

Telmessus

Xanthus

Antalya

L Y C I A

Limyra
Myra

SCALE

| | | | | | | | |
0   100   200   300   400km

0   50   100   150   200miles

9. Anatolia

225. Gordium-Yassıhüyük. The main city mound, accumulated from the Early Bronze Age through the Hittite period, was levelled and expanded by the Phrygians and provided with systems of fortification that were repeatedly improved and enlarged. The west side of the principal mound, which measures about 500 m × 300 m, is protected by the Sangarius river. The eighth-century fortification wall on the east side was built of limestone masonry on a stepped base. The wall is preserved to a height of nine metres. In front of it, to the east, is the rubble fill serving as a terrace for the next stage of the citadel, whose gate was built on top of the tall remnants of the eighth-century gate. The rebuilt citadel served into the Persian period.

R. S. Young, *AJA* 60 (1956) 257–60.

226. Gordium-Küçük Hüyük. After the Cimmerian raid on Gordium, which led to the alleged suicide of Midas, an outer system of fortification was built of mudbrick. Part of the twelve-metre high fortification wall was preserved in a tumulus to the south east of the citadel mound, the Küçük Hüyük. The mudbrick rampart curved around the main citadel at a distance of about 250 m. It had towers at regular intervals and was crowned by defensive structures. This shows part of an inner corner of the main wall, standing to a height of 120 courses to a total of 12 m. At this point the rampart widens to support a fortress of some

8 metres additional height. This mudbrick rampart was attacked and conquered by Cyrus on his way to Sardis in 547 B.C. The outer face of the wall had hundreds of arrowheads embedded in its mud plaster.

R. S. Young, *AJA* 61 (1957) 324; 63 (1959) 264.

227. Arrowheads from the mudbrick outer rampart at Gordium. The arrowheads found stuck in the mud plaster of the outer (east) face of the wall and its towers are of several kinds. The bronze arrowheads are all socketed. Some are of the two-flanged type with a barb on the socket, others are three-flanged, triangular in section. There is a variety of forms and sizes, from 3 to 5.5 cm in length. Iron points also occur. Arrows were undoubtedly returned by the opposing party if they missed their aim. Several arrowheads in the fill had dented tips. The fighting around the tower of the east fortress crowning the rampart must have been especially heavy.

R. S. Young, *Archaeology* 6 (1953) 164–5.

228. Phrygian Yazılıkaya, 'Midas City'. The most important Phrygian citadel in the western highlands between Eskişehir and Afyon is on a natural rock formation (**a**) measuring about 600 m × 100/200 m. Approached from the east, it has a natural elevation of some 30–50 m above the plain. Its most striking landmark now is the carved rock façade (**b**) with the Midas inscription. The façade, in the shape of the front of a Phrygian gabled megaron, 17 m high, stands at the north-eastern tip of the citadel and is visible from afar. The site was excavated from 1937 to 1939. Traces of eighth- to sixth-century Phrygian habitation were found. Strategic devices are rock-cut staircases and tunnels in the north and south parts of the fortress, presumably connected with cisterns to provide water supplies also in times of siege. A spring exists near the north-west tip of the citadel. The fortress may have been captured by Cyrus during his 547/6 campaign, as is indicated by signs of destruction on the citadel.

C. H. E. Haspels, *The Highlands of Phrygia* (Princeton, 1971) 36–40, 139–44; A. Gabriel, *Phrygie, Exploration Archéologique* IV: *La cité de Midas: Architecture* (Paris, 1965); *CAH* Plates to Vols. I & II, pl. 157b (façade).

229. The Midas tumulus at Gordium. To the north east of the citadel of Gordium, in the cemetery of tumuli containing the burials of Phrygian noblemen, the tumulus of Midas dominates the scenery as a giant monument to the great Phrygian king. It is now about 50 m in height and 300 m in diameter; originally it was higher and steeper. The mound was erected over the wooden chamber that contained the burial and paraphernalia of the king. This chamber was larger and better built than any other known timber grave. It was made of large cedar logs, carefully smoothed on the interior. The roof was gabled. Outer walls of juniper logs protected the inner cabin, a rockpile amassed over the construction was retained by a limestone wall. The tumulus proper was made principally of clay which solidified in its dome shape over the rockpile. There was no entrance or dromos to the tomb; the excavation in 1957 proceeded by making an open trench and a tunnel into the core of the tumulus over a length of 140 m.

R. S. Young, *AJA* 62 (1958) 147–54; *id. Gordion* I.

230. Skeleton of Midas in chamber of the great tumulus. In the tomb chamber, which measures 6.20 m × 5.15 m inside, the king had been laid on a large wooden bed. This was set against the north wall, the head of the king at the east. His height was measured as 1.59 m, and the age at death was over sixty. The skeleton, by archaeological and historical inference, must be that of Midas who ruled Phrygia in the last third of the eighth century and the beginning of the seventh. There was no identification in the tomb, although writing occurred on wax strips applied to some of the bronze bowls (**232**). The king was dressed in textile, leather, and a bronze belt. Many fibulae were found on the bed, some part of the king's costume, others holding the bed cloths together. The equipment in the tomb consisted of wooden furniture, bronze cauldrons and large numbers of other bronze vessels, some pottery, many more fibulae, and large bronze belts. There were no weapons, no precious metal, no ivory; the most precious objects are imported metal vessels such as lion- and ram-headed situlae and figural cauldron attachments.

231. Inlaid wooden screens from tomb of Midas. The most outstanding samples of Phrygian furniture are the two screens that leaned against the north wall of the tomb. They are functionally different from the known types of Near Eastern and Greek furniture. Each screen, measuring about 95 cm in height and 80 cm in width, has a horizontal openwork panel attached to the top at the rear, supported by a vertical leg. The screens therefore were portable and could be set up as freestanding backdrops. The front of a screen consists of light box wood inlaid with ornaments (swastikas and small lozenges) of dark yew. An openwork screen, similar in construction and ornament, was found in the tombchamber of a child buried in Tumulus P at Gordium. Whatever the specific meaning of these elaborate screens is, they are part of a long tradition of Phrygian furniture-making, showing fine technical ability in the making and fitting of miniature inlays of contrasting woods and in the composition of native geometric ornament.

R. S. Young, *Expedition* 16:3 (1974) 9–13; *id. Gordion* I 176–81, pl. 44A, B.

232. Bronze bowl with inscription, Midas tomb. A bronze bowl of typical Phrygian shape, with ring-handles attached to bolsters and reinforced with rods along the rim. On the left of one handle, a wax strip had been applied and incised with an inscription reading Si↑idosakor. There are two other bowls with similar strips of wax for the application of graffiti in the Midas tomb. In addition, an omphalos bowl carried an incised graffito on the base, and one pottery vessel had an inscription on the shoulder. Alphabetic Phrygian writing was evidently

232

in use at the time of Midas; the use of wax strips seems to indicate that wax was a medium familiar and readily available to the scribes at Gordium. No wooden tablets have come to light so far at the site.

(Gordion inv. 4824 B 818. Diameter 22.7 cm, height to rim 7.9 cm.)

R. S. Young, *Hesperia* 38 (1969) 261–2; *id. Gordion* I 130, MM68, figs. 84, 134a; pls. 67D, 97A; Appendix I (C. Brixhe).

233

233. Ivory inlay plaque, Gordium. In the burnt debris left by the Cimmerian destruction of the citadel remnants of furniture with ivory inlay were discovered on the floor of megaron 3. The plaque shows a Phrygian warrior on horseback. The man holds a round shield on his left side, covering most of his body. His left hand holds a long spear. The head is covered by a helmet with a cheekpiece and with a crest that curves forward. There are some details for bridle and reins, but none for saddlecloth or saddle on the horse. A series of such warriors on horseback appeared on a charred wooden frieze from another piece of furniture found in megaron 3. These simple reliefs give us a contemporary representation of Phrygian cavalrymen of the eighth century B.C.

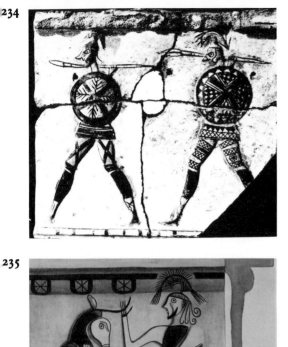

234

235

may be knitted stockings. Several warriors wear greaves and laced boots. These warriors may indeed by Phrygians since the area of the former Hittites of Khattusha and Alaca Hüyük was occupied by Phrygians in the seventh and eighth centuries.

(Ankara Museum. 47 cm × 44 cm. Photograph, after Koşay.)

H. Z. Koşay, *Pazarlı Hafriyatı Raporu. Les Fouilles de Pazarlı* (Ankara, 1941) pls. 21–4, 54; E. Akurgal, *Phrygische Kunst* (Ankara, 1955) 72–8, pls. 45–50; Å. Åkerström, *Die architektonischen Terrakotten Kleinasiens* (Lund, 1966) pls. 90–2, 95–6.

235. Theseus and the Minotaur, terracotta revetment from Gordium. Fragments of revetment plaques illustrating the killing of the Minotaur by Theseus were a somewhat surprising discovery in the Archaic level at Gordium. The drawing shows a reconstruction. Theseus wears a short red tunic. Like all figures on the relief plaques, he is moulded in low relief and rendered more vivid by applied paint. Details vary from plaque to plaque. Theseus' helmet in the best instances has a large double-plumed crest. His weapon is a short sword or dagger with a round pommel. He stabs the Minotaur in the neck while grabbing him by one horn. Both Minotaur and Theseus tend to be provided with garters or leggings. The theme of the hero vanquishing a monster may have taken on special local significance for the Phrygian kings of the sixth century B.C.

(Gordion inv. 5802 BI 333. Height 4.6 cm × 4.8 cm.)
R. S. Young, *AJA* 64 (1960) 240, pl. 60, fig. 25 c; K. DeVries, *From Athens to Gordion* (University Museum Papers 1; Philadelphia 1980) 47, figs. 7–8.

234. Phrygian warriors, terracotta plaques from Pazarlı. Phrygian warriors of the sixth century B.C. are shown on terracotta revetment plaques found at Pazarlı, 29 km north east of the Hittite site of Alaca Hüyük. Like the horsemen from Gordium, they have round shields; their spears are relatively short. The helmets vary in detail according to the whim of the painters who provided the contours and colours. The crests do not project in a forward curve, but sit rather symmetrically on a crestholder. Cheekpieces are indicated in several instances. The short tunics and leggings of the Pazarlı warriors are close-fitting and colourful. The leggings

(Gordion. *c.* 40 cm × 39 cm. Composite drawing by Marian Welker.)
Åkerström, *op. cit.* 145, pls. 78–9.

236. Acropolis, Sardis. The acropolis of Sardis (a) dominates the lower city which stretches to the north of it down to the plain of the Hermus and the East–West highway, with the Pactolus valley as the natural border to the west. The citadel stood on a spur of the Tmolus range, rising 275 m above the level of the Pactolus, with a steep south side, precipices on the east and west, and a more gradual slope in the direction of the lower town. It has been eroded into spectacular crags. In Lydian and Persian times terraces were supported by retaining walls of limestone and sandstone ashlar masonry, some of which have been exposed by the recent excavations of the American Sardis

expedition (**b**). Tunnels lead from the acropolis to the lower north side, perhaps dating back to the Lydian period. The acropolis has extensive building and fortification remains of the Byzantine period. Lydian fortifications are to be postulated.

G. M. A. Hanfmann *et al.*, *Bull. Amer. School Or. Res.* 162 (1961) 32–7; 166 (1962) 35–40; 170 (1963) 31–7; 206 (1972) 15–20; 228 (1977) 48–50; G. M. A. Hanfmann, *Festschrift für Frank Brommer* (Mainz,

1977) 145–54; H. C. Butler, *Sardis* 1: *The Excavations 1910–1914* (Leiden, 1922) 16–25.

237. Tumulus of Gyges(?), Sardis. The large tumulus nicknamed Karnıyarık Tepe may contain the burial chamber of Gyges. This tumulus is one of the three largest in the cemetery Bintepe across the Hermus river north west of Sardis. The largest, eastern tumulus is that of Alyattes. Excavations in the 38 m high 'Gyges'

tumulus in 1964–5 revealed many ancient robbers' tunnels but also came upon a curved limestone retaining wall with a half round moulding (a). This wall would have retained a tumulus of *c.* 90 m in diameter and may have been left unfinished when it was decided to enlarge the tumulus to about twice the original size. Mason's marks or signs to be read as 'Gugu' are engraved in the upper ashlar course of the retaining wall (b). The tomb chamber of the tumulus has not yet been located. The chamber in the Alyattes mound is of fine marble masonry.

G. M. A. Hanfmann *et al., Bull. Amer. School Or. Res.* 174 (1964) 53–5; 177 (1965) 27–35; 182 (1966) 27–30; 186 (1967) 43–6; R. Gusmani, *Neue epichorische Schriftzeugnisse aus Sardis* (Cambridge, Mass., 1975) 67–71.

238. The acropolis of Xanthus is set on a limestone rock formation on the east bank of the Xanthus river, protected by steep cliffs on the river side, and overlooking the alluvial plain to the south. The road to the west crosses the river just to the south of the citadel. The elevation above the river plain is about 50 metres; a saddle to the north separates the Lycian citadel from the higher Roman acropolis, the east slopes of which have Lycian tombs. The modern coastline is about 8 km south of Xanthus, but anciently the formation of the coast and the estuary of the river must have been different. The Lycian dynasty of the eighth to fifth centuries had its residences in an enclosure on the highest point of the citadel. The existing fortification walls date to the fifth century B.C. or later. There is no evidence of pre-eighth-century occupation on the citadel.

Fouilles de Xanthos, Institut français d'archéologie d'Istanbul II: H. Metzger, *L'acropole lycienne* (Paris, 1963).

239. Pillar tomb and rockcut tombs, upper acropolis at Xanthus. On the east spur of the upper (Roman) acropolis of Xanthus, overlooking the southern plain, stand a number of

238

239

Lycian tombs. They are all plundered and therefore difficult to date precisely. The two types represented here are characteristic of Lycian funerary architecture. The pillar tomb is set on a rockcut stepped base. Its monolithic pillar of 4.75 m height supports a chamber partly hollowed out in the pillar and partly constructed of marble slabs; this chamber had a door in the north side. The roof is a slab of stepped profile. There is no trace of decoration left on the marble slabs of the burial chamber. In the rock below the pillar tomb, three tombs were cut with façades imitating Lycian timber

construction. One of the lower panels in each tomb has a sliding door. The chambers have rockcut benches or *klinai* along the walls. These four tombs are traditional in shape although they may date to the fourth century B.C.

P. Demargne, *Fouilles de Xanthos* 1: *Les Piliers Funéraires* (Paris, 1958) 113–22.

240. Carian funerary stela from North Saqqara, Egypt. The Egyptian limestone stela from a Carian cemetery in Memphis was found re-used in the lining of a fourth-century votive pit. It

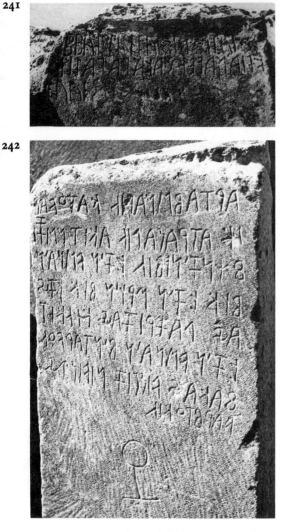

241

242

can discern in the figures or fashions, but the inscriptions identify the figures as Carian. An East Greek–West Anatolian koine is shared by these sixth-century figures representing Carians in Memphis. The two vertical inscriptions, beginning below, are written dextroverse and are partly worn away. Their meaning is obscure, but certainly funerary.

(Cambridge, Fitzwilliam Museum, E 1.1971. Height 91.2 cm, width 37 cm. Drawing, G. Denning.)
    W. B. Emery, *JEA* 56 (1970) pl. 10, p. 6; R. V. Nicholls in *Archaeological Reports 1970–71*, 75–6; O. Masson, *Carian Inscriptions from North Saqqara and Buhen* (London, 1979) no. 3.

241. Old-Phrygian rock-cut inscription at the site Yazılıkaya, 'Midas City' (see **228**). Boustrophedon, undeciphered; probably a dedication.

    J. Friedrich, *Kleinasiatische Sprachdenkmäler* (Berlin, 1932) 125, no. 3.

242. Lydian inscription on a funeral stela from Sardis. The stela had an anthemion finial of Greek type. The twelve sinistroverse lines are well engraved and seem to carry an epitaph for two men: X, son of Artabanas (a Persian name) and Katovas, son of Atrasas.

(Izmir Museum.)
    Sardis VI.2 (Leiden, 1924) 8, pl. 4; Friedrich, *op. cit.* 111, no. 8.

is no earlier than the mid-fifth century in date. Under a winged disk of Egyptian tradition, a Carian man and woman stand facing each other in a scene of affection and farewell. They touch each other's chins and the man grasps the woman's wrist. The woman wears Carian–West Anatolian costume: a long crinkly chiton and a mantle or long veil which is pulled over her head. A kolpos of the chiton hangs over her belt. The man is dressed in a long garment with the hem at ankle-length; over this he wears a short mantle draped over arms and shoulders. There is nothing distinctively Carian that we

243. Trilingual inscription on limestone from the Letôon site, south west of Xanthus. Face A, the top of which is shown here, bears 41 lines in Lycian; face B, 27 lines in Aramaean; face C, 35 lines in Greek. The Lycian is dextroverse. It is dated to year 1 of one Artaxerxes, probably 358 B.C. Lines 1–2 may be translated as follows: 'When Pigesere (Pixodarus) son of Katamla (Ekatomnôs) was satrap of Termis (Lycia) . . .' (after Laroche).

(Height 1.35 m; width 0.575 m.)
    H. Metzger, E. Laroche, A. Dupont-Sommer, and M. Mayrhofer, *Fouilles de Xanthos* VI: *La Stèle trilingue du Létôon* (Paris, 1979).

11. THE THRACIANS

G. MIHAILOV

After the great migrations in the Balkan–Aegean area during the second half of the second and first centuries of the first millennium B.C. the Thracians occupied a broad territory between the Black Sea, the Vardar region, the Aegean and the trans-Danubian countries – quite apart from their presence in the Troad and Bithynia. Their country offered a varied aspect of mountains and plains, watered by many great rivers and their tributaries, rich in forests, fish and game, in places also rich in metals (iron, copper, gold, silver) and with fertile soil (for grain and the vine). The Thracians, the origins of whose name remains unknown, kept their organization in tribes but evolved towards a state with the breakdown of class divisions. This is the time of the formation of the states of the Odrysae, the Bessoi, the Thynoi and the Getae, and of their intertribal conflicts. One of these was between the Apsynthioi and Dolonkoi in the sixth century and it led to the establishment of the Athenian Philaidae on the Thracian Chersonese about 555, which, with Sigeum on the facing Anatolian shore, assured control of the straits (the Dardanelles) for Athens. This activity in the Aegean by Pisistratus and the Philaidae marked the beginning of Athenian expansion into Thrace, a move which partook of the general character of colonization although the Athenians had been anticipated on this coast by other Greek cities, notably Chalcis, Megara and Miletus. At first commercial relations between the Thracians and Greeks were not close and the foundation of the colonies was usually accompanied by struggles, which sometimes proved long and disastrous for them.

The Thracian states were of the archaic type: a king – at first a priest-king – and a privileged nobility. The Thracians were good warriors, on foot or horseback, and particularly famous as peltasts (light-armed troops, so named from the lunate *pelte* shield). The people lived in townships, sometimes fortified, villages and hamlets, and had fortified strongpoints. In their life style, customs, traditions and beliefs there were always tribal peculiarities and social differences, but there was a general practice of polygamy, and concubinage, tattooing and various styles of coiffure were current, while music and the dance played major roles. Their funerary rites admitted both cremation and inhumation. In different areas it was the practice to bury kings and nobles in dolmens (to the seventh century), in rock-cut tombs, in rock mausolea of singular form open to the sky, and especially beneath tumuli. We know little of their religion but it appears that their pantheon was well evolved (there is evidence for Apollo, Bendis, Ares). The characteristic style of their art – pottery, metal vessels, jewellery, etc. – is Geometric and this is found to be common to all social strata and so can be regarded as a truly national style, though beginning to admit influence from Anatolia.

GENERAL BIBLIOGRAPHY

Ch. M. Danov, *Altthrakien* (Berlin, New York, 1976)
R. F. Hoddinott, *Bulgaria in Antiquity* (London, 1975)
G. Kazarov, *Beiträge zur Kulturgeschichte der Thraker* (Sarajevo, 1916)
G. Mihailov, 'Le processus d'urbanisation de l'espace balkanique jusqu'à la fin de l'Antiquité', IIIe Congrès international d'Etudes du Sud-Est européen (Bucarest, 1974)
I. Venedikov and T. Gerasimov, *Thracian Art Treasures* (Sofia, London, 1975)

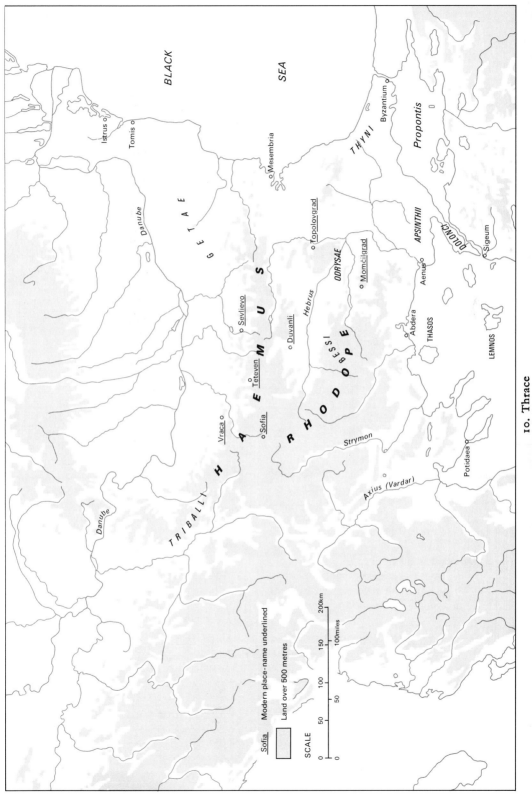

BLACK SEA

Propontis

Danube

GETAE

Istrus

Tomis

Mesembria

THYNI

Byzantium

APSINTHII

DOLONCI

Sigeum

Topolovgrad

Sevlievo

ODRYSAE

Momčilgrad

Hebrus

Duvanli

Teteven

RHODOPE

BESSI

Aenus

Abdera

THASOS

LEMNOS

Sofia

Vraca

HAEMUS

TRIBALLI

Danube

Strymon

Axius (Vardar)

Potidaea

Sofia   Modern place-name underlined

Land over 500 metres

SCALE

0   50   100   150   200km

0   50   100miles

10. Thrace

244. Dolmen near the village of Bâlgarska Poljana in the Topolovgrad district, in the Sakar mountains. Eighth–seventh century B.C. The dolmens are 2 to 4 m long, constructed of big, rough-hewn stones. Some consist of a simple burial chamber while others have more developed forms. There is often a short dromos to the door of the chamber and in some dolmens this is entered through one or two antechambers. The dolmens had been covered with earth and the low mound was often retained by a circular, low rough-stone wall or krepis. This dolmen has a burial chamber measuring 2.2 m × 1.5 m × 2.1 m high, with two antechambers, the larger measuring 1.5 m × 1.6 m × 1.7 m, and something resembling a dromos.

I. Venedikov *et al.*, *Megalitite v Trakija. Megalithi Thraciae; Les megalithes en Thrace*, in *Trakijski pametnici, Monumenta Thraciae antiquae* I (1976) 40–3, drawings, 20–27, pls. 36–44; on dolmens generally, 36–50, figs. 1–66.

There is a stair to the sepulchral niche from which one ascends to a platform where there is another grave cut in the open air. This peculiar plan for a rock-cut tomb is so far unique.

Venedikov, *et al.*, *Megalitite v Trakija*, 94–5, drawings 94–8, pls. 173–9.

245. Rock tomb (seen from the north west) near the village of Tatul in the Momčilgrad district, in the Eastern Rhodope mountains. Seventh–sixth century B.C. Two graves were cut in the rock, hewn in the form of a pyramid.

246. Ritual bronze axe from Teteven (Central Stara planina). Tenth–seventh century B.C. The massive bronze blade is decorated along its rear edge with the heads of a bull, a ram and a goat. There are two small round holes near the

weapons of this period were normally made of iron, indicates their association with cult. There are similar axes of this period in Asia Minor and especially in Persia.

(Sofia Archaeological Museum, Prehistoric Dept. inv. no. 745. Height 12.5 cm.)
Venedikov, *Thracian Art Treasures* 23–5, pls. 4–8.

247. Bronze figurine of a stag (partly damaged) from the Sevlievo District (Central Stara planina). Tenth–seventh century B.C. The almost triangular head is carried by a prismatic neck and body, the edges marking belly, spine and sides. Only the shoulders and thighs have been treated at all realistically. The antlers are stylized as hooks, reminiscent of bird heads. There are isolated figurines of animals – stag, horse, birds – from the Thracian region. Their geometric style at times betrays the influence of Greek art (a statuette from near Philippi) and at times elements from the Near East, especially from Persia of the pre-Achaemenian period (the Sevlievo stag shown here).

(Sofia Archaeological Museum, Prehistoric Dept. inv. no. 747. Height 16 cm.)
Venedikov, *Thracian Art Treasures* 25–6, pls. 5, 9.

248. Bronze headstall found with horse trappings at the village of Sofronievo in the Vraca District. Seventh–sixth century B.C. Elliptical open-work with geometric wings, a bird's tail, a boss with ornamental patterns, a horned animal head (probably a bull) and incised rings with a bold centre point and spirals. Bronze plaques as horse trappings are found in Thrace and neighbouring areas, in the form of a cross, a rosette or the like (usually open-work), in a geometric style. These too show links with the

cutting edge. This belongs to a series of axes whose rear edges, which are straight or crescent-shaped, are wholly decorated with heads or whole figures of animals. These are treated in a formal geometricized style. The axe and handle were cast in one piece, or an iron rod was fixed to the short bronze handle which gave the whole the appearance of a sceptre. Some axes have two or three holes cut in them for attachment to dress or for some other purpose. Others, without a handle, were worn as amulets suspended from a necklace by a hole or ring. The very fact that these axes were not provided with a shaft hole for a solid (wooden) handle and were always of bronze, while real

249a

249b

249d

249. Jewellery from the Mušovica mound near the village of Duvanli in the Plovdiv District. End of the sixth century B.C. (**a**) Gold earring (one of a pair) in the form of a loop with upturned ends. The terminals are short cylinders decorated with gold filigree spirals topped by pyramids decorated with granulation and a gold ball. Height 3.6 cm, weight 26.4 gm (the other, 26.05 gm). (**b**) Gold earring, one of ten of the same type found in a grave. Filigree lines and rosettes on the hoop and granule patterns of lines and triangles, with a pyramid of four balls at the end. Height 3.2 cm, weight 9.9 gm. (**c**) Gold pectoral decorated at the edges with repoussé birds in profile. At the end holes through which are inserted two fibulae (13.1 and 13.5 gm) of semicircular form from which hang three loop-in-loop chains with pine-cone terminals. Length 26 cm, weight 195.8 gm. (**d**) Gold necklace of 19 fluted beads. Weight 11.5 gm.

There is a large group of tumuli at Duvanli containing rich burials of nobles and royalty. The earrings are stylistically closest to finds in Macedonia (P. Amandry, *Collection Hélène Stathatou. Les Bijoux Antiques* (Strasbourg, 1953) 54–5 and figs. 135–42) but the decoration of the pectoral more resembles the art of Asia Minor. The birds are treated in an eastern, Persian manner. Compare, for instance, those on the

arts of the Near East. This find contains several pieces of harness and a geometrically designed belt buckle.

(Vraca Archaeological Museum. Height 7 cm.)
Venedikov, *Thracian Art Treasures* 22–3, pls. 11–20.

250

252a

252b

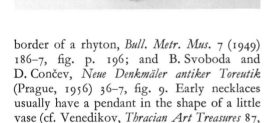

251

border of a rhyton, *Bull. Metr. Mus.* 7 (1949) 186–7, fig. p. 196; and B. Svoboda and D. Končev, *Neue Denkmäler antiker Toreutik* (Prague, 1956) 36–7, fig. 9. Early necklaces usually have a pendant in the shape of a little vase (cf. Venedikov, *Thracian Art Treasures* 87, fig. 204, from the Kazanlâk region).

((a) Sofia Archaeological Museum. (b–d) Plovdiv Archaeological Museum inv. 1537, 1531–3, 1535.)

B. Filov, *Die Grabbügelnekropole bei Duvanlij in Südbulgarien* (Sofia, 1934); Venedikov, *Thracian Art Treasures* 86–93, figs. 179, 180, 204, 214; for the Duvanli jewellery, R. A. Higgins, *Greek and Roman Jewellery* (London, 1961) ch. 12 and 213; for Duvanli, also R. F. Hoddinott, *Bulgaria in Antiquity* (London, 1975) 58–69.

250. Clay basin (*podanipter*) from the village of Široko Pole in the Momčilgrad district, in the Rhodope mountains. Ninth–eighth century B.C. The deep conical bowl on three legs is decorated at the rim with incised triangles

filled with white paste, which appear also on the legs and 'paws'. This is a good specimen of the pottery of the period. There is a great variety in shapes, usually with geometric incised decoration: triangles, circles, spirals or maeanders, never animal motifs. There is no painting in Thrace. The influence of metal techniques, such as the presence of grooves, can be detected.

(Sofia Archaeological Museum, Prehistoric Dept. inv. 2952. Height 33 cm.)

Venedikov, *Thracian Art Treasures* 26–7, pls. 27–9.

251. Gold cup from Kazičane, near Sofia. Probably eighth–seventh century B.C. The deep cup is almost a hemisphere, cut off to a flat bottom. The shallow ribbed rim is decorated with two rows of dotted semicircles. The bowl has 19 repoussé flutes, and on the base within are two concentric circles with eight buds between them and one central, all surrounded by a dotted line. The buds are linked by a dotted line and between them and the outer circle are eight lightly incised dotted circles.

(Museum of the History of Sofia inv. no. MUCA 3012. Height 12.5 cm, diameter 27 cm, weight 1.05 kg, 23.60 carat.)

M. Stančeva, 'Une coupe en or de Sofia', *Thracia. Primus Congressus Studiorum Thracicorum* III (1974) 221–41, figs. 4–6.

252. Thracian town wall and gate (**b**) at Mesambria, on the Black Sea. Seventh–sixth century B.C., or a little earlier, before the foundation of the Greek colony at the end of the sixth century. The town (modern Nesebâr) has a Thracian name of unknown etymology. It is built on a peninsula with a long and very narrow isthmus. The first inhabitants were Thracians, driven out at the end of the sixth century by the Greek colonists from Megara and her settlements at Byzantium and Chalcedon. The Thracian wall enclosed a small area near the isthmus, no more than 2,000 sq. m, a tiny part of the whole peninsula. The excavated stretch, about 40 m long, is at the north west, about one metre wide and high; the original height was no more than three metres. It was constructed of rough stones. There was more careful masonry and mudbrick at the gate which had two leaves outside and one like a portcullis within. There were two rectangular towers (3 m × 2.8 m) flanking the gate.

I. Venedikov *et al.*, *Nessèbre* I (Sofia, 1966), II (Sofia, 1980) 75–80, figs. 51–65, 69, 70; Hoddinott, *op. cit.* 41–9.

12. THE SCYTHIANS

T. SULIMIRSKI

The Scythians met by colonizing Greeks on the shores of the Black Sea, were not an indigenous people, and the tribes with whom the Greeks dealt in south Russia were comparatively new arrivals. The Cimmerians, who ravaged Phrygia in the seventh century, had long been at home in the Ukraine (the Catacomb culture) from which they were displaced by the Scythians. The principal tribes of the latter moved north from north-west Iran, across the Caucasus into the Kuban and south Russia. Their animal-style art is closely related to that of other nomad peoples, of Iran and the farther Asian steppes, but it carries too the mark of their sojourn in the neighbourhood of the Mesopotamian empire of the Assyrians, and eventually confronts Greek Archaic art, itself 'orientalizing' but in a markedly different manner, in the sixth century B.C.

GENERAL BIBLIOGRAPHY

CAH III².2, ch. 33*a*
M. Artamonov, *Treasures from the Scythian Tombs* (London, 1970)
Boardman, *GO* 256–64
From the Lands of the Scythians (Metr. Mus. of Art and Los Angeles County Mus. of Art, not dated)
E. Minns, *Scythians and Greeks* (Cambridge, 1913)
Or des Scythes (Paris, 1975)

253a

253b

254

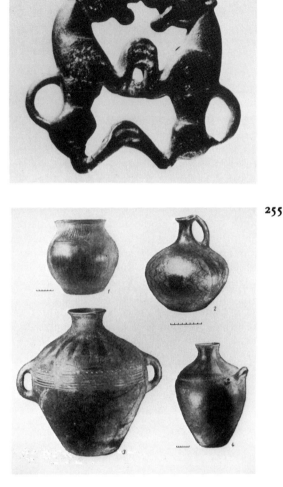

255

253. (a) Clay 'incense-burner' or lamp from a burial of the Catacomb culture in the Ukraine. (b) A similar object from Alishar Hüyük in Phrygia (Anatolia). Found in the level which may mark the Cimmerian destruction of 680 B.C. (Stratum V). The latter is an important find which supports the identification of the Catacomb culture with the Cimmerians. Such vessels, on a cross-foot and with the partition within the bowl, represent a type very common in graves of the Manych group of the Catacomb culture in the north Caucasus and on the Don. According to written records the Cimmerians lived formerly in the Ukraine, east of the Dnepr. Around 1400–1200 B.C., chased by the Scythians, they retreated partly into the Crimea and partly into the central part of the Caucasus. New Scythian pressure around 900–800 B.C. forced them to move again southwards, into Soviet Armenia and ancient Cappadocia, and farther west. The incense-burner from Alishar Hüyük marks their presence there.

((b) Diameter 15.6–16.8 cm. Photograph after Schmidt.)

E. F. Schmidt, *The Alishar Hüyük 1928–9* II (Chicago, 1933) 53, fig. 65, a 127.

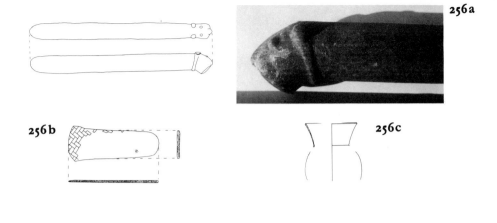

256a

256b

256c

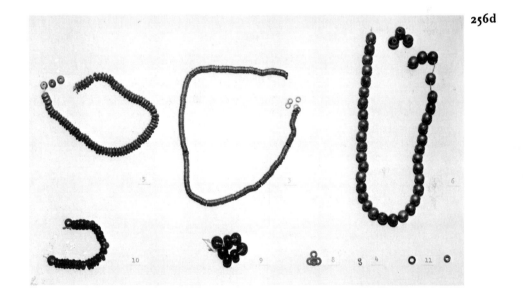

256d

254. Bronze belt clasp or bridle decoration in the form of two lions, from the Tsukur Liman barrow grave (considered Cimmerian). Openwork, in the form of two upright lions, recalling the heraldic figures on pole-tops from Cappadocia and from other sites in Anatolia.

(Leningrad, Hermitage Museum, T 1913, 55. Height 4.3 cm. Photograph after *Or des Scythes*.)
  Artamonov, *Treasures . . . Scythian Tombs* 15, fig. 14; *From the Lands* no. 39; *Or des Scythes* no. 32.

255. Pottery from the grave of a Scythian chief (21 vessels) in the Small Barrow at Kyamil Tepe in the eastern part of Azerbaijan. Seventh century B.C. The burial formed part of the Scythian group, the best known site of which was Mingechaur on the Kura. Mingechaur was seized first by the Early Iranians (presumably early Medes and/or Persians) in about the eleventh or even the twelfth century B.C., and then, in the ninth–eighth century, by the early

256e

256f

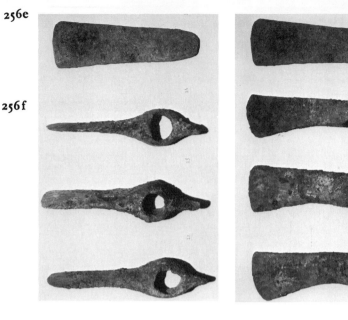

Scythians advancing southwards. The country had then been called 'Sacassene'. Early in the sixth century these were forced by the expansion of the Medes to retreat northwards into the northern Caucasus. Late in the fifth century, under pressure from the Sarmatian Siraces, these Scythians had to abandon the Caucasus and move farther northwards. All the circumstances suggest that they had reached as far as the afforested part of the Ukraine east of the Dnepr, where they contributed to the formation of the Sula group of the Scythian culture.

(Photograph, after Iessen.)

A. A. Iessen, *Materialy i Issledovaniya po Arkheologii SSSR* 125 (1965) 26, fig. 8.

256. Objects from two tombs at Sé Girdan near Hasanlu, south west of Lake Urmia. From Tumulus III: (**a**) a whetstone sceptre (length 37 cm); (**b**) a bronze flat adze (length 13.4 cm); (**c**) a silver vessel. From Tumulus IV: (**d**) 565 gold and 38 carnelian beads; (**e**) a bronze flat adze (length 13.8 cm); (**f**) three bronze axes (lengths, 14.3, 14.5, 13.9 cm). See note after the next item.

(Iran Bastan Museum, Tehran. Photographs and drawing, O. Muscarella.)

O. W. Muscarella, *Metropolitan Museum Journal* 2 (1969) 21, figs. 25–9; 4 (1971) 14, figs. 13–14.

257. Cheekpieces of bone and silver. (**a–c**) Three bone cheekpieces from Kaplantu, east of Ziwiye. Seventh century B.C. Carved with animal-head terminals. (**d**) Flat silver cheekpieces from the barrow grave Ulskii 2, in the north-west Caucasus. With cut-out and incised animal decoration. (**e–j**) Six bone cheek pieces from the Ukraine. Sixth century B.C. Four are carved with animal-head terminals.

((**a–c**) New York, Metropolitan Museum 58.131, gift of Khalil Rabenou. (**d**) Leningrad, Hermitage Museum. Length 22 cm. After Rostovtseff. (**e–j**) Warsaw, State Archaeological Museum.)

(**d**) Artamonov, *Treasures . . . Scythian Tombs* pl. 56; M. Rostovtseff, *The Animal Style* (Oxford, 1929) 27–8, pl. 8.1.

The objects shown in **256–7** come from the centre of the ancient country of Mannai (Kaplantu), or from its western border (Sé Girdan). Tumuli of the latter site formed a small cemetery of six mounds of the Iron IIIb or IV period, of the seventh century B.C. They were presumably associated with the Scythian branch which ultimately reached Mannai via Azerbaijan. They seem to have belonged to the branch subsequently ruled by King Bartatua. The Kaplantu cheekpieces illustrate well the gradual adoption by the early Scythians of zoomorphic decoration.

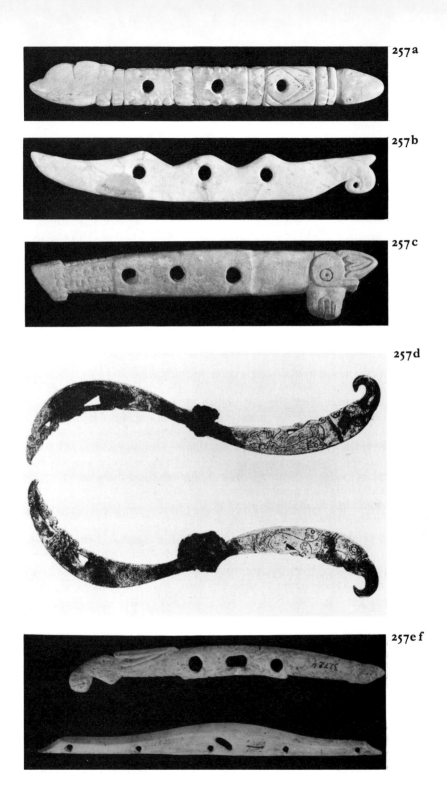

257a

257b

257c

257d

257e f

189

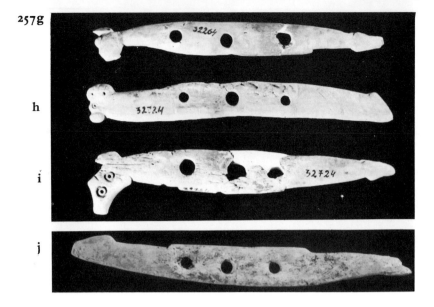

257g

h

i

j

The decoration of one of the specimens is geometric, like that of the cheekpieces of the Srubnaya and Andronovo cultures, although their patterns and manner of execution are different. Notable is the way their tops are given the shape of fish heads. Another specimen was evidently carved to imitate the common eastern cheekpieces of the type from Ulskii 2 barrow, shown in **257d**. Another Kaplantu cheekpiece is of the type which eventually was generally accepted for use by Scythians in Europe (**257e–j**).

258. Gold belt cover from Ziwiye. Interlace with facing lion heads at the joints, recumbent stags and goats in the interstices. Seventh century B.C.

(Iran Bastan Museum, Tehran, 12516.)
   Bull. Inst. Arch. London 1978, 23 with fig. 11 (detail).

259. Gold sheet from a gorytus case from barrow 4–1903, Kelermes, south-west Caucasus. Curled quadrupeds (panthers?) along the edges, recumbent stags in the panels. Sixth century B.C. The decoration was evidently based on the patterns represented on the belt cover, **258**, which is earlier by at least a few decades. Both may serve as examples, out of many, to indicate the derivation of the early Royal

Scythian art from that bred several decades earlier in north-west Iran. Recent archaeological discoveries have revealed abundant evidence in this area for a vigorous animal style of the early centuries of the first millennium B.C., in the provinces Gilan and Mazaderan. It is no longer necessary to assume that the origin of all sophisticated animal-style art lay north of the Caucasus.

(Leningrad, Hermitage Museum, Ku 1904, 1/28. 40.5 cm × 22.2 cm. Photograph, after *Or des Scythes*.)
   Artamonov, *Treasures . . . Scythian Tombs* pl. 21; *From the Lands* no. 26; *Or des Scythes* no. 19.

260. Assyrian silver calf's head, decoration from a table, from a cremation burial at Alekseevka-Krivorozhe on the Kalitva, a tributary of the Don. The burial also yielded a gold circlet, possibly from a helmet, and the top of an East Greek clay oinochoe, in the form of a ram's head, of the end of the seventh century B.C.

(Photograph, after Mantsevich.)
   A. P. Mantsevich, *Arch. Ertesito* 88 (1961.1) 79, fig. 2; Boardman, *GO* 244.

261. Assyrian gilt silver leg shoe (from a set of four) for a small table or stool, from the Melgunov Barrow, the Ukraine. Late seventh to sixth century B.C.

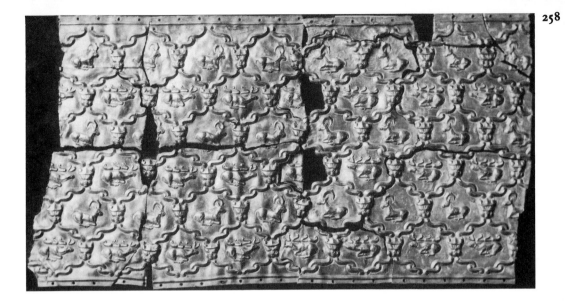

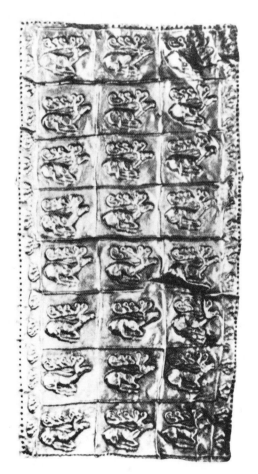

261

(Leningrad, Hermitage Museum 1763. 1/23. Height 11 cm. Photograph, after *Or des Scythes*.)

R. D. Barnett, *Iranica Antiqua* 2 (1962) pl. 6; *From the Lands* no. 17; *Or des Scythes* no. 33.

262. Gold chain from Ziwiye.

(Iran Bastan Museum, Tehran, 11606. Length 50 cm.)

Bull. Inst. Arch. London 1978, 24, fig. 12.

263. Gold and other objects from a find at Witaszkovo (Vettersfelde) in western Poland. About 500 B.C. The most notable object was the gold fish, shown in **375**. The other finds are shown here (apart from a number of bronze 'Scythian' arrowheads): a gold chain; a gold hoop with soldered ends (diameter 21 cm); gold

262

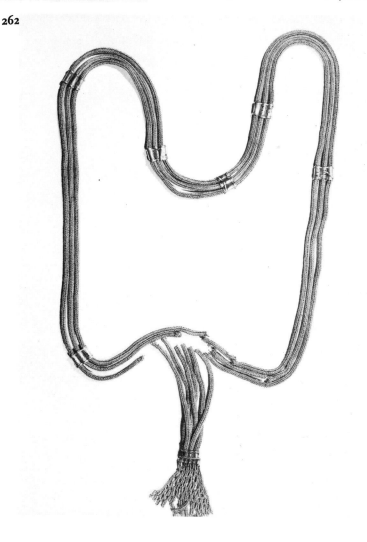

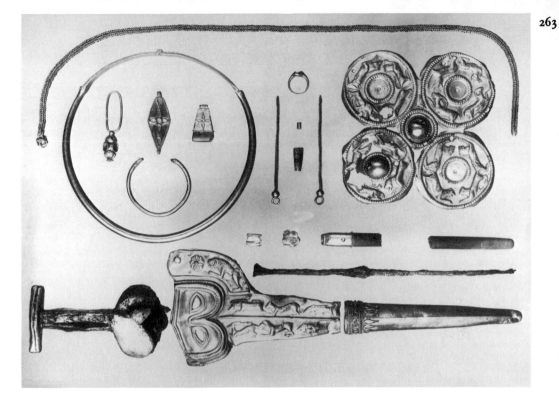

pendants, one perhaps an earring, and bracelet; a pectoral for a horse (?) of four circlets decorated with animals; a finger-ring; a whetstone in a gold mount; short sword and scabbard of Scythian type (*akinakes*) decorated with animals. The articles appear to represent grave goods from a cremation burial of around 500 B.C., evidently of a Scythian princeling or chief, who presumably fell during a plunder raid into Central Europe.

(Berlin, Staatliche Museen (West), Misc. 7839–7855.)
   A. Greifenhagen, *Schmuckarbeiten in Edelmetall* I (Berlin, 1970) pls. 41–4; *From the Lands* 153–5; A. Greifenhagen, *Antike Welt* 13.3 (1982) 3–9.

Articles shown in **258–9, 262**, found in various parts of eastern Europe, and some (**263**) in Central Europe, represent either genuine 'Scythian' types or their direct successors, modelled upon them and presumably made in Kerch (Panticapaeum, the Greek colony) or in workshops of ancient Scythia. Some authors wrongly consider them Scythian spoils, taken during Scythian plunder raids in western

Asiatic countries, or as acquired by way of trade. The map showing the geographical diffusion of the articles (**264**) and the distances separating the sites, demonstrates the nonsense of such allegations. No traces have been found of any trade at that time in such precious goods between the areas concerned. These were evidently the property of west Asiatic Scythians, acquired around the turn of the seventh and sixth century, during their stay in western Iran or in the Caucasus area; while those of later date were imitative works made by local artisans for their heirs.

264. Map showing the supposed northward migrations of the early Scythians of the west Asiatic Kuban group and the east Caucasian group. The sites plotted have yielded remains of the west Asiatic Scythians and of their successors of, approximately, the seventh century (1, 2), the early sixth century (3–6), the first half of the sixth century (7–13), the late sixth century (14–17). The presumed route into Europe of the west Asiatic Scythians is marked, and the direction of migration northwards of the east Caucasian Scythians.

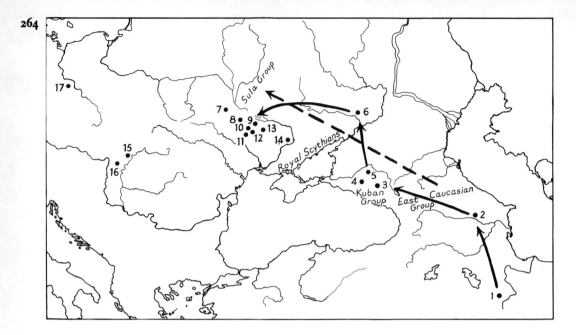

List of sites plotted:

1. Ziwiye	6. Alekseevka-Krivorozhe	10. Makeevka	14. Tomakovka
2. Mingechaur	7. Mala Ofirna	11. Zhurovka	15. Zoldhalompuszta
3. Kostromskaya	8. Syniavka	12. Osytniazhka	16. Tapioszentmarton
4. Kelermes	9. Zhabotin	13. Litoi	17. Witaszkovo
5. Ulskii			(Vettersfelde)

13. THE GREEK WORLD

JOHN BOARDMAN
(325 *by Mervyn R. Popham*)

The Greek lands

The geography of Greece – its long coastline, many islands, land masses partitioned by ridge and river into self-contained enclaves with few and small open plains – determined the history of Greece and, no doubt, contributed to determination of the character of its people. For some sites considerations of defence and sustenance worked together to ensure long continuity of occupation; others enjoyed briefer periods of prosperity determined by the temper of the age. Broader geographical areas, like counties or provinces dominated by one city, begin to emerge as cultural units even in this early period, though their validity as political units is more apparent with some (Attica, Thessaly) than others (Boeotia, the Argolid). Common characteristics of the Greek landscape and agricultural conditions were recognized on other Mediterranean shores, and where settlement rather than trade was the prime concern,

it is generally sites of Hellenic aspect or climate that are preferred, where vine or olive can flourish and there is safe access to the sea. The pictures in this section offer a selection of the types of setting chosen for settlements in Greek lands.

GENERAL BIBLIOGRAPHY

M. Grant, *The Ancient Mediterranean* (London, 1969)
A. Philippson and E. Kirsten, *Griechische Landschaften* I–III (Frankfurt am Main, 1950–9)
R. Schoder, *Ancient Greece from the Air* (London, 1974)
V. Scully, *The Earth, the Temple and the Gods* (New Haven, 1962) argues that landscape and setting could determine the placing of Greek sites and sanctuaries, but he does not allow adequately for other factors and for the changes effected by time and chance
C. Vita-Finzi, *The Mediterranean Valleys* (Cambridge, 1969)

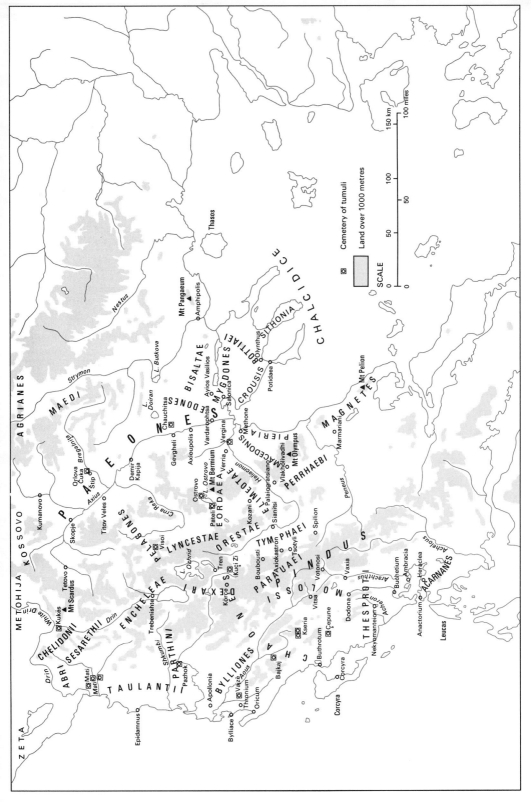

11. North Greece

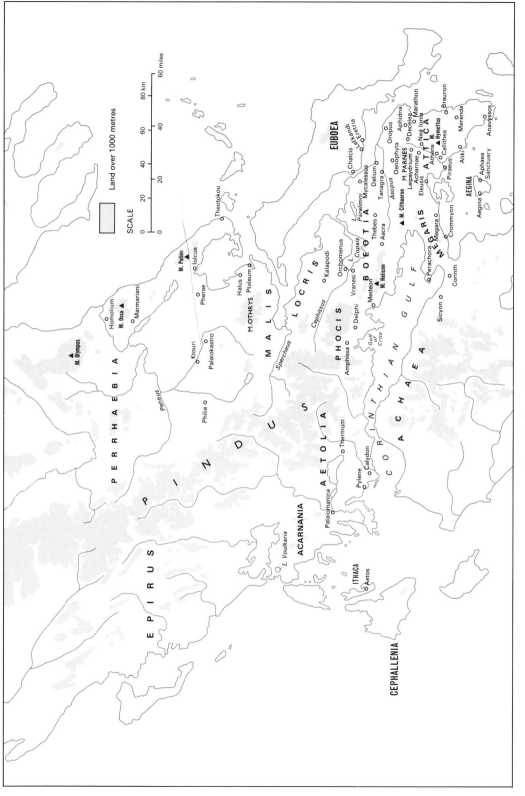

12. Central Greece

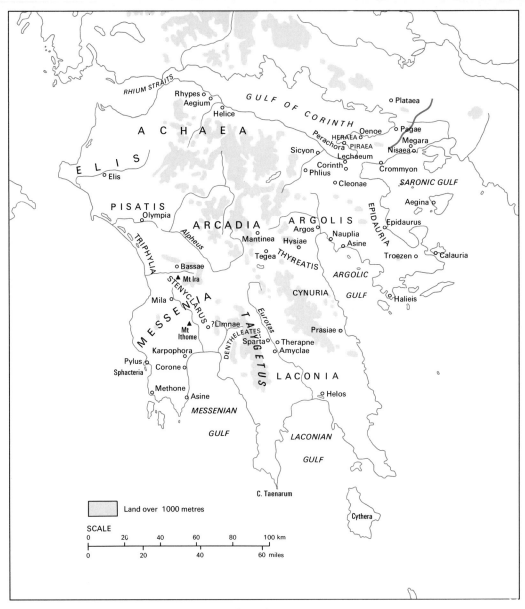

13. The Peloponnese

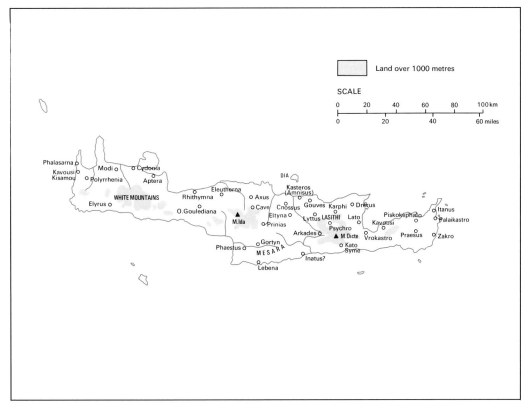

Land over 1000 metres

SCALE

| 0 | 20 | 40 | 60 | 80 | 100 km |
| 0 | | 20 | | 40 | 60 miles |

Phalasarna

Kavousi
Kisamou

Modi

Cydonia

Polyrrhenia

Aptera

Eleutherna

DIA

Kasteros
(Amnisus)

WHITE MOUNTAINS

Rhithymna

Axus

Elyrus

O.Goulediana

Cave

Cnossus

Gouves

Karphi

Dretus

Itanus

Eltyna

Lyttus

LASITHI

Lato

Piskokephalo

Palaikastro

M.Ida

Prinias

Psychro

Kavousi

Arkades

M.Dicte

Vrokastro

Praesus

Zakro

Phaestus

Gortyn

M E S A R A

Kato
Syme

Inatus?

Lebena

14. Crete

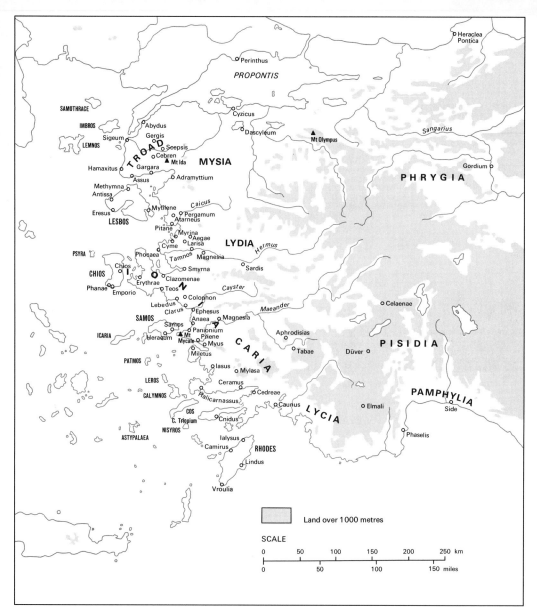

Heraclea
Pontica

Perinthus

PROPONTIS

SAMOTHRACE

Cyzicus

IMBROS
Abydus
Gergis
Sigeum
LEMNOS Scepsis
Cebren
T R O A D Mt Ida
Hamaxitus Gargara
Assus
Methymna Adramyttium
Antissa

Eresus Mytilene *Caicus*
Pergamum
LESBOS Atarneus
Pitane
Myrina
Aegae
Cyme Larisa
PSYRA Phocaea Tamnos Magnesia
CHIOS Chios Smyrna
Phanae Erythrae Clazomenae
Emporio Teos *Cayster*
Lebedus Colophon
SAMOS Clarus Ephesus
Anaea Magnesia
Samos Panionium
ICARIA Heraeum Mt Phene
Mycale Myus
Miletus
PATMOS
Iasus
LEROS Mylasa
Ceramus
CALYMNOS Cedreae
Halicarnassus
Caunus
COS
C. Triopium Cnidus
NISYROS
ASTYPALAEA Ialysus
Camirus RHODES
Lindus

Vroulia

Dascyleum

Mt Olympus

Sangarius

Gordium

P H R Y G I A

MYSIA

LYDIA *Hermus*

Sardis

Maeander

Celaenae

Aphrodisias

Tabae Düver

C A R I A

Elmali

PISIDIA

PAMPHYLIA

Side

LYCIA

Phaselis

Land over 1000 metres

SCALE

0   50   100   150   200   250 km

0   50   100   150 miles

15. East Greece

265. The site at Lefkandi (Xeropolis), near the mouth of the River Lelas, between Chalcis and Eretria in the island of Euboea. In the Dark Ages the broad, low site, well served by anchorages at either side, was one of the most prosperous in Greece (see **325**) and possibly the starting point of the overseas ventures which brought Euboeans and islanders to the coasts of Syria and of central Italy. It was not fortified and had access to rich farmland, the Lelantine plain. The Lelantine War may have been the occasion for its abandonment at the end of the eighth century, by which time its role in the island appears to have been taken over by Eretria, where major Iron Age settlement begins only in the first half of the eighth century.

CAH III².1, 754–65; *Lefkandi* I.

266. The site at Zagora, on the west coast of Andros in the Cyclades, from the east. The township was occupied through the eighth century B.C. The Cyclades offer little by way of agricultural wealth and their inhabitants looked inevitably to the sea. The broad, steep peninsula of Zagora was fortified on its landward

side, against the rest of the island it would seem, which has encouraged the suggestion that it was a non-Andrian foundation, from Euboea. It was possible to beach ships at either side of the promontory. See the plan, *CAH* III².3, 768, fig. 81.

A. Cambitoglou *et al.*, *Zagora* I (Sydney, 1971).

267. Drerus, in north-west Crete, from the south west. The centre of the Archaic and Classical site lies on the saddle of the twin-peaked hill in the middle distance. Here lay the agora and a temple of Apollo Delphinius (see **276** and *CAH* III².1, 777, fig. 85; one of the earliest written lawcodes had been inscribed on its walls). There was a shrine and wall also on the right (eastern) eminence. The setting closely resembles that of other Archaic sites in Crete (Lato, Prinias, Axus, etc.), a hill with a fair-sized upper area to occupy and cultivate but not easy to approach in force or with speed. The hill top is 470 m above sea level (250 m above the plain) and 6 km from the coast.

CAH III².1, 778; III².3, 230, 237; *Princeton Encyclopedia of Classical Sites* (Princeton, 1976) s.v. for bibliography and description of site.

266

267

268a. 1

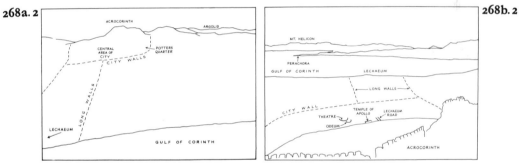

268a. 2

ACROCORINTH   ARGOLID

CENTRAL
AREA OF   POTTERS
CITY   QUARTER
        CITY WALLS

L
O
N
G

W
A
L
L
S

LECHAEUM

GULF OF CORINTH

268b. 2

MT. HELICON

PERACHORA

GULF OF CORINTH   LECHAEUM

LONG WALLS

CITY WALL

                 TEMPLE OF
        THEATRE APOLLO   LECHAEUM
                           ROAD
        ODEUM

                      ACROCORINTH

268b. 1

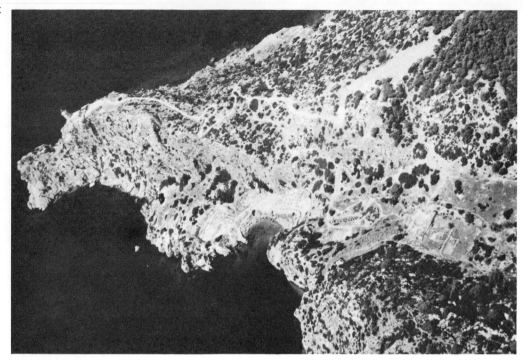

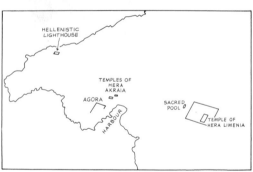

269. Perachora, from the south east. The site lies at the western end of Mt Gerania promontory (see **268b** for a view from Acrocorinth). Though in Megarian territory its fortunes were soon determined by Corinth. The small, secure harbour must have been much visited, to judge from the rich and varied dedications in the sanctuaries – the temples of Hera Akraia (ninth and sixth century) and of Hera Limenia (eighth century), by the harbour. The fortified Heraeum acropolis site lies 1 km from the harbour.

H. Payne and T. J. Dunbabin, *Perachora* I, II (Oxford, 1940, 1962); J. Salmon, *BSA* 67 (1972) 159–204.

268. Corinth. (a) The city and acropolis (Acrocorinth) seen from the shore of the Gulf of Corinth, looking south. The northern port of Corinth, Lechaeum, lies just to the east. (b) Looking NNW from Acrocorinth, over the lower town, to the shore of the Gulf of Corinth and the port of Lechaeum, about 3.5 km away. The Gerania ridge projects into the Gulf from the east, with Perachora (see **269**) at its tip. On the skyline is Mt Cithaeron in Boeotia. The whole city area and acropolis was not walled until the fourth century when there were also Long Walls to embrace Lechaeum, but there was local fortification in the lower town or assembly of villages in the Archaic period.

270. The site at Emporio on the south-east coast of Chios, looking south. The islands of Ionia are more fertile than the Cyclades and Emporio enjoyed access both to good farmland and to a good harbour and beaches, unlike Zagora (**266**). The acropolis beside the harbour and the adjacent area were occupied at the end of the Bronze Age (*CAH* II³.2, 663, 667). Resumption of occupation in the eighth century was at first confined to the steep slopes of the hill Prophetes Elias (from which this view was taken), in the right foreground of the

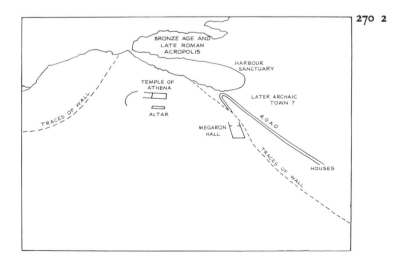

BRONZE AGE AND
LATE ROMAN
ACROPOLIS

HARBOUR
SANCTUARY

TEMPLE OF
ATHENA

LATER ARCHAIC
TOWN ?

TRACES OF WALL

ROAD

ALTAR

MEGARON
HALL

TRACES OF WALL

HOUSES

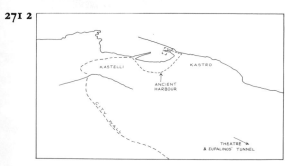

their prosperity dependent on both land and sea resources.

CAH III².1, 753, fig. 76 (plan); J. Boardman, *Greek Emporio* (London, 1967).

picture. The peak and saddle of the hill (centre) were enclosed in a fortification wall leaving the houses outside and with only a shrine to Athena (the visible structure is sixth-century) and a megaron building (centre and centre right) within. It can be seen that the town was just out of sight from the harbour and to this degree protected from surprise attack. In the seventh century occupation moved down to the harbourside where there was already a sanctuary area, but the Athena temple on the old site was not forgotten. The ancient name is not known but the setting must be typical of many flourishing Archaic townships in the islands,

271. Samos. The city site from the north (modern Tigani, or Pythagoreion). The site is on the east coast of the island, less than 2.5 km from the Asia Minor coast. For plan see *CAH* III².3, 444, fig. 55. The Archaic acropolis (Kastro) beside the harbour carried Polycrates' palace. The main circuit wall, 7 km long, was built first in the sixth century, embracing port, acropolis and the steep slope of the adjacent inland hill (height 235 m), through which Eupalinus drove his kilometre-long tunnel to supply water. (The hill Kastelli may not have been included until later.) The Heraeum lies 6 km away to the west, at the mouth of the River Imbrasus.

R. Tölle, *Die antike Stadt Samos* (Mainz, 1969); F. Winter, *Greek Fortifications* (London, 1971) 108–9.

272. Sparta. The city area from the east, looking across the plain to Mount Taygetus. It is overlaid by modern Sparta. The site is low lying, with no very distinctive physical features and without any city wall until the Hellenistic period. Even the 'acropolis' (at the north) is a barely defined hillock. The plain of the Eurotas valley (about 14 km × 5 km) is extremely fertile and there was easy access to the sea at Gythium, 46 km away. There were important, and older, out-of-town settlements and sanctuaries at Amyclae and the Menelaeum.

P. Cartledge, *Sparta and Laconia* (London, 1979) ch. 2; L. F. Fitzhardinge, *The Spartans* (London, 1980) ch. 2.

Greeks and barbarians

Greece in the Bronze Age had been open to the goods and influences of the older civilizations of the Near East and Egypt. In the ensuing Dark Ages these links with the 'barbarian' became tenuous, and a symptom if not in large part also a cause of the Greek renaissance of the ninth century and later was the renewal of these links, soon to be more strongly forged by the foundation of trading posts in east and west (Al Mina, Ischia). The physical effect can be measured in part by the foreign objects introduced to the Greek world in the ninth to sixth centuries, in part by the evidence for the immigration of foreign craftsmen, in part by the nature of the changes wrought in the technology, arts and life style of the Greeks themselves.

GENERAL BIBLIOGRAPHY

CAH III².3, ch. 36
E. Akurgal, *The Birth of Greek Art* (London, 1968)

Boardman, *GO*
Coldstream, *GG*
T. J. Dunbabin, *The Greeks and their eastern Neighbours* (London, 1957)

P. J. Riis and J. N. Coldstream in *Madrider Beiträge* 8 (1982) on Greeks in Phoenicia and Phoenicians in Greece

273. Two gold earring pendants from a rich woman's grave of the mid-ninth century, found on the slopes of the Areopagus in Athens. The burial also contained a clay model of a multiple granary; pins, fibulae and rings in gold and bronze; a necklace of faience beads; two ivory seals; many painted vases, simpler incised pots and toys and a handsomely decorated burial urn (see *CAH* III².1, 666, fig. 61). Much of the metal and the ivory attest import or influence from the east. The earrings are executed with an elaboration of filigree and granulation not seen in Greece since the Bronze Age. Their shape is not easy to parallel in either the east or Greece at this date (except in the unique ivory seals from the same burial) but the new techniques and the alternating twisted and straight wire patterns, which recall Cypriot bronze work, suggest an eastern studio, perhaps in Cyprus. The whole assemblage presents a formidable display of wealth, both agricultural (the granaries) and luxury goods.

(Agora Museum J 148a, b. Height 6.5 cm.)
 E. L. Smithson, *Hesperia* 37 (1968) 77–116, for the burial; Coldstream, *GG* 55–6; R. A. Higgins, *BSA* 64 (1969) 144–5.

274. Two gold pendants of the later ninth century from a grave at Khaniale Teke, near Cnossus. The gold is worked in filigree and granulation, with repoussé for the heads and birds on (**b**), the snake-head terminals to the chain on (**a**). There are round and oval cloisons for inlays on both, and amber was said to have been found in some of them. The big crescent inlay in (**a**) is of rock crystal, a stone which was available in Crete, but harder than anything worked in Greek lands since the Bronze Age. These are likely to be of local manufacture by immigrant craftsmen whose work in Crete can be traced, in gold jewellery, impressed gold

bands, bronze weapons (a belt and quiver at Cnossus) and the Drerus figures (**276**) from the late ninth century to at least 700. The style also informed work in other materials – stone relief and vase decoration (the Protogeometric B style at Cnossus). The Teke tomb, a reused Minoan tholos, is a rich source for the work of this guild of craftsmen. The jewellery shown was buried in two plain vases just inside the door of the tomb, perhaps consecrating it to its new use. The jewellery forms – the crescents and crescent-with-disk – find parallels in near-contemporary jewellery from Tell Halaf in upper Mesopotamia, and the craftsmen may hail from this general area. A snake-head terminal of the type on (**a**) has also been found in Ithaca.

(Heraklion Museum. Width of (**a**) 6.8 cm; width of (**b**) 5.5 cm.)
 R. W. Hutchinson and J. Boardman, *BSA* 49 (1954) 215–28, the tomb; J. Boardman, *BSA* 62 (1967) 57–70, nos. 1 and 2, the jewellery and parallels, and *GO* 56–7; R. A. Higgins, *BSA* 64 (1969) 150–1.

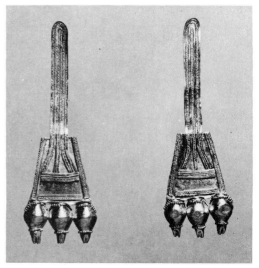

273

274a

74b

275

276

275. Five gold plaques from a grave at Eleusis of about 750–725 B.C., fittings for a pectoral or belt. There was orientalizing goldwork in Attica comparable to that in Crete (see **274**) with similar techniques and themes but differently applied, and presumably also inspired by immigrant eastern craftsmen, from about 800 into the second half of the eighth century. In these plaques we recognize the new techniques, including cloisons for glass, but the patterns are by now largely Greek, including a simple 'battlement' maeander, swastikas, a 'Dipylon shield' and zigzags, as well as the eastern wave pattern.

(Athens NM 3534–3538. Width of rectangular plaque *c.* 4.0 cm.)

Coldstream, *GG* 125f. and 78f. for earlier jewellery of this class from Eleusis; Higgins, *op. cit.* 147f.

276. Three bronze statues, less than half life size, which may have stood as cult images in the small temple of Apollo Delphinius at Drerus in east Crete (see **267**). They are made of bronze sheet hammered over a core (*sphyrelaton*) with eyes hollowed for inlay. Stylistically they belong to the series of orientalizing works in gold, bronze and stone which appear in Crete from the end of the ninth century on and culminate in these statues, which could have been created for the small temple, itself built some time in the second half of the eighth century. The style seems to have been introduced to Crete by immigrant eastern craftsmen, and may not survive the eighth century. Other examples of their work are the jewellery from the late ninth- and eighth-century burials at Teke near Cnossus (**274**) and a cast bronze figurine, like the male here, from a late eighth-century context at Arcades. In the temple they appear to have stood on a bench at the back, while near the centre of the room there was a hearth (*CAH* III².1, 777, fig. 85). We might readily identify them as Apollo with Leto and Artemis in any later group, but there are other divine triads in Archaic Crete and we cannot be certain of the importance of the whole divine and Olympian family at Archaic Drerus.

(Heraklion Museum 2445–7. Heights 0.80, 0.45, 0.40 m.)

Boardman, *GSAP* fig. 16, cf. fig. 17, the cast figure from Arcades, and *BSA* 62 (1967) 61; R. Willetts, *Cretan Cults and Festivals* (London, 1962) 263f.; S. Marinatos, *BCH* 60 (1936) 214–85; I. Beyer, *Die Tempel von Dreros und Prinias A* (Freiburg, 1976); Richter, *Korai* figs. 70–5.

277. Bronze tympanon of the later eighth century, from the Idaean Cave, Crete. The way in which it was used is indicated by the two eastern demons who clash similar disks in the repoussé decoration of the bronze. Here they flank a god or hero who swings a lion over his head and strides over a bull. The style is oriental, North Syrian or Assyrian, and closely related to other bronzes from Greece, at Olympia and Dodona, as well as in Etruscan graves. That the Cretan tympanon was made in the island is suggested by the activity depicted, which recalls how the cries of the infant Zeus were drowned by the Couretes who clashed shields, and the way the tympanon is used, which seems not eastern (where they are used singly, like a gypsy tambourine). This, then, should be the work of another immigrant studio, serving local cult.

(Heraklion Museum 9. Diameter 0.55 m. Photograph, after Kunze.)

E. Kunze, *Kretische Bronzereliefs* (Stuttgart, 1931) no. 74, pl. 49; Boardman, *GO* 58–60, on the workshop, fig. 26.

278. Bronze shield from the Idaean Cave, Crete. The central boss is a lion head in the round. The repoussé friezes are part oriental – types of armour, lions trampling men (for the lion eating a man, however, compare **343**), the vulture; part Greek – the Dipylon shield. Pieces of nearly one hundred bronze shields of this general type were found in the cave, and examples reached other parts of Greece – Delphi, Dodona and Miletus. They may be related to the cult in the cave (see on **277**) and are not for martial use though the type with the animal-head boss is attested in the east. The style is oriental (cf. **90, 100**), introduced by immigrant craftsmen perhaps as early as 800, becoming increasingly hellenized. The workshop was probably working still through the first half of the seventh century.

(Heraklion Museum 7. Diameter 0.83 m.)

Kunze, *op. cit.* no. 6, pls. 1–2, Beil. 1; Boardman, *loc. cit.*; F. Canciani, *Bronzi orientali e orientalizzanti a Creta nell' VIII e VII sec. a. C.* (Rome, 1970) for the class, but deriving many from Cyprus; Coldstream, *GG* 286–8.

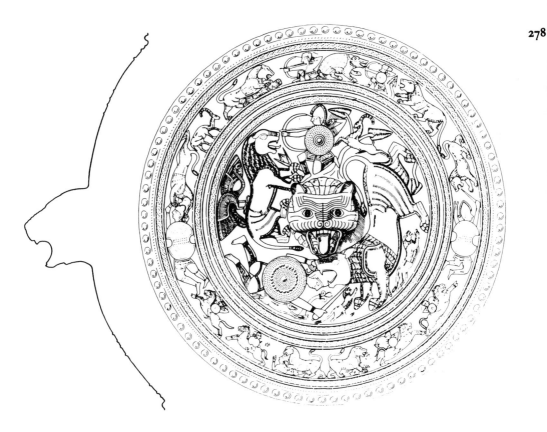

279. Clay vase in the form of a recumbent lion holding a bowl between its forelegs, from Afrati (Arcades) in Crete, Tomb R. Pieces of similar Cretan examples have been found in Cnossus and in the Dictaean Cave (Psychro) and one of the same general type, but in faience, in the Idaean Cave. The type can be traced in both Egypt and the Near East. In the form of a stone lion-head and forelegs holding a bowl examples from Syria reached Greece, and there is a Cretan clay imitation of one also (Heidelberg; see *CAH* III².3, 226, fig. 36). This, and the full-figure vases, were made in central Crete in the mid-seventh century and attest a lively orientalizing school, imitating foreign goods which had usually been executed in other materials (also griffin cauldrons, of which there are clay copies in Crete but no bronze originals).

(Heraklion Museum. Length 32.6 cm.)

D. Levi, *AS Atene* 10–12 (1927–9) 239f., fig. 281, pl. 19; and 460f., fig. 588, faience, Idaean Cave; J. Boardman, *BSA* 57 (1962) 33f. (similar examples); in *Dädalische Kunst* (Hamburg, 1970) 19, and *GO* 115, fig. 132; R. Hampe, *Kretische Löwenschale des siebten Jahrhunderts v. Chr.* (Heidelberg, 1969) pls. 7.2, 8, 10.2, and passim for the type and the Heidelberg vase.

280. 'The Cesnola crater', of Greek island manufacture (Euboean, but more Naxian in style), found at Curium in Cyprus, of the third quarter of the eighth century. Greek Geometric pottery had a limited distribution in the Near East, where pottery was not a normal field for elaborate painting. This is one of three vases by the same artist (the Cesnola Painter) found at Curium. The motif in the central panels between the handles, showing goats at either side of a tree, returns to the east an old oriental motif, occasionally copied by Greek island artists in the Geometric period. This big vase was probably a gift from a Greek plying the eastern route via Cyprus to north Syria, where Euboeans and islanders had established trading posts (notably at Al Mina, as early as the end of the ninth century).

(New York, Metropolitan Museum 74.51.965. Height 1.15 m.)

J. N. Coldstream, *Greek Geometric Pottery* (London, 1968) 172ff., as Naxian, and *BICS* 18 (1971) 1ff., as Euboean; Boardman in *Lefkandi* 1 74–6, the Euboean character challenged; Arias–Hirmer, pl. 24; Simon–Hirmer, pls. 5 below, 7.

281. Ivory girl from a grave in the Dipylon cemetery at Athens, of the third quarter of the eighth century. One of a group of five, of different sizes. She appears to have served as a handle, for a mirror or flywhisk, to judge from her plumper Egyptian or Near Eastern (Nimrud) counterparts. That she was made in Greece is indicated by her slim, Geometric proportions and the pattern on her hat. She is the earliest example of sophisticated carving in ivory, now

practised in Greece again for the first time since the Bronze Age, and being used for purposes other than simple stamp seals.

(Athens, NM 776. Height 24 cm.)
E. Kunze, *Ath. Mitt.* 55 (1930) 147ff., for the group; M. Weber, *Ath. Mitt.* 89 (1974) 27f., their use; Richter, *Korai* figs. 16–19, cf. 20–2.

282. Ivory group from Delphi of a man with a spear holding a lion by its forelock. The date is uncertain but it is probably of the first half of the seventh century. The dress and lion are strongly Assyrianizing but other features, the face and the base pattern, recall Lydia, and this may be its source. The pose is as that for an eastern hero with a lion, such as Gilgamesh, but not, perhaps, altogether inappropriate for an Apollo, at least in the eyes of an Anatolian donor or craftsman. Both Phrygian (Midas) and Lydian (Croesus) kings are recorded as sending gifts to Delphi.

(Delphi Museum. Height 24 cm.)
P. Amandry, *Syria* 24 (1944–5) pls. 10–11; K. Schefold in *Festschrift G. von Lücken* (Rostock, 1968) 769ff. and *Arch. Anz.* 1970, 574ff., proposing an early date; F. Salviat, *BCH* 86 (1962) 105, the base; Boardman, *GO* 62–3, orientalizing ivories in Greece.

283. Ivory head from Corfu, seventh century. The rest of the head and figure was supplied in other pieces, probably other materials (wood), making this an early example of the use of ivory for flesh parts of figures only, which is met again in the sixth century at Delphi (**310b**) and later in the Classical chryselephantine cult statues. The work is eastern though this 'acrelephantine' technique is rare among eastern ivories. A similar head, but with the ears carved in one piece with the features, also with eyes cut for inlay, was found at Perachora

and is datable to about 700; another, from Sardis, has carved eyes, ears and earrings, and cheek tattoos. All are possibly Lydian.

(Corfu Museum MR 710.)

G. Dontas, *Arch. Delt* 22 (1967) Chr. 364, pl. 272; Boardman, *GO* 63, fig. 38 (fig. 37, the Perachora head); R. D. Barnett, *JHS* 68 (1948) 23 and E. Akurgal, *Die Kunst Anatoliens* (Berlin, 1961) pl. VII, the Sardis head.

284. Ivory fitting for the arm of a lyre, early sixth century. The upper terminal is a swan's head and neck, the 'arm' a woman wearing a bulbous headdress and long pigtail, her hands and whatever she held having been added separately and now missing. She stands on the back of a sphinx with sweeping 'Hathoric' coiffure. An analogous lyre-fitting in the form of a kneeling boy, of late seventh-century date, was found on Samos – see **285.** Ours is in a plumper, rather later style, close to that of some ivories found at Ephesus, where the headdress too is met. This must be Lydian work also, representing a style current and influential in the richer cities of Ionia.

(Berlin, Staatliche Museen (West) 1964.36. Height 22.5 cm.)

A. Greifenhagen, *Jb. Berliner Museen* 7 (1965) 125 ff., and for comparanda; Boardman, *GSAP* fig. 53; L. Bonfante in *In Memoriam Otto J. Brendel* (Mainz, 1976) 13–20, pl. 5, the hair style.

285. Restoration of a lyre with ivory fittings, from the Samos Heraeum. Late seventh century B.C. One of the kneeling youths is preserved. He had inlaid eyes, ear-lobes and earrings, pubic hair. This is probably East Greek work, like **284** which is the fitting from a similar lyre, despite the angularity of the features in profile. These can, however, be matched in ivories of possible Lydian provenience.

(Athens, National Museum (Samos E.88). Height of youth 14.5 cm. Drawing, after Ohly.)

D. Ohly, *AM* 74 (1959) 48–56, Beil. 87–93; B. Freyer-Schauenburg, *Elfenbeine aus dem samischen Heraion* (Hamburg, 1966) 19–26; Greifenhagen, *op. cit.* 284; Boardman, *GSAP* fig. 54.

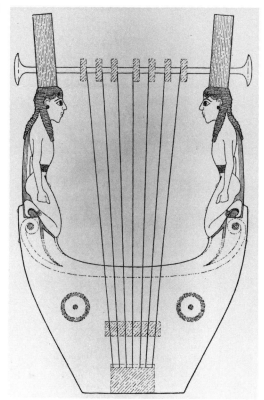

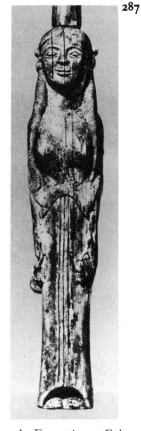

286

D. G. Hogarth, *Excavations at Ephesus* (London, 1908) pl. 25.12. E. Akurgal, *Die Kunst Anatoliens* (Berlin, 1961) 193, fig. 151.

287. The handle of an ivory wand, tipped by a bird (not shown), in the form of a girl, wearing a chiton, and holding a jug and a dish of a type well attested in Phrygia and Lydia. This is one of the latest (*c.* 560 B.C.) of the orientalizing ivories from Lydian or Ionian studios, the finest of a rich series excavated by Hogarth in the temple of Artemis at Ephesus. The rounded forms of head and body recall contemporary Ionian monumental sculpture (the Samos kore dedicated by Cheramyes, for example, and the head type is common from Samos to Rhodes).

(Istanbul Museum. Height of girl 10.7 cm.)

Greifenhagen, *op. cit.* figs. 9–12; Akurgal, *op. cit.* 204ff., figs. 169–73; Boardman, *GSAP* fig. 88, cf. figs. 87, 89–92; Richter, *Korai* figs. 259–62.

286. Ivory lion from the temple of Artemis at Ephesus, late seventh century B.C. The lion head has the square, Hittite features, but the lively, twisting pose seems not oriental, yet it is notably different from the more Assyrian lion type represented in the ivory from Smyrna (**314**). It was apparently set between an upper and lower border, so perhaps an attachment to furniture and if so not rendered as comparable eastern furniture plaques (as **205**) which are in very flat, low relief.

(Istanbul Museum. Length 7 cm.)

288. Clay mould from Corinth, early seventh century. The mould was made locally but

clearly derives from an eastern work. The east introduced to Greece the use of the mould for works in clay. This led to mass-production of relief clay plaques in southern Greece and Crete, and it helped determine and stereotype the 'Daedalic' forms introduced with the eastern technique; see on **289**. This piece is unusual in showing a profile head but it usefully demonstrates the adoption of the mould technique in Greece.

(Corinth Museum KH 1. Height 6 cm.)
    T. J. Dunbabin, *The Greeks and their Eastern Neighbours* (London, 1957) pl. 8. 6, 7; Boardman, *GSAP* fig. 24, cf. fig. 23; *GO* 76, fig. 73.

289. Plaster casts of two seventh-century statues, possibly near-contemporaries of around 640–630 B.C., but significantly different in scale and material despite their superficial similarity in style (the miscalled 'Daedalic'). The small figure (**a**) is typical of the decorative small-scale statuary in soft stone (here limestone), wood or clay (see **316, 322**) which carried the orientalizing Daedalic style (on its origin see on **288**) through much of the seventh century. Greek experience of Egyptian statuary, life size or larger and executed in hard stone, around the mid-century, led to experiments with their own hard, island marble, first from Naxos, then Paros (from Pentelicum in Attica only from the sixth century on). The larger figure (**b**) is of the new scale and material, but stylistically is

still Daedalic since the Greek artists borrowed only superficial details (for their *kouros* statues) from Egypt or the east. Its relatively primitive appearance, compared with (**a**), is due to the problems of technique and scale and does not necessarily reflect any earlier date of carving.

    (**a**) Limestone statuette, possibly Cretan (the 'Auxerre statue'). The Daedalic style is typified by the angular frontal head with its flat top and wig-like hair, comparatively formless body (though well-developed bust) and a type of shawl and belt seen on comparable figures. It was highly coloured in the patterns incised on the dress and on the features. The type may derive from the naked frontal relief figures of Astarte, the eastern goddess, observed in Greece on imported clay plaques. From these

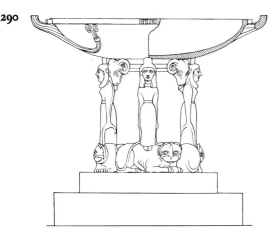

local craftsmen learned both the use of the mould for mass-production in clay (see **288**) and the figure type, which they soon clothed.

(**b**) Marble statue from Delos, sanctuary of Artemis. She may have been holding a wreath, bow or the lead of a lion (compare **290**). A dedicatory inscription is incised along her skirt: 'Nikandre dedicated me to the far-shooter of arrows, the excellent daughter of Deinodikes of Naxos, sister of Deinomenes, wife of Phraxos n(ow?).' Naxos, as well as being the prime source for white statuary marble in this period, also dominated the religious and political life of the Delos sanctuaries.

(Casts in Oxford, Ashmolean Museum Cast Gallery. Originals in (**a**) Paris, Louvre 3098 (once in the Auxerre Museum). Height 65 cm. (**b**) Athens, National Museum 1. Height 1.75 m.)
Richter, *Korai* figs. 76–9 (**a**), figs. 25–8 (**b**). On the Daedalic style, R. H. Jenkins, *Dedalica* (Cambridge, 1936); C. Davaras, *Die Statue aus Astritsi*

(Bern, 1972); Boardman, *GSAP* 13–25 (fig. 128 for (**a**) coloured); L. Adams, *Orientalizing Sculpture in soft limestone* (Oxford, 1978) 32–4; B. S. Ridgway, *The Archaic Style in Greek Sculpture* (Princeton, 1977) ch. 2; Jeffery, *LSAG* 291 (for (**b**)).

290. Marble *perirrhanterion* (laver or basin of a type found in sanctuaries and houses) from the sanctuary of Poseidon at Isthmia, near Corinth, late seventh century. A series of these objects, all of much the same date, is known, from Isthmia, Sparta, Samos, Rhodes, Olympia, Delphi, the Ptoon (Boeotia). The supports are invariably women holding lions by leads and their tails, sometimes standing on their backs. Supports of this general type are oriental, and the eastern 'potnia theron', Mistress of Animals, could be assimilated to a Greek Artemis. They may not all have been made in one centre and the style, which is not Daedalic, is uninformative, but Laconia seems to have been an important source and Sparta was an important centre and market for orientalizing art in the seventh century.

(Corinth Museum. Height restored 1.26 m. without the stepped base.)
O. Broneer, *Hesperia* 27 (1968) 24ff., pls. 10–11 and in *Charisterion A. K. Orlandos* III (Athens, 1966) 61ff. On the type, J. Ducat, *BCH* 88 (1964) 577ff.; F. W. Hamdorf, *Ath. Mitt.* 89 (1974) 47ff.; Boardman, *GSAP* 25f., 243; Richter, *Korai* figs. 35, 37–56.

291. Bronze cauldron from Cyme, with cast bull-head attachments, early seventh century B.C. The cauldron shape, with inturning rim, is eastern (cf. **203** and *CAH* III².3, 448, fig. 58) in contrast to the hemispherical, open Geometric Greek cauldrons (as *CAH* III².1, 788, fig. 89). The type with bull-head attachments was made in Urartu, north Syria and possibly Cyprus, and was very widely copied in Greece. This is a Greek version, carried west at an early date to the Euboean colony of Cyme.

(Copenhagen NM 4952. Height 28 cm. Photograph, after Amandry.)
P. Amandry in *The Aegean and the Near East* (Studies, H. Goldman, New York, 1956) 239ff., pl. 28; O. Muscarella, *Metropolitan Museum Journal* I (1968) 7ff.; H. Kyrieleis, *Ath. Mitt.* 92 (1977) 71ff.

292. Cast bronze attachment from a cauldron, in the form of a 'siren' with spread wings, early

292 3

seventh century. These are the commonest form of cast bronze attachment to oriental cauldrons introduced to the Greek world and found in many seventh-century sanctuaries. They were imitated in Greek studios and this is a Greek version, replacing the plump eastern features with more angular and alert Greek ones. The form derives more from the eastern deity supported by a winged disk than from anything related to the monster later identified as a Siren by Greeks.

(Olympia Museum B 28. Width 20.3 cm.)
 H.-V. Herrmann, *Die Kessel der orientalisierenden Zeit* (Olympische Forschungen VI.1; Berlin, 1966) A 22, pl. 32; Boardman, *GO* 64–5 for the type.

293. Hammered bronze griffin protome, from a cauldron, from the Athenian Acropolis, early seventh century. The inspiration for this type of attachment must be eastern but in this form it is wholly Greek, the early examples being of beaten bronze, the later ones cast. They may appear on cauldrons with siren attachments (as **292**; but contrast **203** where the sirens are beaten, the griffins cast) but were not necessarily all attached at one time and the Greek griffins might have been added to eastern siren-

cauldrons. The later, cast griffins, take a more elegant serpentine form, and exaggerate the forehead knobs, spiral tendrils and animal ears (as **308a, b**). It was an 'Argive crater' of this type, with relief griffin heads, that Colaeus' Samians dedicated as a tithe of their profits from their voyage to Tartessus (Hdt. IV.152).

(Oxford, Ashmolean Museum 1895.71. Length 12.8 cm.)
 U. Jantzen, *Griechische Greifenkessel* (Berlin, 1955) 105, no. 1; Herrmann, *op. cit.* 142ff.; Boardman, *GO* 66–7, for the type.

294. Corinthian ('Early Protocorinthian') flask for perfumed oil (aryballos) of the late eighth century. The trade in perfumed oil was one result of renewed contact with the east, and Corinth in particular was not slow to produce small, luxury containers such as this. The Corinthian painters, with no tradition in Geometric figure-drawing, were more susceptible to the new subjects and styles of drawing suggested by eastern work. On this aryballos the effect is demonstrated by the outline technique of drawing used for some figures, the presence of a lion, floral patterns in the field and the stylized eastern 'tree of life' motif before the horseman. It is not clear whether any unity of theme was intended, beyond the couplets of lion-chasing-deer, and hoplite-with-squire.

(London, British Museum 1969.12–15.1. Height 6.8 cm.)
 Archaeological Reports for 1971–2 61f.; *British Museum Quarterly* 36 (1971–2) 42ff.

295. Corinthian ('Transitional') olpe, third quarter of the seventh century B.C. Animal-frieze decoration had been a subsidiary feature in Greek Geometric vase-painting. With the orientalizing period it becomes dominant, especially on Corinthian vases, with a new range of fauna – lions and sphinxes as well as the more familiar goats and birds. The 'black-figure' technique, with incised detail on silhouette figures, seems also to have been

296

inspired by the incised decoration of eastern bronzes and ivories. The animal frieze remains an important decorative feature on all Greek wares until well into the first half of the sixth century, when narrative, human- or divine-figure subjects take over (see on **356**).

(Munich, Antikensammlungen 8764. Height 34 cm.)

For this style in Corinth see H. Payne, *Necrocorinthia* (Oxford, 1931) and *Protokorinthische Vasenmalerei* (Berlin, 1933; Mainz, 1974); Cook, *GPP* 46ff.

296. East Greek, perhaps Milesian, 'Wild Goat' style oinochoe. A distinctive orientalizing animal-frieze style was adopted in Ionia and the Dodecanese around the middle of the seventh century, goats and deer being the most popular creatures and the style one of outline and silhouette with little added colour, rather than the incising black-figure style of Corinth (**295**). The rich variety of background patterns suggests that the source of inspiration may have been eastern textiles and embroidery.

(Tübingen, Arch. Inst. inv. 1237. Height 33.5 cm.)

On the origins and development of the style, Cook, *GPP* 115ff.

297. Egyptian bronze statuette of a woman, from the Heraeum, Samos, seventh century.

Minor Egyptian imports to Greece appear in the ninth and eighth centuries but it is not until the seventh century that they arrive in any numbers and Samos is one of the most prolific sources for them. The Samian captain Colaeus was on his way to Egypt when he was blown off course (he said) to the western Mediterranean in *c.* 638 B.C.: Hdt. IV.152.

(Samos Museum B 1216. Height 17.3 cm.)

U. Jantzen, *Samos* VIII (Bonn, 1972) pl. 15.2, 3; Boardman, *GO* 112–15 on Egyptian imports to Greece.

298. 'Faience' flask in the form of a man squatting before a pot, topped by a frog, from Camirus in Rhodes, late seventh century. 'Faience' is a sandy composition covered with glaze – an Egyptian technique practised also in the Near East. By the mid-seventh century a studio was set up in Rhodes, to be supplemented at the end of the century by one at Naucratis. These mass-produced flasks and figurines were made mainly for the East Greek world, some (like the one illustrated) with Egyptian motifs, some with Greek.

(London, British Museum 1860.4-4.75. Height 9.5 cm.)

V. Webb, *Archaic Greek Faience* (Warminster, 1978) 13, no. 1, pl. 1, also for a general study of the ware; and Boardman, *GO* 126–8.

299. Painted wooden plaque from the Isaeum, Saqqara, Egypt, about 500 B.C. This was found in recent British excavations. The colours are reds, yellow, buff, brown and black on white. The subject, men leading cattle, is executed in a purely East Greek style, very closely matched on vases painted by East Greek émigrés in Etruria – the masters of the 'Caeretan hydriae' (who also betray knowledge of Egyptian art; see **362**). This is a precious example of the type of wooden panel painting which must have been extremely common in Greece, but which has usually never been preserved (an exception, **323**) and it is vivid evidence for the probable presence of Greek artists of quality living and working in Egypt, since the subject is even more familiar in Egypt than Greece, though executed in a profoundly different style by Egyptian artists.

(Cairo Museum. Excavation no. H5-2571. Width 46 cm. Watercolour by Helen Ward, after Nicholls pl. 1.)

R. V. Nicholls in G. T. Martin, *The Tomb of Ḥetepka* (London, 1979) 74–8.

300. (a) Spartan flask imitating the Lydian ointment vase (so-called *lydion*), from Orvieto, mid-sixth century. The Lydian vase, perhaps for the perfume *bakkaris* (mentioned already by Semonides, fr. 16 and Hipponax, fr. 104, 21; West) was normally decorated with a marbling pattern (b). The shape is also imitated in Athens, East Greece and Etruria, and is one of the few eastern vase shapes to be adopted in Greece, beside the phiale and figure-rhyton.

((a) Philadelphia University Museum MS 4856. Height 24.3 cm. (b) Hamburg, Museum für Kunst und Gewerbe 1962.40. Height 13.7 cm.)

(a) E. H. Dohan, *Phil. Mus. Journal* 23 (1932) 61–3, fig. 1, as a Lydian imitation of Laconian; E. A. Lane, *BSA* 34 (1933–4) 135 as probably Laconian. For such imitations see C. Greenewalt, *California Stud. Class. Arch.* 1 (1968) 148; Boardman, *GO* 99.

(b) H. Hoffmann, *Arch. Anz.* 1969, 340–1.

301. Athenian black-figure alabastron decorated by the Amasis Painter, from the Agora, Athens, about 560 B.C. The Egyptian stone (alabaster) shape was imitated in clay first in East Greece. The earliest Athenian example known is this, made by a potter (probably potter/painter) with a hellenized Egyptian name (Amasis = A-ahmes) shared by the pharaoh of these years, though probably not inspired by his name which was common in Egypt. The lip and one lug handle are missing.

(Athens, Agora Museum P 12628. Height 9.2 cm.)
Beazley, *ABV* 155, no. 64; E. Vanderpool, *Hesperia* 8 (1939) 248ff.; Amasis' name, J. Boardman, *JHS* 78 (1958) 1–3.

302. Impression of a serpentine seal made in the Greek islands, probably Melos, about 600 B.C. The remains of the Bronze Age world, the Greek Mycenaean and the non-Greek Minoan, were an intermittent source of inspiration to Greek artists in the orientalizing period. Minoan stone seals, found accidentally in the islands and prized as amulets, inspired a class of 'Island Gems' which copy the Bronze Age shapes (this is a so-called amygdaloid) and occasionally Bronze Age schemes (as the contorted body of the goat, here) though the style remains contemporary, Greek Archaic. The

floruit for the class is the later seventh and early sixth century, and it enjoyed a limited distribution in the Greek world.

(London, British Museum, Walters, no. 162. Length 2.5 cm.)
Boardman, *Island Gems* (London, 1963) pl. 2, no. 45; id. *Greek Gems and Finger Rings* (London, 1970) pl. 247.

303. Impression of a cornelian scarab, mid-sixth century. One of the latest borrowings of the Greeks in the east was the technique of cutting hard stones as seals, which appears to have been learnt from the Phoenicians, probably in Cyprus, in the second quarter of the sixth century. They also copy the scarab shape and the remainder of the history of hard-stone seal engraving in the Archaic period is confined to the East Greek world and Greek studios in Cyprus. The example illustrated shows a gorgon, with snake hair and winged feet, and with a horse body, which is a rare but acceptable (cf. **350**) variant on the usual form

(Medusa was a mate of a horse-Poseidon and gave birth to the winged horse Pegasus). Her dress, however, the wing shapes and her behaviour with the lion are eastern, and many of these early Greek scarabs betray in this manner the eastern source of inspiration for the whole series.

(Unknown whereabouts. Length 1.4 cm.)

Boardman, *Archaic Greek Gems* (London, 1968) pl. 2, no. 31; *id. Greek Gems and Finger Rings* (London, 1970) pl. 282.

Sanctuaries and religion

Some of the so-called 'national' sanctuaries of Greece acquired an importance which derived from the functions they served – the games at Olympia, the oracles at Delphi and Dodona – rather than the wealth or influence of the state in whose territory they lay. They were open at all times, however, to political manipulation. Their size and complexity reflected the attention paid to them not only by homeland Greek states, but also by Greeks overseas and by foreigners – Olympia, by the western Greek colonists; Delphi, for a while, by eastern kings. Other sanctuaries of purely local importance, as the Heraeum at Samos, may also reflect the interests of the state's friends as much as those of the state itself. Since temples and their subsidiary buildings represent almost the only monumental architecture of this period, and since votive deposits offer us more of the luxury goods of Archaic Greece than its cemeteries, the major sanctuaries are important sources for our appreciation of the higher arts, quite apart from what they have to tell us about religious practices. The layout and some of the finds of four major sanctuaries are discussed here, followed by an account of typical evidence from some of the smaller local shrines.

GENERAL BIBLIOGRAPHY

B. Bergquist, *The Archaic Greek Temenos* (Lund, 1967)

H. Berve and G. Gruben, *Greek Temples, Theatres and Shrines* (London, 1963)

A. W. Lawrence, *Greek Architecture* (Harmondsworth, 1973)

R. A. Tomlinson, *Greek Sanctuaries* (London, 1976)

304. The sanctuary of Zeus at Olympia lies by the confluence of the rivers Cladeus and Alpheus, on flat ground with adjacent low hills, nearly 15 km from the sea. The heart of the sanctuary was the 'grave of Pelops' with its enclosure. To its north is the peripteral Temple of Hera, built in the early sixth century replacing a seventh-century temple. (The Classical Temple of Zeus was to be erected south of the Pelopion.) The Prytaneum is conjectural (this is its later position) and at the south is the apsidal Bouleuterion, also to be extended in the fifth century. The Stadium ran on into the sanctuary and was only cut off from it by the construction of the Echo Stoa in the fourth century. Overlooking its end, on a long terrace, is a row of Treasuries (Paus. VI.19) and, at the west, smaller sanctuaries of Eileithyia and Aphrodite Urania (Paus. VI.20.2, 4).

((**a**) View of the sanctuary (bottom right) from the north west, along the valley of the R. Alpheus. (**b**) Plan of the Archaic sanctuary (after Herrmann).)

(**c**) Model of the terrace of Treasuries at Olympia. The Treasuries were dedications by individual states to house rich dedications by these states, and others. They overlooked the

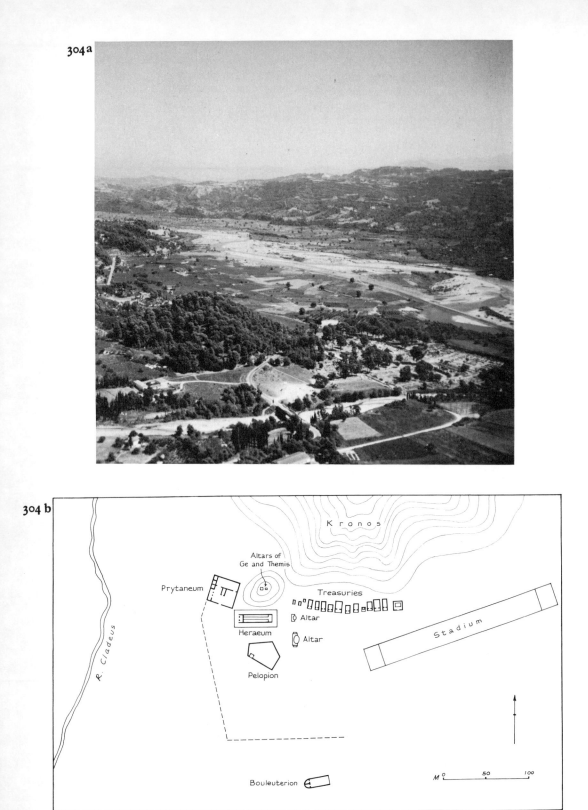

304 a

304 b

Kronos

Altars of
Ge and Themis

Prytaneum

Treasuries

Altar

Heraeum

Altar

R. Cladeus

Stadium

Pelopion

Bouleuterion

M 0   50   100

end of the Stadium when they were built but this model shows the sanctuary in its later form. Pausanias (VI.19) saw Treasuries of Sicyon, Carthage (really Syracuse; he was misled by the dedicated spoils), Epidamnus, Byzantium, Sybaris, Cyrene, (the next structure is an altar, it seems), Selinus, Metapontum, Megara and Gela. Apart from those of Syracuse and Sicyon, all were erected in the Archaic period. It is noteworthy how many are the gift of western colonial cities (and it is possible that the Megarian Treasury was the gift of the Sicilian city and adopted by its mother city some time after the colony's destruction by Gelon in 483).

H. V. Herrmann, *Olympia: Heiligtum und Wett-kampfstätte* (Munich, 1972) and in *Gymnasium* 80 (1973) 172–205; B. Bergquist, *The Archaic Greek Temenos* (Lund, 1967).

305. The foundations and replaced lower column drums of the Temple of Hera at Olympia. This was the first monumental temple on the site, replacing a simpler one in the same position early in the sixth century. It was perhaps dedicated to Zeus and Hera jointly at first, Zeus only receiving his own temple in the fifth century (see **304**). Pausanias (VI.16.1) saw an oak column still in its rear porch, and the great variety of stone capitals from the building suggests that all its columns were originally of wood, gradually replaced by stone as need arose. It is a hekatompedon (32.64 m = 100 long feet). For its cult statue see **306**.

Herrmann, *op. cit.* 92–7.

307

306. Limestone head of Hera, from the Temple of Hera at Olympia, early sixth century. Pausanias (v.17.1) saw in the temple a statue of Zeus, standing, bearded and helmeted, and beside him Hera seated on a throne, 'simple works': ἔργα δέ ἐστιν ἁπλᾶ. The head, found in 1878, bearing still traces of colour, is likely to be from the Hera, who must have been rather more than twice life size. This view, from slightly below (as in antiquity), emphasizes the heaviness of the features.

(Olympia Museum. Height 52 cm.)
Herrmann, *op. cit.* 96; Richter, *Korai* no. 73; Boardman, *GSAP* 25, fig. 73.

307. Bronze blazon from a shield dedicated at Olympia, first half of the sixth century B.C. Arms dedications were particularly common at Olympia and many of the Archaic period have been excavated from the fill of the backing of the Classical Stadium. The blazon was fastened to a hoplite shield. The monstrous figure is an original creation designed to confound an enemy at close quarters, reminiscent of the Phobos on the shield of Heracles (*Aspis* 144–8) or the Gorgo, Phobos and Deimos on Agamemnon's shield (*Iliad* XI.36–7). The head is a gorgon's, wearing a transverse crest, as of a helmet. Her body is winged and she holds two snakes. Below she has the body of a sea serpent (*ketos*) with lion forelegs.

(Olympia Museum B 4990. Height 56 cm.)
Herrmann, *op. cit.* 110–11, pl. 36a and n. 426.

308. Fragments of bronze cauldron attachments and stands, from Olympia. The early orientalizing cauldrons carried hammered animal protomes (as **293**), cast siren attachments (as **292**), and stood on conical, hammered stands (cf. *CAH* III².3, 448, fig. 58). In the seventh century the animal protomes become the only decorative feature on the bowls themselves, and are almost exclusively cast protomes of griffins, as (**a**) and (**b**) here (about third quarter of the seventh century), the necks becoming more serpentine, the ears and forehead knobs longer, the beaks more menacing. The type continues into the sixth century when there is more evidence for the rod tripods on which the cauldrons were placed. These tripods are embellished with anthemia, as (**c**), animal figurines and lion-paw feet, as (**d**). For a

308a

308b

reconstructed cauldron with stand see *CAH* III².3, 359, fig. 53. In the sixth century the flat rims may also be decorated with figurines.

((**a**) Athens, National Museum 6159 (G 71). Height 35.5 cm. (**b**) Olympia Museum B 145+4315 (G 104). Height 27.8 cm. (**c**) Olympia Museum B 6115 (S 14). Height 15.8 cm. (**d**) Olympia Museum B 6101 (S 39). Height 24 cm. The G and S numbers refer to the catalogue in H.-V. Herrmann, *Die Kessel der orientalisierenden Zeit* (Olympische Forschungen XI; Berlin, 1979), q.v. for illustrations and discussion.)

309. The site at Delphi faces south towards the Gulf of Corinth, at the foot of mount Parnassus. The sanctuary of Apollo was established in the eighth century, to judge from offerings. A smaller terrace sanctuary of Athena (Pronaia) lay further down the hillside, and is of comparable antiquity. Two stages in the Archaic development of the Apollo sanctuary are shown in the plans.

(**a**) About 550 B.C. The temple (which was destroyed by fire in 548) stood on a central terrace north of the enclosure for the 'rock of Leto' and a primitive apsidal building. There were also a council house (*bouleuterion*) and a number of Treasuries of which the location of the Corinthian is known and the existence of one or two Sicyonian is attested by sculptural remains (found in the later Sicyonian Treasury). A prominent dedication was the column of the Naxians, surmounted by a sphinx (**311**).

(**b**) About 475 B.C. The new temple of Apollo, partly financed by the refugee Athenian Alcmaeonids, was given a broader terrace and at its east the Chians erected a new altar. The temenos was extended to the south embracing a path to a new entrance, at the south east. There are several new Treasuries including those of Siphnos (about 525), Sicyon, Athens (around 500–490, over an earlier Treasury, possibly also Athenian), Potidaea (?), Cnidus, Acanthus.

(**c**) View of Delphi from the east, with the Pleistos gorge, plain of Krisa and Gulf of Itea (top left).

(**a**, **b**, after Bergquist.)
Fouilles de Delphes for the definitive excavation reports. Bergquist, *op. cit.* 30–2.

310. Two pits were excavated beneath the Sacred Way in 1939 and found to contain a mass of fragments of gold, silver, bronze, iron and ivory, all from damaged or discarded votives. The burial may have taken place in the

309a

309b

Temple of Apollo

Altar

Naxian Column

Bouleuterion

Tr. of Athens

Tr. of Corinth

0 10 20 30 40 50 M

Temenos of Dionysos

Tr. of Acanthus (?)

Temple of Apollo

Altar

Naxian Column

Tr. of Athens

Bouleuterion

Tr. of Potidaea

Tr. of Cnidus

Tr. of Corinth

Tr. of Boeotia(?)

Tr. of Siphnos

Tr. of Sicyon

0 10 50 M

309c

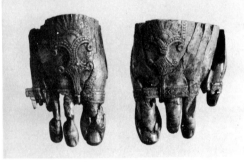

last quarter of the fifth century, no earlier, but the bulk of the objects are Archaic and represent some of the richest Archaic offerings to have survived from any Greek sanctuary. They include the ivories of our **357**.

Preliminary report: P. Amandry, *BCH* 63 (1939) 86–119 and *BCH* Suppl. 4 (1977) 273–4, 292–3. There will be a full publication in *Fouilles de Delphes*. For the bibliography of the pieces so far published see below.

(a) Life-size statue of a bull, in silver and gold, found crushed at the bottom of one of the pits beneath the Sacred Way, probably Ionian, sixth century B.C. The body is of hammered sheets of silver mounted on strips of silvered copper over wood. Gilt silver for the hairy

(b) Ivory head and sandalled feet from chryselephantine figures, Ionian, about 540 B.C. These are from figures of up to life size. In the find there were fragments of some nine ivory heads of various sizes, of feet and hands.

(Delphi Museum. Two-thirds life size.)

(c) One of a pair of matching gold plaques, probably designed for attachment to the dress of a figure, possibly one of those with the ivory head and feet. Probably Ionian.

(Delphi Museum. Height 35 cm. Painting by E. Gilliéron fils.)

The ivories – P. Amandry, *BCH* 63 (1939) 86–119; Boardman, *GSAP* fig. 127. The gold plaques – P. Amandry, *Ath. Mitt.* 77 (1962) 35–71. The ivory heads have now been restored and one mounted as part of a seated figure to which the gold plaques were attached.

frontlet, dewlap and genitals. This must have been one of the most spectacular of the Archaic offerings but was overlooked by Herodotus in his account of gifts from eastern kings and the lavish use of silver rather than gold may point to a Greek source rather than Anatolian.

(Delphi Museum. Restored 2.59 m × 1.46 m.)

P. Amandry, *BCH* Suppl. 4 (1977) 273–93.

311. Marble figure of a sphinx standing on an Ionic column east of the Temple of Apollo at Delphi, about 560 B.C. The column capital is one of the earliest extant examples of the Ionic order, its upper part being generally restored as a continuous concave channel (a Naxian

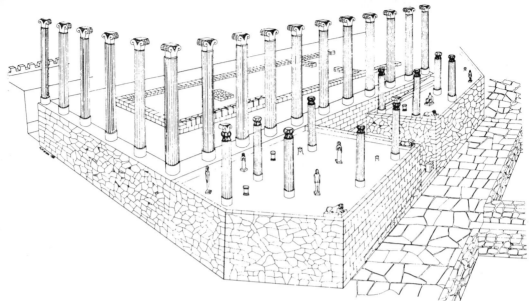

feature; the Parian have a central floral). The many flutes and cylindrical base are also primitive Ionic features. On the base a later inscription rewards the Naxians with priority at the oracle (*promanteia*) indicating the original dedicators, whose gifts are even more prominent at Apollo's other major sanctuary on Delos. Naxos, as source of the marble for much early statuary in Greece, was also the home of a distinctive sculptural studio and the sphinx head defines its style for this period very well.

(Delphi Museum. Height of sphinx 2.32 m. Height of the whole column with sphinx, *c.* 10 m.)

Fouilles de Delphes IV.1 (Paris, 1909) 41ff.; Boardman, *GSAP* fig. 100.

312. Old Smyrna (Bayraklı). Reconstruction of the temenos and unfinished Temple of Athena, overthrown by Alyattes' sack of the city in the early sixth century. (See *CAH* III².3, 197; Boardman, *GO* 97 for the siege mound by which it was taken; *CAH* III².1, 445–6 for the city at this time and for its houses and a granary.) Much of the structure and its votive deposits were uncovered in joint excavations of the British School at Athens and Ankara University in 1948–51, and excavations have continued under Professor Akurgal, to whom is owed this reconstruction of the site. He detects repair of the temenos before further destruction by the Persians in the mid century.

(After Akurgal.)

E. Akurgal, *Bayraklı* (Ankara, 1950); J. M. Cook et al., *BSA* 53–4 (1958–9); Akurgal, *Ancient Civilizations and Ruins of Turkey*³ (Ankara, 1973) 119–21; Akurgal, *Alt-Smyrna* 1 (1983) for the latest reconstruction.

313. Capital from the unfinished temple at Old Smyrna. Limestone. See **312.** This is perhaps the earliest extant stone capital with floral decoration from the East Greek world. When excavated the capitals bore traces of red and

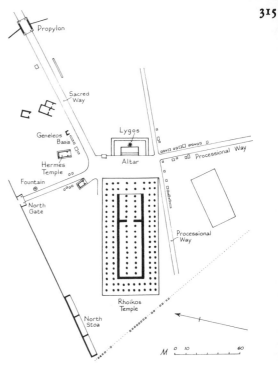

yellow paint. There are eastern antecedents for comparably decorated architectural mouldings but this use of a ring of leaves as a capital is peculiarly Greek. Combined with a volute top, the volutes either springing from the shaft and leaf ring ('Aeolic') or joined across the leaf ring ('Ionic'), it is the basis of the second most important of all the Greek architectural orders.

(Izmir.)
    E. Akurgal, *Die Kunst Anatoliens* (Berlin, 1961) 282, fig. 251; *id. Ancient Civilizations and Ruins of Turkey*[3] (Ankara, 1973) pl. 42a; *id. JHS* 72 (1952) pl. 6.3; *Anatolia* 5 (1960) pl. 1a.

314. Ivory lion from the temple deposits at Old Smyrna, later seventh century B.C. Anatolian ivories (see also here, **282–7**) offer an intriguing blend of the eastern and the Greek – eastern in subject and in detail of execution, Greek in freedom of pose and often in function. This lion's head is typically Assyrian but the body is rendered in a supple and vivacious manner, far removed from the rather hieratic treatment of the Mesopotamian and Syrian studios. Lydia is a likely home for such a blend of styles and may be the source of several of the finer ivories on East Greek sites, as well as of some carried to mainland Greece.

(Once Ankara. Length 5.6 cm. After Akurgal.)
    E. Akurgal, *Die Kunst Anatoliens* (Berlin, 1961) 188–9, figs. 140–2.

315. The site of the sanctuary of Hera on Samos lay 6 km away from the city (**271**) on low-lying ground close to the sea at the mouth of the R. Imbrasus. There had been a Bronze Age site here, reviving in the ninth century and centred on the goddess' sacred *lygos* tree. In the eighth century the earliest known colonnaded temple in Greek lands was added to a sequence of early altars. To the seventh century belongs a simple stoa, another forerunner of an important architectural type in Greece (*CAH* III².3, 204, fig. 32). In the sixth century a colossal Ionic temple was built by Rhoikos and Theodorus, with a double colonnade of columns at the sides and deep colonnaded porches, measuring 102 m × 51 m, and provided with a monumental altar. This was destroyed by fire and work started on a replacement for it later in the century. The earlier temple inspired emulation at Ephesus and Didyma (cf. *ibid.* 204–5).

(After Bergquist, *op. cit.* pl. 26, and Walter, fig. 66.)
    H. Walter, *Das Heraion von Samos* (Munich, 1976).

316. Wooden statuette of a goddess, probably Hera, from the Samos Heraeum, about 630 B.C. Her tall headdress, a version of the more familiar low 'polos', may be related to Hera's famous 'tower'-headdress, the *pyleon*. The damp conditions of the Heraeum site have proved favourable to the preservation of wooden objects (which otherwise require the utter dryness of, for example, Egypt) and such finds tell us of an art medium which must always have

been much exploited in Greece. From the Archaic Samian examples it seems that techniques and styles were closely related to those of the contemporary ivories, which is not surprising. There is no hint yet of really large-scale work in wood executed with any sophistication.

(Samos, Vathy Museum H 41. Height 28.7 cm.)

G. Kopcke, *Ath. Mitt.* 82 (1967) Beil. 43–7. *Ibid.*

100ff., and D. Ohly, *Ath. Mitt.* 58 (1953) 77ff.; H. Kyrieleis, *Ath. Mitt.* 95 (1980) 87ff., for other examples in wood from Samos (and Boardman, *GSAP* figs. 49, 50).

317. A group of marble statues, by the artist Geneleos, about 560–550 B.C. The signature is on the legs of the seated figure, Phileia. The next figure was probably a boy, then three girls (two named, Philippe and Ornithe). The reclining figure was the dedicator, named

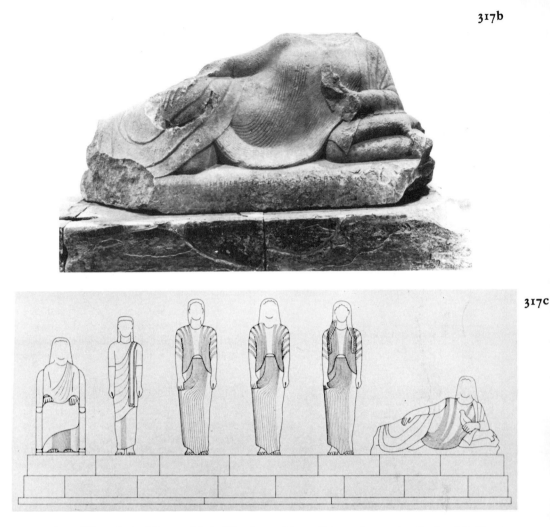

... arches. Though holding a bird (Hera's cuckoo?) and rotund in build, this is probably a male – East Greek sculpture is franker about male obesity and often clothes its men. The whole scheme then resembles a symposion, though perhaps here a sacred occasion if not heroic, at which the man reclines, the woman (wife here) is seated and children or attendants stand.

(The group is restored in B. Freyer-Schauenburg, *Bildwerke der archäischen Zeit und des strengen Stils* (*Samos* XI; Bonn, 1974) nos. 58–63. The surviving figures (all but the boy and one girl) are in Samos and Berlin (East), slightly over life size. The figures shown here are: (**a**) Ornithe (Berlin, Staatliche Museen (East) 1739; height 1.68 m); (**b**) ... arches (Samos 768; length 1.58 m). Photograph (**c**) after Freyer-Schauenburg.)

Freyer-Schauenburg, *op. cit.*, for full literature and illustrations; Richter, *Korai* figs. 217–24; G. Schmidt, *Ath. Mitt.* 86 (1971) 31–41, on the sculptor; Jeffery, *LSAG* 329.

318. Head of a colossal marble *kouros*, about 550–540 B.C. Several enormous *kouroi*, three to four metres high, were dedicated in the Heraeum – rather unexpectedly, given the sex of the patron goddess: contrast the dearth of *kouros* dedications on Athena's acropolis. The rounded head and swept-back hair is characteristic of central and southern Ionia and sufficiently unlike island and mainland Greek head-types to make us look for other sources of inspiration, perhaps neo-Babylonian (and compare the ivory **287**).

318

(Istanbul Museum 530. Height 49 cm.)

Freyer-Schauenburg, *op. cit.* no. 47, and for pieces of the body (one joining the head) in Samos. Another, recent *kouros* find is *Archaeological Reports for 1980–81* 41–2, fig. 78.

On East Greek sculpture of this period N. Himmelmann, *Istanbuler Mitteilungen* 15 (1965) 24–41; Boardman, *GSAP* 68–70.

319. Ivory relief, late seventh century B.C. The subject is Perseus decapitating the Gorgon Medusa, encouraged by Athena (at the left). The hero's helmet-like headgear is his magic cap of darkness. He carefully looks away from Medusa's petrifying head. This head-type for the monster was devised by Greek artists in the mid-seventh century and is based on a lion's mask – animal nose, open jaws with tusks and lolling tongue – observed on eastern demons. The style resembles that of ivory reliefs from the Peloponnese but at this date it is not easy to judge whether this relief could be Ionian in origin. It does not particularly resemble the more distinctly orientalizing types in ivory,

319

found in East Greece and elsewhere (as **282–7**) and iconographic details are more readily matched in the homeland.

(Athens, National Museum S. 201,726. Height 10.6 cm.)

B. Freyer-Schauenburg, *Elfenbeine aus dem sami-* *schen Heraion* (Hamburg, 1966) 30–9; Schefold 1, pl. 17.

20 1

320 2

320. Bronze cauldron dedicated to Hera at the Heraeum, Samos. Second quarter of the sixth century B.C. The dedication is incised on the rim: Βρύχωμ μάνέθηκεν ὁ Τιμόλεω 'Brychon, son of Timoleos, dedicated me.' Brychon is named as father of Aiaces on the latter's dedication to Hera found in Samos town (a seated figure; Boardman, *GSAP* fig. 96). The date of this Aiaces and his statue has been open to argument on epigraphical and historical grounds (Jeffery, *LSAG* 330; R. Meiggs and D. M. Lewis, *Greek Historical Inscriptions* (Oxford, 1975) no. 16) since the temptation had been to identify him with the father of the Samian tyrant Polycrates. The name on the cauldron, whose date has some archaeological support, might seem to justify the stemma – Timoleos, Brychon, Aiaces, Polycrates.

(Samos, Vathy Museum B 1759. Height 41 cm. Schmidt, Beil. 4.)

G. Schmidt, *Ath. Mitt.* 87 (1972) 165–85; (G. Dunst, *ibid.* 116–21, 137–8, still upholds the late date for the Aiaces of the dedication, supposing repetition of names).

321. Bronze aryballos from the Menelaion, near Sparta. Second quarter of the seventh century B.C. The shape is more familiar in clay (cf. **336**) and can be dated by reference to clay

321 1

321 2

specimens. On lip and handle is the incised dedication: Δεῖνι[ς]) τάδ' ἀνέθεκε) Χαρι[.]) ϝελέναι) Μενελϝο 'Deinis (son of Charias?) dedicated this to Helen [wife of] Menelaus.' This is the earliest known Laconian inscription and has already the distinctive Laconian punctuation between words. From the later eighth century on, hero-sanctuaries of royal figures of prehistory (in our terms) begin to appear: of Agamemnon at Mycenae, of Menelaus and Helen at Sparta. Here, as in other sanctuaries, the dedications, either humble or more costly like this bronze oil-flask, may be incised with the names of donor and deity.

(Sparta Museum. Height 7.5 cm.)

H. W. Catling and H. Cavanagh, *Kadmos* 15 (1976) 145–52; *ibid.* 153–7, for a bronze 'meathook' dedicated to Helen alone. On 'Homeric' (not to be taken too literally) hero-shrines of this and earlier date see J. N. Coldstream, *JHS* 96 (1976) 9–17.

322

322. Clay votive plaque from Lato, Crete. Mid-seventh century B.C. The subject is a sphinx, its head rendered in the Daedalic style (see **289**) and wearing a high headdress with a flower tendril springing from it. For the early history of this technique see on **288**. It was much used for the mass-production of trivial dedicatory (and no doubt purely decorative) objects, either figures in the round or relief plaques, as this. Usually the plaques are provided with a hole or holes for suspension or nailing, and there were probably even more made of wood, but if these were elaborately painted (as **323**) they must have been regarded as more expensive than the clay votives, which were generally only summarily painted before firing. The subjects on them may be the deity honoured, the adorant, or decorative, even narrative. The sphinx used to be no more than

323

decorative, but in some contexts the creature could have a protective, funerary (on grave stelai, as **332a**, **b**) or minatory function.

(Oxford, Ashmolean Museum G.488. 10.4 cm × 8 cm.)

J. Boardman, *The Cretan Collection in Oxford* (Oxford, 1961) 110, 116, no. 500, pl. 39.

323. Wooden plaque from a sacred cave at Pitsa, near Sicyon, second half of the sixth century B.C. This is the best preserved from a find of several plaque fragments made in 1934. Others were from larger plaques, apparently measuring up to 40 cm in height. They are precious evidence for an art form which must have been very common in Archaic Greece (compare too **299**). The style of painting resembles that of the latest Corinthian figure-decorated vases of the mid-sixth century. (Production of these decorated vases ceased at about that date, for no clear reason though Attic competition is generally blamed. The plaques show the medium in which such painted figure decoration was still practised.) The subject, a family leading animals to sacrifice, recurs on much later votive reliefs of stone. The wood surface had been prepared with plaster; colours are red, blue, pink.

(Athens, National Museum. Length *c*. 30 cm. This is a photograph of a copy of the plaque by E. Gilliéron fils.)

A. K. Orlandos in *Enciclopedia dell' Arte antica* s.v. 'Pitsà' for the fullest account of the find. On plaque painting, J. Boardman, *JHS* 100 (1980) 205–6.

324. A scene of sacrifice and preparation, from a vase made in Etruria by an immigrant East Greek artist, about 540 B.C., from Caere. In a vine and ivy bower the priest of Dionysus, holding a kantharos-cup (often associated with the god), approaches from the left, followed by a piper, a boy with a cup, and (out of sight here) boys dismembering a goat, ram and deer (?). Over the altar flames two youths cook meat, held on spits, while a third seems to deal with something being consumed in the flames themselves. The latter is the portion of the gods (fat, bones, entrails, the tongue, the tail), but the meat on spits is presumably for mortal consumption, borrowing the sacred fire for cooking. It reminds us that animal-sacrifice did more for the dedicator's appetite than the deity's (even in the view of a believer) and that sacrifices, especially state sacrifices, had as important a social and nutritional function as a devotional one. The rest of the frieze is also devoted to preparation for the feast which regularly followed such sacrifice: a boy dips for wine from an amphora perched on a stand (wine amphorae have pointed feet), holding a strainer in his other hand; another ladles broth or stew into a bowl from a deep cauldron standing over a fire; two prepare food on a standed table (or shallow basin); and (out of sight here) two load spits at a table and bellows are worked for the fire.

(Rome, Villa Giulia.)

G. Ricci, *AS Atene* 24–6 (1946–8) 47–57, pls. 3–6; J. Boardman, *JHS* 78 (1958) 10–11, with remarks on the style of the vase; for which, more fully R. M. Cook and J. Hemelrijk in *Jahrbuch der Berliner Museen* 5 (1963) 107–20.

Greek burials

Many, probably most sites of early Greece are better known from their cemeteries than from their walls, temples or houses. The early period is marked by diversity of practice – inhumation or cremation – and generally by reluctance to furnish the grave itself extravagantly, although there are some notable exceptions. However, the manner of burial could be spectacular, especially in the Geometric period if we judge from the representations on Athens' funeral vases, and there is an increasing interest in supplying the grave with a distinguished and sometimes extravagant marker.

GENERAL BIBLIOGRAPHY

M. Andronikos, *Totenkult* (*Archaeologia Homerica*; Göttingen, 1968)
Kurtz–Boardman
G. M. A. Richter, *The Archaic Gravestones of Attica* (London, 1961) and *Kouroi* (London, 1970)

325 (by M. R. Popham). British excavations at Lefkandi in Euboea have revolutionized our knowledge of the Greek Dark Age and earlier Geometric period (see *CAH* III².1, 754–64). Both town and cemetery have been explored, and the latter not only illustrates an unusual combination of cremation on pyres with offerings placed in separate cist- (and later shaft-) graves, but has also yielded a so-far unique royal burial and heroon. Moreover, the grave finds demonstrate even more clearly than those of the settlement the chequered history and overseas relations of the site, as the following selection shows.

Lefkandi 1.

(a) Some thirty tombs and fifteen pyres, after excavation, at Palia Perivolia, part of one of the cemeteries at Lefkandi. The lack of any

325a

325b

325c

over the whole of the Dark Ages, from Sub-Mycenaean, around 1100 B.C., to about 825 (Middle Geometric I in Attic terms, early Sub-Protogeometric III at Lefkandi), when these cemeteries are abandoned, perhaps because their users moved away to another site.

Lefkandi I, pl. 197a.

(b) Bichrome flask (red and black) decorated with concentric circles. Evidence that the Lefkandians were in communication with Cyprus and the Near East at an early stage is one of the most important aspects of these cemeteries. Perhaps intermittent at first, trade of a more regular kind with that region is clearly demonstrated at least by LPG, and it continues until the burials cease late in the ninth century. This is clearly a Cypriot Bichrome vase: the potters at Lefkandi imitated both this type and other Cypriot pots which they must have seen at home. The offerings in the LPG burial where it was found, and others in contemporary tombs, show that the Euboeans were in touch with other areas too. Close connexions with Attica are not surprising since the two states are virtually neighbours. Not only were vases imported from that region but potters at Lefkandi took over so many features of them that at one stage, early in LPG, it looked as though local individualism might be swamped. In fact it survived, to produce among other things the distinctive two-handled skyphos decorated with sets of semicircles pendent from the rim (*CAH* III². 1, 758, fig. 78), a type which we can recognize as an Euboean export in the Near East and which even reached Sicily and Italy. Two burials of Attic type, cremations contained in urns and buried in pits, may even reflect the actual presence of Athenians at Lefkandi, one of whom was a warrior with sword and spear.

(Eretria Museum, Lefkandi P22, 19. Height 14 cm.)
Lefkandi I, pl. 270a.

(c) More unexpected are imports from north Greece which include a handmade and burnished jug with its cutaway spout, a type familiar in the north but alien to central Greece. These look as though they may be the forerunners of an enterprise which resulted later in the establishment of Euboean colonies in Chalcidice, just as the Near Eastern contacts

consistent orientation in the burials is typical of the four main burial grounds which are clustered on the rising ground just above the modern seaside village and some 600 m distant from the ancient settlement (**265**). So far (1982) some 150 tombs have been excavated extending

325 d

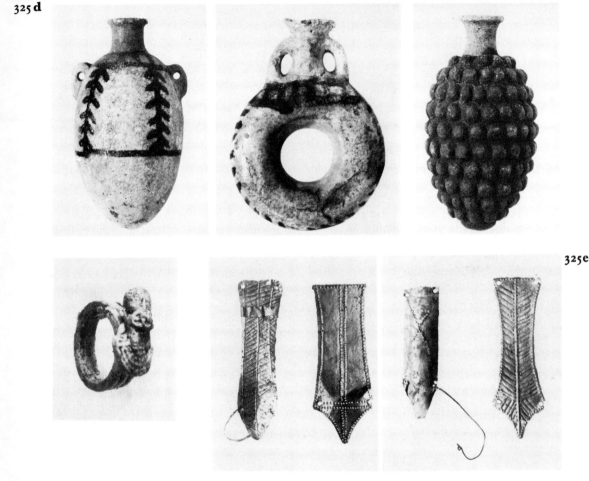

325e

325f

led to Euboean participation in the founding of the north Syrian emporium at Al Mina (*CAH* III².3, 9–14).

(Eretria Museum, Lefkandi T 41, 12. Height 22 cm.)
M. R. Popham *et al.*, *BSA* 77 (1982) pl. 22.12.

(**d**) Collection of faience objects, including these three vases and ring, deposited in a LPG tomb containing another northern jug, as (**c**). Such finds are usually thought to be Phoenician, made under Egyptian influence, but some of the objects from the Toumba cemetery are more likely to be of Egyptian manufacture. The ring is one example, with its depiction of the ram-headed god of Egypt. This same burial, and a neighbouring one, have each produced a squat-bodied bronze jug with cast handle in the form of a lotus flower, a type thought to have been made in Egypt, while a further tomb contained a bronze situla of Egyptian shape and engraved in an Egyptian manner. We can see now that at an earlier date than has hitherto been suspected for any Greek state, Euboea was playing a leading role in extensive overseas activities. It may be that we still underestimate

the extent of this early Euboean enterprise, and that it may have included direct trade with Egypt.

(Eretria Museum, Lefkandi T39, 42, 39, 40, 37. Height of grapes 9.2 cm, of flasks 8.9 cm and 8.5 cm; diameter of ring hoop 2 cm.)
Popham, *op. cit.* pls. 20, 31, 32.

(e) Gold attachments. Some items of jewellery may well be imported but by at least 900 B.C. objects such as these appear in the tombs of Lefkandi. They are cut from sheet gold incised with simple designs and often have loops fastened to the upper and lower parts. They occur in varying numbers and are usually accompanied by a long gold band. Their purpose remains obscure. But, since they are found only in Euboea (and in the neighbouring island of Skyros, which shares its culture) we may be reasonably certain that they were made in Euboea by resident goldsmiths.

(Eretria Museum, Lefkandi T39, 24–7. Heights 5.3 to 4.3 cm.)
Popham, *op. cit.* pls. 17, 30.

(f, g) The prosperous community of Lefkandi must have required soldiers to protect it from envious neighbours, and, in fact, warrior burials occur, with swords, spears and a single instance of arrows and a shield boss. Curiously, two such burials are inhumations made in wooden coffins. But one tomb is outstanding, not least in closely resembling a hero's burial as described in the Homeric poems. Its date is PG and not later than 950 B.C. (f) shows the collapsed bronze crater in which the cremated remains of the Lefkandian hero or king were buried, together with his linen cloak: its cast rim is decorated with bulls, lions and other animals being hunted by archers. A Cypriot origin for it is likely. Iron sword, spear and whetstone had been placed beside the crater and attest the dead man's warrior status. On the other side of his burial shaft lay the outstretched skeleton of a woman (g) decked out with gold jewellery and ornaments, while the bodies of at least three horses had been cast into an adjacent shaft. After the burials, a large apsidal 'temple' or heroon (some 50 m long and 10 m wide) was erected over the site with the burial shafts at its centre. The rich Toumba cemetery lay just outside this building, and it seems likely that it was here that the descendants of the heroic king of Lefkandi and his consort were later buried.

H. W. Catling, *Archaeological Reports for 1981–2* 15–17; M. R. Popham, E. Touloupa and L. H. Sackett, *Antiquity* 56 (1982) 169–74.

326. Part of a burial beneath a tumulus at Vergina in Macedonia, ninth–eighth century B.C. The head lay at the right, a jug and triple-axe pendant of bronze beside it. Other ornament here includes bronze spirals (a group of three), beads and three gold hair-rings. A bronze spiral ('spectacle') fibula fastened the dress at each

shoulder, with a cut-out ornament and beads from a necklace. There are three spiral bracelets of bronze (two on the left arm) and six rows of bronze studs from the back of the belt. The skeleton had disintegrated and the leg area had been disturbed. This is typically rich assemblage for the inhumation of a woman.

M. Andronikos, *Vergina* I (Athens, 1969) 67, pls. 12 and 23; A. M. Snodgrass, *Dark Age of Greece* (Edinburgh, 1971) 160–3 on the cemetery.

326

327. Detail of an Athenian burial crater, from the Dipylon cemetery at Athens, about 740 B.C. This vase marked a grave. It, and similar vases, regularly carry scenes of the laying out of the body (*prothesis*) or its carriage to the grave (*ekphora*), as here. We see the body of a man on a four-legged bier with a chequered shroud lifted over it, set on a cart. To the left and under the handle stand mourning women, with their breasts shown by blips on the torso, their hands raised to their heads. In the register above are three men and a child. At the right stand men wearing swords, one of them holding the horses, and in the panel above are more women mourners. There is no good reason to doubt that this depicts a contemporary burial, with a degree of pomp which was restricted by sumptuary legislation in the time of Solon, and at intervals subsequently. For the chariot frieze, see below, on **334**.

(Athens, National Museum 990.)

J. N. Coldstream, *Greek Geometric Pottery* (London, 1968) 41ff., pl. 8b, by the Hirschfeld Painter; Arias–Hirmer, pl. 5; Simon–Hirmer, pls. 8, 9, for the whole vase, whose height is 1.23 m. On

327

burials in Geometric Athens, Kurtz–Boardman, chapter 4; G. Ahlberg, *Prothesis and Ekphora in Greek Geometric Art* (Stockholm, 1971).

328. Rough-hewn gravestone from the cemetery on Thera, second half of the seventh century B.C. It is inscribed with the name Eteokleia (Ἐτεοκλήια). For marking graves vases like **327** were exceptional, and the position of a grave was more commonly, if at all, indicated by a plain slab or stone. This, in the seventh century, may sometimes be inscribed with the name of the dead, as in the Thera cemetery. There may also be a tendency to anthropomorphize the slab, but there are no certain gravestones carrying carved or incised human figures until the sixth century (slabs from Prinias in Crete are often thought to be exceptions: see *CAH* III².3, 228, fig. 38).

(Thera Museum. Height 70 cm.)

Jeffery, *LSAG* 317f., pl. 61.3.ii; Kurtz–Boardman, chapter 12, for early grave-markers.

329. Clay model of the carriage of a body to the cemetery (*ekphora*), from Vari in Attica, first half of the seventh century B.C. The bier stands on a low, four-wheeled cart. The body is totally covered by a shroud (contrast the way it is exposed on **327**), but in the model the shroud can be lifted to display it. There are mourners around the bier and a child has crept onto the shroud. At the right stands the driver of the horse-team (missing) which pulls the cart. This is a unique rendering in the round of the scene shown on earlier, Geometric grave-marking vases (as **327**).

(Athens, National Museum.)

328

329

330

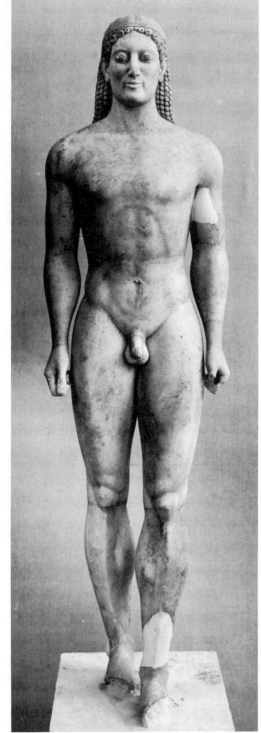

M. Andronikos, *Totenkult* (Göttingen, 1968) pl. 4a; Kurtz–Boardman 78, pl. 16, and pls. 10–15, 17, 18, for other early Athenian grave furniture.

330. Life-size marble figure of a youth, which served as a grave-marker in the cemetery at Anavyssos in Attica, about 530 B.C. From the end of the seventh century, beginning in the Greek islands where monumental statuary in white marble was first attempted, such kouroi served as grave-markers. Except for an occasional early island example, wearing a belt, they are invariably naked with no attribute to indicate warlike or athletic prowess. They are usually shown in their prime, beardless, and apparently far less closely identifiable with the dead whose grave they marked than the figures on the relief stelae (**332**). This one has an inscribed base:

στ̃ε̄θι : καὶ οἴκτιρον : Κροίσο παρὰ σε̃μα θανόντος hόν ποτ’ ἐνὶ προμάχοις : ὄλεσε θο̃ρος Ἄρες.

‘Stay and mourn at the monument for dead Kroisos, whom violent Ares destroyed, fighting in the front rank.’ The young man was apparently named after the Lydian king, deposed in 546.

(Athens, National Museum 3851. Height 1.94 m.)
  G. M. A. Richter, *Kouroi* (London, 1970) no. 136, figs. 395–8, 400–1; E. Mastrokostas, *AAA* 7 (1974) 215ff., the base; Boardman, *GSAP* fig. 107 and 22ff.; B. S. Ridgway, *The Archaic Style* (Princeton, 1977) chapter 3; Kurtz–Boardman 88f., 237f., on statues as grave-markers.

331. Marble statues of a *kouros* and *kore* which marked graves at Merenda (Myrrhinous) in Attica, about 550 B.C. They had been buried in antiquity, together with a grave *kouros*, presumably to escape destruction in a time of trouble, or possibly after damage (the *kouros* had a broken arm). Political animosities could be exercised even on the graves of opponents’ families, even by Greeks. *Korai* as grave-markers are rarer than the *kouroi* (as **330**) which are found in many parts of Greece in this role. The *kore* is for Phrasikleia and is elaborately dressed, wearing a floral headdress, earrings and necklace. The statue was found in 1972 but the base had been known long before. It carries the signature of the artist Aristion of Paros, and the epitaph

332a 1

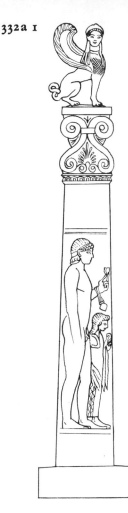

332a 2

332a 3

σῆμα Φρασικλείας · κόρη κεκλέσομαι αἴει,
ἀντὶ γάμο παρὰ θεῦν τοῦτο λάχος᾽ ὄνομα.

'Marker of Phrasikleia, I shall ever be called maiden (*kore*), the gods allotting me this title in place of marriage.' The grandeur and quality of the tomb monuments were not matched in the Archaic period by richness of offerings placed in the tomb itself.

(Athens, National Museum.)

E. Mastrokostas, *AAA* 5 (1972) 298ff.; Boardman, *GSAP* fig. 108a and 24f.; Ridgway, *op. cit.* chapter 4; the full publication of the find has not yet appeared.

332. The most elaborate grave-markers of Archaic Greece are Athenian stelae of the years around and just after the mid sixth century B.C.

(a) Stela from Attica, of the most elaborate form, topped by a sphinx carved in the round, seated on a volute capital. On the shaft a boy athlete, with flower and oil flask, and a girl with a flower. On the base the inscription

μνῆμα φίλοι: Με[   ] πατὲρ
ἐπέθεκε θανόντι χσὺν δὲ φίλε μέτερ.

'To dear dead Me. . . . his father and dear mother raised this monument . . .' Some associate this with the Alcmaionid family (Megacles) and think that it was overthrown by the Pisistratids in 514. On such stelae the panels above and below the figure may be painted or carved also.

(New York, Metropolitan Museum 11.185, and Berlin, Staatliche Museen (West) 1531 (the girl's head). Height restored 4.23 m. Drawing, Marion Cox.)

G. M. A. Richter, *Archaic Gravestones of Attica* (London, 1961) no. 37, figs. 96–109, 204.

(**b**) Sphinx and capital from a grave stela found in Attica. Much of the elaborate painting (green, blue, red, black) is preserved.

(Boston, Museum of Fine Art 40.576. Height 1.42 m.)

Richter, *op. cit.* no. 38, figs. 110–14.

(**c**) Fragment of a grave stela from Athens, found in the Themistoclean Wall (cf. Thuc. 1.93.2), showing a boxer with cauliflower ear, broken nose and his bound hand raised. Unlike the *kouroi* the figures on stelae display differences of age and interest: for the young, athletics (as our (**a**); the boxer is rather older); for the mature, soldiering; and for the elderly, a relaxed pose leaning on a stick, with a dog.

(Athens, Kerameikos Museum. Height 23 cm.)

Richter, *op. cit.* no. 31, fig. 92.

Warfare

Homer is a poor guide to the military practices of early Greece. Some of his descriptions of armour derive from older formulae which accompanied the story-telling embedded in the epics. His chariot teams generally make better tactical sense if understood as horsemen with squires rather than heroes with charioteers, but he knew how chariots behaved, and in battle, being an Ionian and neighbour to peoples who still used war chariots (the Lydians). Archaeology and representational evidence tell us all we can now know of Greek armour and weaponry and we may, with caution, project back classical accounts of the conduct of hoplite battles to the seventh century, in which hoplite armour and tactics were first in common use.

GENERAL BIBLIOGRAPHY

CAH III².1, 761, 786; III².3, 454–7, on warfare and weapons
H.-G. Buchholz *et al.*, *Kriegswesen* (*Archaeologia Homerica* E; Göttingen, 1977–)
D. Gray, *Seewesen* (*ibid.* G; 1974)
P. A. L. Greenhalgh, *Early Greek Warfare* (Cambridge, 1973)
A. M. Snodgrass, *EGAW*, and *Arms and Armour of the Greeks* (London, 1967)

333. Bronze figure of a warrior, from Karditsa in Thessaly, early seventh century. This is a good example in the round of the Geometric warrior more familiar on Geometric vases, especially in Athens. The cap-like helmet is more a support for an impressive high crest than usefully protective. The highly stylized 'Dipylon shield' is a light shield, slung from a baldric, but some scholars regard it as unreal – a heroic throwback to the Bronze Age figure-of-eight shields, which it does not, in fact, closely resemble. It persists in both this (see **327, 336**) and its more sophisticated hoplite form (the 'Boeotian shield') into the Classical period. Many Geometric bronze warriors wear a broad belt only, which looks real and no substitute or abbreviation for a corselet or other dress.

(Athens, National Museum 12831. Height 27.6 cm.)
S. Karouzou, *Ath. Mitt.* 91 (1976) 23–30, pls. 5,

6, as an Achilles. On the 'Dipylon shield' – Snod-grass, *EGAW* 58ff. and *Ath. Mitt.* 95 (1980) 51–8, disbelieving; P. A. L. Greenhalgh, *Early Greek Warfare* (Cambridge, 1973) 63ff.; J. Carter, *BSA* 67 (1972) 55–7; G. Ahlberg, *Fighting on Land and Sea in Greek Geometric Art* (Stockholm, 1971) 59ff.; Boardman, forthcoming (Madison Symposium).

334. See **327**, lower frieze. In Bronze Age Greece chariots were used in battle, as they were by the Egyptians and Hittites. By Homer's time this practice is forgotten and the poet uses them as a taxi-service for heroes on the battle-field, a role more plausibly filled then, and cer-tainly later, by horse-riding with a squire. In Geometric art they appear very rarely in battle scenes but more often, as here, in procession on grave vases. The Geometric conventions are not always readily interpreted but in the examples shown we should probably recognize a two-wheeled chariot driven by a warrior

336 1

carrying a 'Dipylon' shield and wearing a helmet (the crest only is apparent). These pro-cessions are honorific but sometimes the chariots race and then funeral games must be implied. The chariot continues in use for racing and ceremonial occasions, though never again in the battle line in the Greek homeland.

Greenhalgh, *op. cit.* chs. 1, 2. On the use of chariots by Iron Age Greeks see J. K. Anderson, *AJA* 69 (1965) 349–52 and 79 (1975) 175–87; and Boardman, forthcoming (Madison Symposium).

335. Bronze helmet and corselet from a tomb at Argos, late eighth century. It also contained fire-dogs and spits. The helmet, of the 'Kegel-helm' type, is made of five pieces of bronze, rivetted together, and provided with a high crest-holder which closely copies an Assyrian form. The corselet is made in two pieces, hinged along one side, and is the 'bell corselet' which continues in use through the sixth century, while the helmet is soon replaced by more advanced types (**338a, 339**). The corselet is lightly decorated with the forms of the body beneath, an early sculptural rendering of anatomical detail. Its shape derives from Cen-tral European types of body armour. The hoplite soldier, relying on discipline in the ranks to come to close grips with his enemy, required heavier body-armour than his more independent and mobile predecessor. The Argos panoply represents some of the basic equipment, to which has to be added the hop-lite shield, a large round shield fastened to the left forearm by arm and hand grips (*porpax, antilabe*) and not held by a single handle like earlier light shields, including the 'Dipylon'. See *CAH* III².1, 781, fig. 86, for the grave group; and 706, fig. 72 for a Dark Age helmet.

(Argos Museum. Heights, 50 cm and 46 cm.)
P. Courbin, *BCH* 81 (1957) 322–86; Snodgrass, *EGAW* 13ff. (helmet), 73ff. (corselet), and in J. Boardman, M. A. Brown, T. G. E. Powell, edd., *The European Community in later Prehistory* (Studies

336 2

in honour of C. F. C. Hawkes; London, 1971) 31ff., on the first European body-armour.

336. Corinthian ('Middle Protocorinthian') aryballos from a grave at Lechaeum, port of Corinth, about 680 B.C. In the battle Corinthian helmets are worn, two with high crests. The three shields shown side-on are of the light type with single handgrip – the 'Dipylon' shield of the Geometric vases (**327**) – one of them worn at a warrior's back as he is attacked from behind. The shield seen from the inside is a regular hoplite shield with arm- and hand-grip. The hoplite, supported by an archer, has a thrusting spear, but holds another, to throw. Of his opponents two have two throwing spears, while the third turns to his secondary weapon, a sword. So this is a skirmish involving a warrior dressed as a hoplite, not a hoplite battle.

(Corinth Museum CP 2096. Height 4.6 cm.)
   C. W. J. and M. Eliot, *Hesperia* 37 (1968) 348–50, pl. 102.2; Snodgrass, *EGAW* 60, 138, 197f.; Greenhalgh, *op. cit.* 69f.

337. Hoplite fighting, on a frieze from the 'Chigi vase', a Corinthian ('Middle Protocorinthian') olpe by the Macmillan Painter, made about 650–640 B.C. and found at Veii in Etruria. This, with another work by the same artist on an aryballos in London, is the earliest clear representation of the hoplite phalanx in action. The ranks are closing. For the two at the left a piper between them plays to help them keep step. The extreme right of the rear rank here is lagging, a common tendency since the right-hand marker's right side is unguarded, and behind two men are still arming (notice the throwing loops on the two spears stuck in the ground). The front ranks raise their spears to thrust overarm, but carry a second spear for an underarm thrust, while the rest carry theirs at the slope. All wear Corinthian helmets, bell corselets, greaves, and carry fully blazoned shields.

(Rome, Villa Giulia Museum 22679. Height 26 cm. Drawing after *Antike Denkmäler* 2, pls. 44–5.)
   Snodgrass, *EGAW* 138, 198, pl. 36; Arias–Hirmer 275f., pl. IV; Simon–Hirmer 49, pl. VII.

338. Pieces from an important find of Cretan armour at Arcades (Afrati) in Crete, late seventh century, now dispersed in museums in Heraklion and Hamburg, and in private collections in New York and Crete. The inscriptions on several items show that they were spoils dedicated from a battle. These distinctive types are found elsewhere in Crete, and at Olympia and Delphi. See *CAH* III².3, 227. The definitive publication is H. Hoffmann, *Early Cretan Armorers* (Mainz, 1972).

337

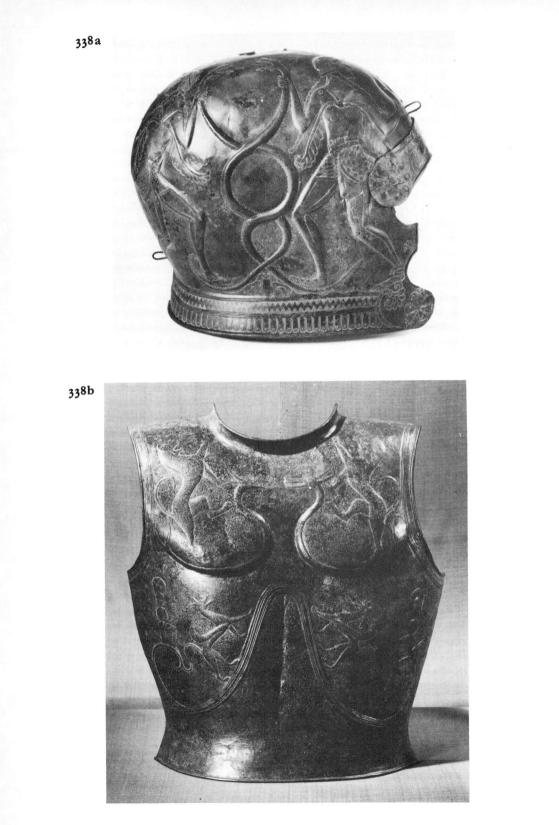

338a

338b

(a) Bronze helmet. The decoration is repoussé and the linear patterns are also traced (i.e. hammered, not incised). Two youths, with winged shoulders and heels, grasp two entwined serpents; beneath is a two-bodied lion. The main part of the helmet is made in two pieces with separate peak and two hoops to fasten a crest. The Cretan helmet is one of the earliest to be evolved in Greece. It offers less protection to the face and neck than other types of helmet developed for hoplite warfare (339). There is an inscription over the frontlet – Νεόπολις.

(New York, Norbert Schimmel Collection. Height 21 cm.)
Hoffmann, *op. cit.* H 1.

(b) Bronze corselet front. The outline of the pectorals takes the form of serpents with rampant lions; on the rib cage appear two griffins and two kneeling warriors; on the stomach traces of felines. This is a standard bell corselet but the decoration is a Cretan speciality only paralleled by comparable examples (though possibly not of Cretan manufacture) found at Olympia (including the Crowe corselet, now in Athens).

(Hamburg, Museum für Kunst und Gewerbe 1970.26a. Height 45.5 cm.)
Hoffmann, *op. cit.* C 1.

(c) Bronze belly guard ('mitra') decorated with the foreparts of two horses. This is a peculiarly Cretan piece of armour, clearly meant to hang from the waist, but Cretan corselets are not provided with holes for the attachment loops, so they must have been hung either from the corselet lining or from belts (not of bronze). They are not the Homeric 'mitra' though the name is commonly used for them. This example is inscribed Συνήνιτος τόδε ὁ Εὐκλῶτα ('Synenitos, son of Euklotas [gave or captured] this'; Synenitos also gave a helmet).

(New York, Norbert Schimmel Collection. Width 24.2 cm.)
Hoffmann, *op. cit.* M 1.

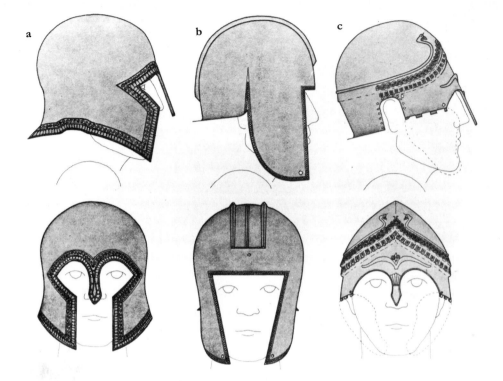

339. Reconstructions of three different helmet types are shown, based on originals in the Newcastle University Collection and indicating how much of the warrior's face and neck was protected.

(a) The Corinthian helmet, developed by about 700 B.C., offered the fullest protection. At first it was made in two pieces (like the Cretan, **338a**), then hammered out of one piece and provided with a tall or low crest. The low crest is the rule later since it was less of a liability in fighting at close quarters.

(b) The 'Illyrian' helmet, also a Peloponnesian invention but most popular in Illyria in the Classical period, whence its name. It is the direct descendant of the Geometric 'Kegelhelm' (**335**) with long cheek pieces and a fore-and-aft groove to fit the crest. Early examples, like the Corinthian, are two-piece in construction.

(c) The 'Chalcidian' helmet appears in the sixth century, again misnamed since it had wide currency, including south Italy. It leaves the ears exposed – useful for communication in battle, if vulnerable, and the cheek pieces may be angular or rounded, or even hinged (as here).

Archaic and Classical helmets are seldom any more elaborately decorated than the examples shown here. The Cretan (**338a**) are exceptional in this respect. The 'Attic' helmet is more of a simple cap, usually with neck guard and hinged cheek pieces.

(Drawings taken from *Greek Arms and Armour* (The Greek Museum, Newcastle upon Tyne, 1978) by B. B. Shefton and P. Foster.)

On the helmet types see Snodgrass, *EGAW* ch. 1 and *Arms and Armour of the Greeks* (London, 1967).

340. Battle scenes on an Attic crater dedicated on the Acropolis about 570 B.C. The presence of chariots in the battle on the main frieze indicates a heroic occasion, perhaps Troy – the chariot is of the usual racing type, the charioteer wears the traditional long chiton and has a light

shield (a version of the 'Dipylon'–Boeotian type) slung at his back. The hoplites wear contemporary armour. Helmets are Corinthian with high crests. Notice the elaborate crest-holders – a swan head and neck, a wheel, antlers; one has no crest but spikes. The hoplite shields show *porpax* and *antilabe* within and blazons on the outside, to be thought of as painted on the wood or hide, or exceptionally as bronze cut-outs such as have been found at Olympia (**307**). Bell corselets are worn with a tunic or nothing beneath, and greaves. Armour attached to arms, thighs and ankles is shown on other vases (**359**). In the smaller frieze Greek cavalrymen with throwing spears (notice the throwing thong, *amentum*) face mounted eastern bowmen wearing soft, pointed caps usually associated with Scythians.

(Athens, National Museum, Acr. 606. After Graef–Langlotz.)

Beazley, *ABV* 81, no. 1, Painter of Acropolis 606; B. Graef and E. Langlotz, *Akropolis Vasen* (Berlin, 1925–33) I, pl. 31; cf. Greenhalgh, *op. cit.* 115f., the horsemen; S. Vos, *Scythian Archers in Archaic Attic Vase Painting* (Groningen, 1963).

341. Athenian vase of about 560 B.C., painted by Lydos. A hoplite, with Corinthian helmet, bell corselet and hoplite shield, rides beside his squire who wears only a tunic and carries a spear. The fully armed hoplite, with his shield fixed to his arm and in heavy armour, could not have fought on horseback but, if a nobleman – cavalier (*hippeus*) – he could ride to line of battle with a squire to attend his horse during the action. This recalls the role of the chariot in Homer, and these aristocratic pairs are seen on vases into the second half of the sixth century. Armed cavalrymen may also be identified on vases, but then only with helmet and corselet, and no shield.

(Naples, Museo Nazionale 2770 (81292).)

Beazley, *ABV* 109, no. 23; *CVA* Naples 1, pl. 6; Simon–Hirmer, pl. 67; Greenhalgh, *op. cit.* chapters 5 and 6 for mounted warriors in the seventh and sixth centuries.

Narrative and art

The changes which were effected in the visual arts from the eighth century on can be in part attributed to the example set by the arts of foreigners, as we have seen, in part to a general increase in prosperity and demand for luxury goods. The subject matter of the decorative arts changed, as did their form and style, and in the Archaic period the Greeks developed conventions in narrative art which were to lie at the heart of both Classical Greek and all subsequent classicizing art in the western world. The Greeks were surrounded by images – icons – on their public buildings and temples, on objects of everyday use. They gave visual expression to stories which were well known to the ordinary man, and which were receiving more sophisticated expression for a more restricted audience from poets. Through their art we may come closer to the Greeks' own view of their gods and heroes and the meaning for them of their rich mythological tradition, rooted in the Bronze Age and developed through the oral tradition of the Dark Ages – an oral tradition which, of course, did not die when Greeks learned to write.

GENERAL BIBLIOGRAPHY

J. Carter, *BSA* 67 (1972) 25–58
Fittschen
Schefold, I, II
Lexicon Iconographicum Mythologiae Classicae 1– (Zurich, 1981–)
M. Robertson, *History of Greek Art* (Cambridge, 1975)

343 2

342. Clay model from a tomb at Archanes, near Cnossus, of the later ninth century B.C. The circular building with a pitched roof and centre 'chimney' had a movable door. It is decorated in the 'Protogeometric B' style, inspired by the patterns of eastern metalwork. Within it is seated a woman with raised hands – a gesture of epiphany or adoration. From the roof she is inspected by two men, accompanied by a dog. Various explanations have been offered – the rape or rescue of a goddess; spying on a goddess of mysteries (but there are no circular shrines that we know in Crete of these years); the discovery of a Bronze Age tholos tomb, taken for an underground shrine, of the type used as a family tomb in this period (*CAH* III².1, 775, fig. 83). Whatever its message, it is one of the earliest groups in the round to attempt to tell a story, and it is not readily matched in Greek art for another hundred years – until the bronze figurines showing a hero fighting a centaur or lion. Earlier, there is the clay 'centaur' from Lefkandi (*CAH* Plates to Vols. I and II, pl. 170b; it is not clear what narrative content there may be in the figure, but a nick in one leg has been identified as Chiron's famous wound; it may not, however, be a 'centaur' at all in the later Greek sense of the term).

(Heraklion Museum. Height 22 cm.)

S. Marinatos and M. Hirmer, *Crete and Mycenae* (London, 1960) pls. 138–9; S. Alexiou, *Kretika Chronika* 1950, 455ff.; 1958, 280ff.; J. Boardman, *BSA* 62 (1967) 64–6, a tomb discovered. For the Lefkandi centaur see now *BSA* 65 (1970) 21ff. and *Lefkandi* I, pls. 251–2.

343. Crater from a tomb at Cnossus (Teke Tomb E), ninth century B.C. Crete is the one area in Greece where there is demonstrable continuity in the tradition of figure decoration on vases through the Dark Ages. One side of this vase shows two sphinxes and a bird. The monsters are orientalizing but were already familiar in Greece in the art of the Bronze Age. The side shown has two lions attacking a man. The motif can also be traced, though with more difficulty, in the east (Cyprus) but it recurs in eighth-century Greece both on an Idaean Cave shield (**278**) and in Attica – on gold bands and painted on vases (cf. *CAH* III².1, 686, fig. 69).

(Heraklion Museum 21147. Height 31.4 cm. Drawing, L. H. Sackett.)

L. H. Sackett, *BSA* 71 (1976) 117ff.; N. Cold-

stream in *Acts of the International Archaeological Symposium* 'The Relations between Cyprus and Crete, *ca.* 2000–500 B.C.' (Nicosia, 1979) 259f.

344. Clay tetrapod from the Dipylon cemetery at Athens, late eighth century B.C. The warriors in the upper frieze carry either 'Dipylon' or round shields, of various sizes. On two legs of the vessel a man is shown attacking a lion, with sword and spear (as shown) or a weapon and bare hands. On the other two legs the lion appears in the same pose but faced by a man carrying an animal over his shoulders. The lion-fights follow an oriental scheme but it is possible that the Geometric artist and/or viewer took this to represent Heracles' encounter with the Nemean lion. (Only later did artists observe those details of the story which require him to tackle the invulnerable beast without weapons.) The shepherd facing the lion on the other two legs might then be taken to reflect another aspect of the story, that Heracles was ridding Nemea of a monster which was ravaging their flocks. The lion was not known in central Greece in this period and is copied from eastern works, but its form here is thoroughly geometricized.

(Athens, Kerameikos Museum inv. 407. Height 17.8 cm.)

K. Kübler, *Kerameikos* 5.1 (Berlin, 1954) pl. 69; Schefold 1, pl. 5a; Fittschen 81ff.

345. Cast bronze tripod leg, from Olympia, about 700 B.C. In the upper panel two warriors fight with a tripod between them. The tripod can be shown in this position as a prize for a contest, but this seems a mortal duel, not wrestling or boxing, and the tripod is so prominent, perhaps even held by the contestants, that a scene of Heracles fighting Apollo for his tripod has been suspected. If so, this is the earliest evidence for the story, which does not appear again in Greek art for over a century.

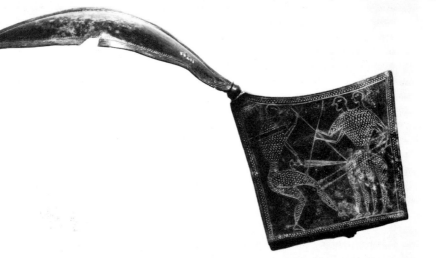

But this was a Delphic, not Olympian story, and the scene might still be of some unrecorded heroic fight *over* a prize rather than *for* a prize. The rampant lions in the lower panel seem to mirror the heroic scene above.

(Olympia Museum B 1730. Height 46.7 cm.)

F. Willemsen, *Olympische Forschungen* III (Berlin, 1957) pls. 62–3; Schefold 1, pl. 4b; Fittschen 29–32 on the subject.

346. Bronze fibula (safety-pin) of Boeotian manufacture, found in the Idaean Cave, Crete, of the early seventh century B.C. The flat catch-plates and sometimes the flat crescent-shaped bows of fibulae served as fields for incised decoration from the late ninth century on. This is an example of after 700. A warrior is shown attacking two others – or a double warrior. The ungainly convention of showing two men side by side, showing a single body (a convention applied more successfully and regularly to teams of horses), was adopted in the third quarter of the eighth century. It was under-standably rare but examples occur in the arts of Athens, Corinth, Argos, Boeotia and on a bronze from Phigaleia. It has been thought by some scholars that all such figures are of the Molione or Actorione, Siamese-twin warriors encountered by Nestor and Heracles; or that the Geometric convention was in time recog-nized as a way of depicting them; or that none

are mythological figures since the convention, and alleged mythological representations, die with Geometric art. The other side of this catch-plate shows two bowmen poised over a warship.

(Athens, National Museum 11765. Catch-plate 9 cm × 9 cm.)

R. Hampe, *Frühe griechische Sagenbilder in Böotien* (Athens, 1936) pl. 14, no. 28, and passim for the fibulae; Fittschen 68ff. on the subject, 213ff. on the fibulae. For the Actorione twins, Hampe in *LIMC* I (1981) s.v.; Boardman, forthcoming (Madison Symposium).

347. Scene from an amphora which served as a child's grave at Eleusis, second quarter of the seventh century B.C. Vase-painters in Attica ignored the miniaturist, black-figure styles of their contemporaries in Corinth (**295, 349**) Their first vases are large, in the tradition of the Geometric grave-marking vases (**327**) and now they carry a variety of orientalizing pat-terns and big-figure mythological scenes. Here the dead Gorgon (Medusa) lies decapitated at the left in an orientalizing shrubbery. Her two sisters pursue Perseus, of whom we see only the booted legs. Between pursuers and quarry stands Athena holding a sceptre – she is not shown as a warrior goddess in Attica until the sixth century. The elements of the story are set out with graphic simplicity. The Gorgon heads are interesting experiments in the grotesque,

348

resembling bronze cauldrons with animal protomes attached (cf. **203**), here serpentine with
lion- or snake-heads, while the nose, eyes and
teeth painted on the bowls recall a griffin's head.
Soon after this a Corinthian artist fixed on the
frontal lion's head, with gaping tusked jaws
and lolling tongue, for the Gorgon head, the
type which was to persist in Greek art through
the Archaic period. In other respects the scheme
of this pursuit remains unchanged for as long
as it is figured in Greek Art. The drawing is
executed in 'black on white' with some added
white paint, streaky application of 'black' on
limbs (which were not certainly covered with
white paint) and minor touches of incision.

(Eleusis Museum. The whole vase is 1.42 m high.
After Mylonas.)

G. E. Mylonas, *Protoattikos Amphoreus apo Eleu-
sinos* (Athens, 1957); Arias–Hirmer, pls. 12, 13;
Simon–Hirmer, pls. 15, IV; Schefold I, pls. I, 6; on
Gorgon heads, J. Boardman, *Archaic Greek Gems*
(London, 1968) 37–9 and *GO* 79.

348. Fragment of a crater from Argos, second
quarter of the seventh century B.C. The scene
is of the giant Polyphemus, reclining on the
rocky floor of his cave which is stylized into a
scale pattern (a device met also in eastern art),
being blinded by Odysseus and his companions

who wield a thin pole. The drawing is closer to the Attic (**347**) than the Corinthian, but a wash of colour is used within the figure outlines, a technique also employed by island artists. The subject has an unusual currency at this time and in widely different studios. It appears on the neck of the Attic vase whose body is shown in **347**, on the other side of the western Greek vase shown in **367** (the scheme is much the same in all), and a little later on a bronze plaque from Samos. Moreover, there is an Attic scene of the sequel, the escape from the cave with the men clinging to the bodies of Polyphemus' flock, on a vase found in Aegina. This is the only *Odyssey* episode taken seriously by Greek artists in the seventh century, and if Homer's epic did not inspire it, it was probably through widespread knowledge of the Polyphemus story on its own. That it should have attracted artists to express it in such similar schemes attests early and 'international' dissemination of iconographic themes, on vases or in other media.

(Argos Museum. Height 24.5 cm.)
   P. Courbin, *BCH* 79 (1955) 1ff.; Schefold 1, 48, fig. 15; Fittschen 192–4 for the subject.

349. Fragment of a Corinthian ('Middle Protocorinthian') cup (kotyle) from Aegina, second quarter of the seventh century B.C. Bellerophon, riding Pegasus, confronts the Chimaera. The subject is one of the most popular in seventh-century Greek art. Here the monster has been given pride of place, at the front of the vase, and the hero is confined to the area beneath the handle. The Chimaera takes its canonical form (we lack the serpent tail, which appears on

other works of this date). It is a Greek invention, perhaps inspired by the eastern winged lion, with the wing growing an animal head (an eastern conceit; and the wing-goat Chimaera is not forgotten in Greek and Etruscan art), and the tail given a bird's head tip rather than a snake's. A few late seventh-century works make the whole hindpart of the monster into a snake, closer to the epic formula (*Iliad* VI.181), but this looked implausible and was soon abandoned by artists.

(Aegina Museum inv. 1376. Height 14.7 cm.)
   H. Payne, *Necrocorinthia* (Oxford, 1931) pl. 4.1–2; W. Kraiker, *Aigina* (Berlin, 1951) no. 253, pl. 18; Schefold 1, pl. 22; Fittschen 157ff. for the subject; and on the later seventh-century Homeric Chimaera, J. Boardman, *Island Gems* (London, 1963) 56 and *JHS* 88 (1968) 3.

350. The neck of a clay relief vase from Thebes, mid seventh century B.C. Perseus decapitates the Gorgon Medusa, carefully looking away from her petrifying head. He wears the three special gifts he received for the encounter – a cap of darkness, a bag for the head (*kibisis*) and magic boots. Like the creator of the slightly earlier Athenian Gorgons (**347**) the artist is not aware of what is to be the canonic head-type and offers here a villainous human face. And like the artist of the sixth-century scarab (**303**) he presents her with a horse's body. These relief vases begin by about 700 in the islands, notably Tenos, and a daughter studio is established in Boeotia during the seventh century. They carry a range of myth scenes which are often original, some of them difficult to identify. (This centaur-like structure for the Gorgon is, for example, also used for a Minotaur with Theseus on one of these vases.)

(Paris, Louvre CA 795; there is also a fragmentary replica, CA 937.)

Hampe, *op. cit.* (**346**), pls. 36, 38; Schefold 1, pl. 15b (pl. 24a, the Minotaur); Fittschen 152; on the class, M. Ervin-Caskey, *AJA* 80 (1976) 19ff.

351. Clay metope from a temple of Apollo at Thermum in Aetolia, around 625 B.C. As soon as temple buildings receive a canonic architectural form – in this case early Doric – they

receive fine decoration, often of narrative content. The Thermum series of metopes, the earliest of which we have substantial remains, are of Corinthian manufacture, and the style of painting on them is close to that on Corinthian vases, but enlarged and eschewing incision, which would have been too feeble for detail at this scale. The scene is of two women undressing, a motif which appears also at about this time in an ivory group. They are probably the daughters of King Proitus of Argos, maddened by Hera. The principles of the choice of subsidiary decoration for temples are not always clear – at Thermum we find also a Gorgoneion, Chelidon and Aedon with the murdered Itys, a hunter, Perseus running with the Medusa head, love-making.

(Athens, National Museum. Height *c.* 88 cm. After Schefold.)

J. Dörig, *AM* 77 (1962) 72ff., pl. 23, the subject; Schefold 1, 37, fig. 6.

352. Bronze plaque from Olympia, late seventh century B.C. Plaques of this type may have been attached to larger wooden objects, furniture or the like, or have served as independent dedicatory pictures, again probably mounted on panels. After the fight at the wedding of Pirithous, in which the Centaurs attacked the

268

Lapiths and their women, a pitched battle developed. The Lapith Kaineus was invulnerable, and is therefore dealt with by the Centaurs by being beaten into the ground with boulders and tree-trunks, their natural weapons. Kaineus needs no shield so can use two hands, as he does here to some effect, though he is normally given a shield in Greek art. He has, however, already been hammered down, half way up his greaved shins. The workmanship of the plaque has been thought island or East Greek, even South Italian, but there are no very sure stylistic criteria at this date. It is an interesting demonstration of how a heraldic, symmetrical man-and-monsters pattern can be turned to the service of narrative and myth.

(Olympia Museum BE 11a. Height 22.5 cm.)
    R. Hampe–U. Jantzen, *Olympia-Bericht* 1 (Berlin, 1937) pl. 28; Fittschen 118, with views on its origin; Schefold 1, pl. 27c.

353. Corinthian oil vase (flat-bottomed aryballos), early sixth century B.C. This unusually ornate little vase carries two mythological scenes. One involves a ship and perhaps shows Odysseus with the sirens. The other, shown here, has Heracles' encounter with the Hydra. He attacks it with a sword while Iolaus uses a sickle. The crab, sent by Hera to distract him, nips Heracles' heel. Behind him stands Athena, in mufti, holding a small phial, perhaps to catch the venomous blood of the Hydra, which Heracles will use to tip his arrows. The subject, set in the Lernaean swamp in the Argolid, is an unusually common one on Corinthian vases and the details of the iconography, well displayed here, are followed quite closely in the many

353

354

355a

355b

later Athenian vase-representations of the scene. It is only much later, however, that artists accept any form of 'cycle' of Heracles' labours, and in this period individual exploits are chosen, and often repeated, while others, popular later, are wholly ignored.

(Basel, Antikenmuseum BS 425. Height 14.5 cm.) *CVA* Basel 1, pl. 11.10; D. A. Amyx and P. Amandry, *Ant. K.* 25 (1982) 102–16, pl. 19; J. Boardman, *Oxford Journal of Archaeology* 1 (1982) 237–8, on the phial.

354. The principal scene from a Corinthian column crater from Caere, about 560 B.C. The subject is the departure of Amphiaraus, leader of the Seven against Thebes, and it is a good example of the way a Greek artist could allude to events in a story which precede or follow that depicted. The subject appeared also on the Chest of Cypselus (see on **357**) and on an Athenian vase in a slightly less detailed manner. Before the palace façade Amphiaraus leaps onto his chariot looking back to his family who appeal to him, rather than bid him farewell. Farthest is his wife Eriphyle, veiled, clutching the necklace with which she had been bribed by Polynices to persuade her husband to join the fateful expedition. The many small animals are perhaps omens. Closest to him is his son Alcmaeon, who will avenge him and kill his mother. At the far right a seer, hand to head in a gesture of despair, is well aware of the outcome of the expedition. This was one of the finest of the Late Corinthian craters, designed mainly, it seems, for the export market to Etruria. Soon after it was made figure-decorated vases of this type disappear from the Corinthian potters' quarter.

(Once Berlin, Staatliche Museen F 1655. After Furtwängler–Reichhold.) A. Furtwängler–K. Reichhold, *Griechische Vasenmalerei* (Munich, 1904–32) pls. 121–2; Schefold 1, pl. 67a.

355. Limestone pedimental sculpture from the temple of Artemis on Corcyra (Corfu), early sixth century B.C. The primitive Doric temple at Thermum carried painted metopes of clay (**351**). Soon, relief sculpture in stone was to be accepted as temple decoration, for metopes and for pediments on Doric temples. This is the earliest near-complete assemblage to have survived. The field is an awkward one and unity of scale is not observed; not even unity of subject, and the relevance of the subjects to the cult is not in every case obvious. The centre group is of the Gorgon Medusa (**b**), fulfilling an apotropaic function at the temple façade (a role she or her kind exercises elsewhere) and in a narrative setting with her children Pegasus and Chrysaor at either side (though they are to be born *after* her death and decapitation). The leopards beside her suit her or Artemis, as mistresses of animals, and are guardians too. The fights at the corners are not so readily explained. At the right Zeus blitzes a Titan or giant; at the left a seated figure is threatened, possibly Rhea; dead giants fill the corners.

(Corfu Museum. Pediment 3.15 m × 22.16 m.) C. Rodenwaldt, *Korkyra* II (Berlin, 1939); Schefold 1, 52f., fig. 16, pls. 42–3; on the subject, J. L. Benson in *Gestalt und Geschichte* (Festschrift K. Schefold; Bern, 1967) 48ff. and R. Hampe, *Göttingische Gelehrte Anzeigen* 220 (1968) 22ff.; Boardman, *GSAP* fig. 187.

356. Athenian volute crater found at Chiusi, made by the potter Ergotimus and the painter Cleitias (who both sign it, twice) about 570 B.C. This is the best preserved of a new group of vases made in Athens after about 570 on which the old zonal treatment of the body is retained, but now all for figure scenes and not the animals which had hitherto occupied all zones except the principal one. From this time on animal-frieze vases are of secondary importance and within fifty years they disappear from Athens. Yet finer vases by these artists and their companions were dedicated on the Athenian Acropolis, but we know them only from fragments. The François Vase, shown here, named after its finder, carries eleven different mythological subjects and only one frieze of animal and floral patterns. The main subject is the procession of gods visiting the newly married Peleus and Thetis. Recurrent themes seem to be the life of Achilles (marriage of his parents, killing Troilus, at the games for Patroclus, his own death) and Theseus (rescuing the Athenian youths and girls from Crete, fighting centaurs); there is also the Calydonian boar-hunt, the return of Hephaestus to Olympus and the fight of pygmies and cranes; Heracles is conspicuous by his absence but he is soon to dominate the narrative interests of Athenian artists.

356

357

(Florence, Museo Archeologico inv. 4209. Height 66 cm.)

Beazley, *ABV* 76, no. 1; Arias–Hirmer, pls. 40–6; Simon–Hirmer, pls. 51–7, figs. 1–3; Schefold 1, pls. 46–52; *Vaso François* (*Bollettino d'Arte* Serie Speciale 1; Rome, 1981), for fullest illustration after restoration.

357. Ivory reliefs from Delphi (see on **310**), mid-sixth century B.C. The scene is part of the story of Phineus. We have the two sons of Boreas pursuing the two Harpies who have stolen the blind king's food. The figure at the left is perhaps his queen and by her is his dining table with, it may be, his hand upon it. The ivories must have been fastened to a piece of furniture, and they remind us that it was not only clay vases that might carry narrative scenes. The Delphi reliefs give a good idea of the decoration of the famous Chest of Cypselus which was dedicated at Olympia and described by Pausanias (v.17–19) – a cedar wood chest with figures in ivory and gold (presumably parts of the dress were gilt; cf. **310c**). It was said to have been the chest in which the baby Cypselus was hidden by his mother. The description suggests that it was of about the same date as the Delphi reliefs and was perhaps an elaborately decorated container for the older, simpler chest. It carried four zones of figures depicting many mythological episodes, some involving several figures, and with inscriptions; the departure of Amphiaraus was shown in a manner closely similar to that on **354**, and there was also 'Phineus of Thrace, with the sons of Boreas chasing the Harpies away from him'. Was there a comparable dedication by the Cypselids at Delphi which did not survive intact to Pausanias' day?

(Delphi Museum. Height 9 cm.)

P. Amandry, *BCH* 63 (1939) 86ff.; 64 (1940–1) 271; Schefold 1, pl. 64b.

358. End of a bronze shield band, from Delphi, mid-sixth century B.C. The arm-grip (*porpax*) of a hoplite shield was fastened to the shield by a bronze band terminating in anthemia. In the later seventh and sixth centuries the bands were decorated with figure panels, fashioned on prepared matrices so that we find the same scenes on different strips. The scenes resemble those on vases but there is not room for many figures. Their principal interest lies in the fact that they offer a rich series of scenes from Peloponnesian studios (mainly Argos and Corinth, it seems from the inscriptions on some of them) to supplement our evidence from our other and richest source in the sixth century – Athenian vases. The panels here show Ajax seizing the naked Cassandra from sanctuary at the statue of Athena during the sack of Troy;

273

and Heracles slaying the triple-bodied Geryon.

(Delphi Museum 4479. Width 6.2 cm. After *Fouilles de Delphes*.)

Fouilles de Delphes v (Paris, 1909) pl. 21; Schefold I, pl. 77 right; for the class, E. Kunze, *Archaische Schildbänder* (Berlin, 1950), ours on pl. 50.

359. Amphora painted in Athens by Exekias about 540–530 B.C. Achilles and Ajax, having set aside part of their armour, are intent on a board game and call the score – 'four:three'. Exekias signs (top left) and at the right the beauty of Onetorides (the archon of 527/6?) is praised. The episode is not mentioned in any extant literary source. It is not uncommon for painters to present unusual variants on standard stories, as do poets, but rare for them to present a story apparently not recorded in any text. Not all episodes of a rich oral tradition may have found literary expression, and it is possible that a new story could have been invented for a special occasion and expressed informally or in art. The scene is popular in Athens for about 50 years. Other versions show

that Athena has to recall the heroes to their duty on the battlefield. The congruence with the Athenians' experience, caught asleep or playing dice by Pisistratus on his return in 546 (Hdt. 1.62–3) has been remarked.

(Rome, Vatican Museums inv. 16757.)

Beazley, *ABV* 145, no. 13; Arias–Hirmer, pls. 62, XVII; Simon–Hirmer, pl. xxv; Schefold II, 245–7, fig. 322. On the theme, Boardman, *AJA* 82 (1978) 11ff.; H. Mommsen in *Tainia* (Fest. R. Hampe; Mainz, 1980) 139–52.

360. Black-figure amphora, painted and made by Amasis, in Athens about 540 B.C. Dionysus, ivy-wreathed and holding his kantharos (a cup shape commonly associated with him) stands between two boys and two girls. The latter hold a wreath, flowers, jug and cup. Amasis was one of the most distinctive and colourful painter/potters (he signs only as potter) of mid-century Athens. The outline-drawn flesh of his girls is an old-fashioned technique, to be revived shortly, but with a black ground, for the new red figure. His name is hellenized

Egyptian, and there are many non-Athenian, even foreign names in Athens' potters' quarter. In this case the Egyptian background might even be detectable, though the painting style is pure Athenian. The god Dionysus is a comparative newcomer to Greek art, whatever his earlier career in cult. He appears often on Athenian vases from about 570 B.C. on and it may be that his rustic festivals had become 'civilized' with new city cults which also accommodated the beginnings of formal dramatic productions, the first steps towards the Classical theatre. Note that the god is accompanied by boys here, not satyrs; the girls could be maenads or mortals.

(Basel, Antikenmuseum KA 420. Height 44 cm.)
  Beazley, *Para* 65; *Ant. K.* 1 (1958) pls. 18, 20; Dionysus in Athens, F. Kolb in *JdI* 92 (1977) 99–138; Amasis and Egypt, Boardman, *JHS* 78 (1958) 1–2 and *GO* 152–3.

360

361. Marble frieze from the east side of the Treasury dedicated by the Siphnians at Delphi, about 525 B.C. In the left half the gods sit in council on Olympus; on the right a duel is fought on the plain at Troy. The pro-Trojan gods, Ares, Aphrodite, Artemis and Apollo sit behind Zeus; before him there may have been a suppliant Thetis, and Poseidon, then – preserved – Athena, Hera, Demeter: the pro-Greeks. The fight is between Hector backed by Aeneas and Menelaus backed by Patroclus, over the body of Sarpedon. The charioteers Glaucus and Automedon attend and at the right is Nestor. The composition and balance of the scenes is Homeric – Olympians and Troy, though the details do not match exactly the encounter and council in Homer (a common circumstance in art). Work on the Treasury (see **309b**) was barely completed when the donor island was sacked by the Samians (Hdt. III.57–8).

361

(Delphi Museum. Height 64 cm. Drawing, Marion Cox.)

P. de La Coste Messelière, *Au Musée de Delphes* (Paris, 1936) part 2; Boardman, *GSAP* fig. 212.2; Schefold II, 214–17, figs. 291–2.

362. Scene from a vase painted by an immigrant East Greek artist in Caere (Etruria) in about 520 B.C. Heracles turns the tables on King Busiris at the altar where he was himself to be sacrificed (Busiris' practice with foreigners). The distinction between the naked Greek hero and the Egyptians is nicely observed, and on the back of the vase the king's Nubian bodyguard hurries along. The painters (probably two masters) of these vases (the so-called Caeretan hydriae) had an original way with myth. Here the iconography of an Egyptian Pharaoh, carrying and trampling on his enemies, has been appropriately borrowed for a scene set in Egypt (compare **372**). The style is closely matched on a painted wooden panel found in Egypt (**299**).

(Vienna, Kunsthistorisches Museum 4593. Height 45 cm.)

J. M. Hemelrijk, *Caeretan Hydriae* (forthcoming); Schefold II, 132–5, fig. 171.

The Greek colonies

The colonizing activities of the Greeks in the Archaic period took them to all the shores of the Mediterranean and the Black Sea, though seldom far inland. Sites were chosen for their suitability for trade with the local population, for defence, and for adjacent farmland, where possible for all three. Some of the earliest foundations seem strongly motivated by considerations of trade: some of the later by their agricultural promise. Many colonies grew as wealthy, or wealthier than their mother cities of the homeland, and imported or sponsored prime works of Greek art and architecture. Where there was a demand there was production in the colonies of sophisticated goods for the local population, and these might to varying degrees reflect local taste or compromise with local artistic traditions (as in the Black Sea colonies, with the Scythians). Otherwise, colonial studios soon developed their own artistic traditions, not always 'provincial' in quality or aspirations.

CAH III².3, chs. 37, 38
Boardman, *GO* chs. 5, 6 and *Pre-Classical* (Harmondsworth, 1967)

T. J. Dunbabin, *The Western Greeks* (Oxford, 1948)
E. Langlotz and M. Hirmer, *The Art of Magna Graecia* (London, 1965)

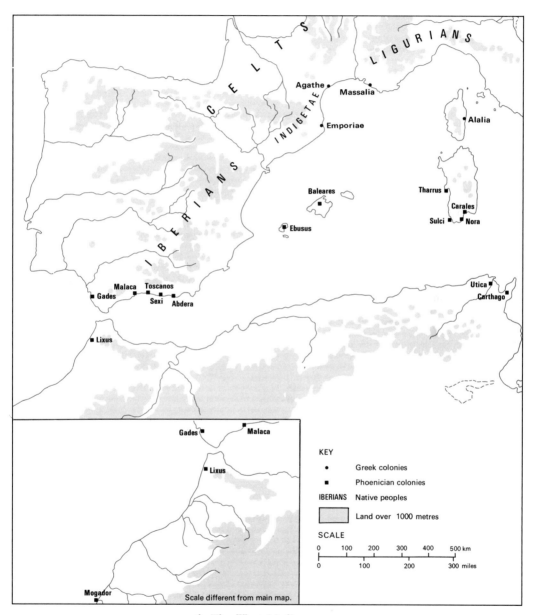

16. The West Mediterranean

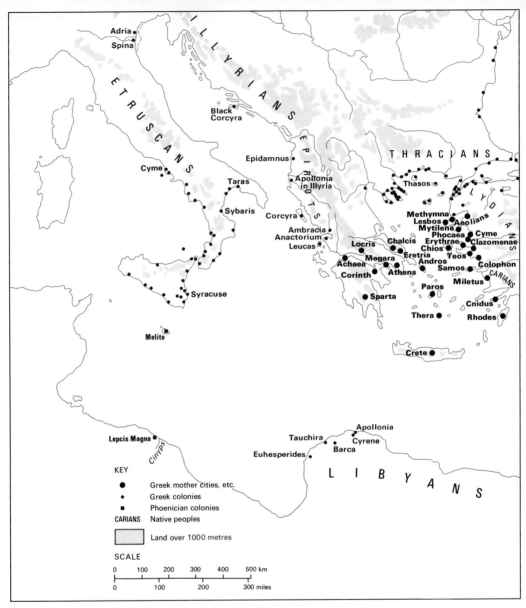

17. The Central Mediterranean

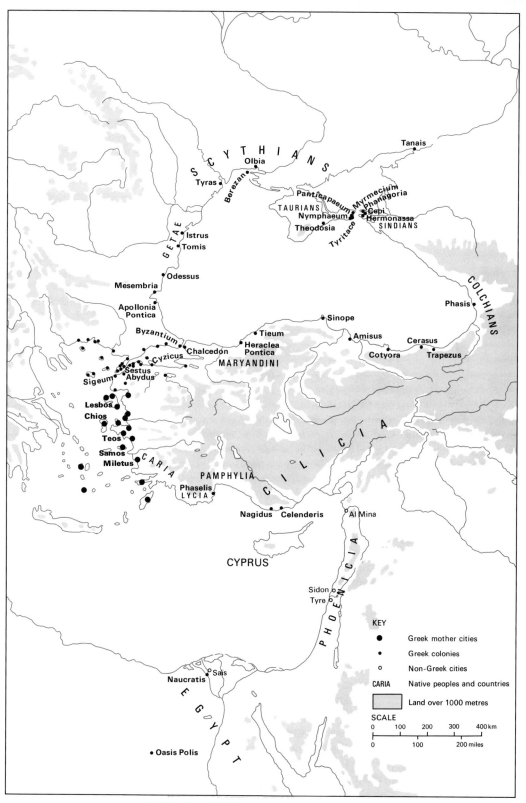

18. The East Mediterranean and the Black Sea

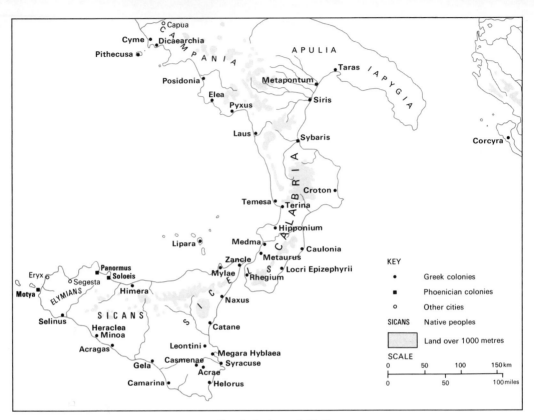

19. South Italy and Sicily

363. The site of Pithecusa on Ischia, from the south. It typifies the sites chosen by Greeks for their overseas settlements: on an offshore island, giving easy access to the mainland but safely distanced from it; and on a steep-sided promontory which could be defended on the landward side and which offered shelter and anchorage for ships at either side. This is the site of the first western settlement by Greeks – Euboeans – after early exploration of these coasts and trading contacts with the natives (Villanovan-Etruscans and other native peoples in Campania) of the Italian mainland. An *emporion* or trading port, it soon becomes a fully fledged Greek city and colony, *apoikia* ('home from home'). Finds betray early contacts with the mainland and with Elba (for its iron) and with Phoenicians, also plying these waters in as yet friendly competition. These small sites (the rocky headland is 750 m wide)

were soon outgrown and at Pithecusa a suburb soon developed on the ridge inland, beyond the first cemeteries which lay in the valley behind the hill. See the plan, *CAH* III².3, 98, fig. 15.

On Pithecusa's role see *CAH* III².3, 97–103, Coldstream, *GG* 225–31, Boardman, *GO* 165–8. The first volume of the publication of excavations at the site (since 1952) is imminent.

364. Aziris was the first coastal site in North Africa settled by Greek colonists – Therans who had spent two unhappy years on an offshore island, Platea. Herodotus (IV.157) describes the site as 'a charming place with a river on one side and lovely valleys on both', but in common with wide tracts of the once fertile Cyrenaica, it is now dusty and windswept. It was identified from the handful of Greek sherds of the brief period of its occupation, for after six years the Greeks were led up onto the

plateau, to the fine site of Cyrene. Here we look east away from the site over the neighbouring stream bed (Wadi-el-Chalig) whose mouth must have offered some shelter for shipping on this exposed coast.

CAH III².3, 134–8 for Therans in North Africa. For the site J. Boardman, *BSA* 61 (1966) 149ff. and *GO* 153–5, with another view from the site, to the west.

365. Thasos. The city lies on the north side of the island some 8 km from the coast of Thrace. It spreads from behind its harbour onto the slopes of a long ridge running parallel to the shore. The colony was established by Parians in about 680 B.C. and its long fortifications (over 4 km) with decorated gateways was first constructed by the end of the Archaic period, but demolished at the insistence of the Persians. It was the most influential of the new Greek cities in the north Aegean throughout the Archaic period, with possessions on the mainland, and rich mineral resources (including gold) both there and on the island itself.

Guide de Thasos (École Française, 1968); *CAH* III².3, 115–17.

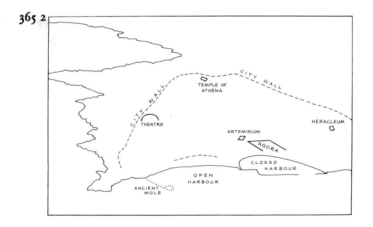

366. Acragas, the southern part of the city seen from the west. The city was a daughter foundation of Gela, of about 580 B.C. The setting, 3 km from the sea, is one of the most ambitious of the western colonies, defended on three sides by steep cliffs. This view is from the west corner along the southern cliff, lined by temples. The acropolis lies a further 3 km north of this cliff, 350 m above sea level, and the main occupied area of the town is of approximately 4 sq.km. The temples on the skyline are, left to right, of Hera Lacinia (mid-fifth century), 'Heracles' (late sixth century), Olympian Zeus (fifth century), and nearer the cliff that of 'Vulcan' (later fifth century).

CAH III².3, 166–7, with plan, fig. 27.

367. Crater from Caere, signed by Aristonothos, second quarter of the seventh century B.C. The script of the signature, Αριστονοθος εποι(ε)σεν, was once thought Argive, but may

well be Euboean. There are, however, traits in the decoration and shape which recall Argos, and which are matched in vases from the Fusco cemetery at Syracuse. One side shows a fight between a warship and a round-bottomed merchantman, perhaps meant for a Phoenician ship. The marines are equipped as hoplites. The other side shows the blinding of Polyphemus by Odysseus and his companions, a subject surprisingly common at this time, which appears also on vases from Attica (Eleusis; the neck of **347**), Argos (**348**) and on a bronze from the Samian Heraeum, while the escape from the cave is seen on an Attic vase from Aegina. Aristonothos was probably an émigré artist, working in a western colony, well in touch with homeland styles and iconography. The best known studios for figure-decorated vases among the western Greeks are in Sicily (Gela, Megara Hyblaea, Syracuse).

(Rome, Conservatori Museum. Height 36 cm.)
    P. Courbin, *BCH* 79 (1955) 21, figs. 12–13; Jeffery, *LSAG* 239; B. Schweitzer, *RM* 62 (1955) 78ff.; Arias–Hirmer, pls. 14, 15; Simon–Hirmer, pls. 18, 19.

368. Limestone statuette of a woman suckling two children, from the cemetery at Megara Hyblaea, mid-sixth century B.C. It was erected over a massive cist (*cella*) tomb. The cemetery is, for an Archaic Greek site, extravagantly furnished with statuary including *kouroi*, one in a Doric naiskos (small shrine), and a group of two horsemen. The suckling mother is not Greek in style and must be regarded as the work of a local craftsman, inspired by the Greek practice but expressing monumentally some native concept – as of a fertility goddess presiding over the dead, rather than simply commemorating a mother of twins. Native works of Greek inspiration are usually in far less exacting techniques.

(Syracuse Museum. Height 78 cm.)
    E. Langlotz and M. Hirmer, *The Art of Magna Graecia* (London, 1965) pl. 17; G. V. Gentili, *Notizie degli Scavi* 1954, 99–103.

369. Metope from the Temple of Hera at the mouth of the River Silaris, just north of Posidonia (Paestum). Limestone; about 500 B.C. Lacking local resources of white marble the western Greeks were obliged to use the poorer limestones, which denied them finesse of detail and often had to be stuccoed over or more drastically painted than the homeland marbles. They also turned the more readily to works in terracotta. They were nevertheless

370 1

370 2

371

very free with sculptural decoration on their temples, on metopes rather than the more demanding pediments. The style tends to be more emphatic, unsubtle, lacking the discipline imposed by working in marble.

(Paestum Museum. Height 85 cm.)

E. Langlotz and M. Hirmer, *The Art of Magna Graecia* (London, 1965) pl. 30; P. Zancani-Montuoro, *Heraion alla Foce del Sele* I (Rome, 1951) and II (1954), with sculptured metopes from an earlier temple.

370. Clay altar (*arula*) probably from Sicily, about 530 B.C. This is a distinctively western Greek artefact, presumably for votive or decorative purposes and not functional. The altars are commonly decorated in relief but this is unusual in being so highly coloured, and in bearing painted scenes at either end. The front shows, probably, Heracles attacking Triton, and the one side shown has the naked witch Circe confronting a part-transmuted companion of Odysseus.

(Paris, Louvre Museum CA 5956. Height 34.8 cm.)
P. Devambez, *Monuments . . . Piot* 58 (1972) 1–23.

371. 'Chalcidian' black figure amphora by the Inscriptions Painter, about 540 B.C. This school of black-figure vases was founded in the mid-sixth century, probably at Rhegium, the Chalcidian colony. The vases have been found in Etruria and in western Greek cities, especially Rhegium. The inscriptions are in Chalcidian letters and the artists were presumably émigrés, though the style is not easy to trace in Euboea. It combines Athenian, Corinthian and Ionian elements. The drawing is accomplished, compositions are decorative and vigorous. The splaying triple body of Geryon, slain by Heracles, would never have been shown thus on an Athenian vase. Moreover, Geryon is

372

given two legs instead of the six in homeland scenes, and wings, which may be an Ionian feature and which appear on another 'Chalcidian' Geryon. The feature in western Greek art perhaps inspired this detail in Stesichorus' description of Geryon (fr. 9 Page; but the poet gives Geryon six legs), rather than vice versa.

(London, British Museum B 155. Height 48 cm.)
A. Rumpf, *Chalkidische Vasen* (Berlin–Leipzig, 1927) pls. 13, 14; on the class, Cook, *GPP* 156–8; Jeffery, *LSAG* 81, 83; J. Boardman, *BSA* 68 (1973) 271–2, 280–2 (analyses and origins) and *Ant. K.* 19 (1976) 13 (Stesichorus).

372. Laconian black-figure cup from Vulci, by the Arcesilas Painter, about 560 B.C. The scene shows a king, named Arcesilas, supervising the weighing of a commodity which is more probably wool than silphion (*pace CAH* III².3, 138). He is shaded by an awning held by a beam on which sit birds and a monkey while a crane flies by. A hunting leopard is tethered to the king's stool. Below, an overseer watches bundles being stacked. The king must be Arcesilas II of Cyrene. The scheme recalls that of weighing and storage in Egyptian painting and, with other vases, once encouraged scholars to believe that the vases were made in Cyrenaica. Many have certainly been found in the Greek cities of Libya (although not this one) but they attest Spartan interest in this area of Dorian colonization, and in relevant subject matter (as here), and not local production.

(Paris, Cabinet des Médailles 189. Diameter 29 cm.)
C. B. Stibbe, *Lakonische Vasenmaler* (Amsterdam, 1972) no. 194; Arias–Hirmer, pls. 74, XXIV; Simon–Hirmer, pls. 38, XV; S. Benton, *Archaeology* 12 (1959) 178–82.

373. Bronze volute crater found in the tomb of a Celtic princess at Vix, the cemetery area of a Hallstatt town on Mt Lassois, near the River Seine little over 100 miles south east of Paris. Probably Spartan work of about 530 B.C. The foundation of Massilia (Marseilles) at the mouth of the River Rhone stimulated trade with the hinterland and on routes from the tin-bearing areas and perhaps even from Britain. The crater is the most spectacular of many luxury gifts of Mediterranean (some Etruscan) origin which made their way up the Rhone, and some on into south Germany (Heuneburg, Asperg, Hochdorf). The crater was carried in pieces with its parts (the cast attachments of foot, handles and rim and the figures on the neck) lettered for reassembly. Other finds in the tomb include three Etruscan bronze vases, two Athenian clay cups and a gold torque of native shape but worked with fine granulation and filigree, and decorated with tiny Greek Pegasi.

(Châtillon-sur-Seine Museum. Height 1.64 m, with lid in the form of a disk with a statuette of a woman as handle.)
R. Joffroy, *Trésor de Vix* (Paris, 1954); E. Gjødesen, *AJA* 67 (1963) 333ff., for a Corinthian origin and earlier date; Boardman, *GO* 216–24, Greek finds in France, north Spain and Germany; Jeffery, *LSAG* 191f., 375.

374. Gilt silver mirror back from Kelermes, mid-sixth century B.C. Objects of Greek workmanship penetrated deep into Scythia from the Black Sea colonies. Some are of native shape, and their subject matter may betray mixed influences. The segments on this mirror, from a rich Scythian site, show – a Greek *potnia theron* with lions; a lion attacking a bull (a Greco-oriental subject) and a boar; heraldic sphinxes and beneath them a crouching feline in a purely Scythian 'animal style'; a lion and a ram; two hairy men fighting a griffin, who must be the Arimasps, set by the Greeks in the distant north (Hdt. IV.27); a bird, a bear and a fox; heraldic sphinxes and a griffin; heraldic lions and a goat. There is a comparably decorated gilt silver rhyton by the same artist from the same site.

(Leningrad, Hermitage Museum. Diameter 17 cm.)
M. Maximova in J. Irmschev and D. B. Schelov, edd., *Griechische Städte* (Berlin, 1961) 35ff.; A. Artamonov, *Treasures from the Scythian Tombs* (London, 1970) pls. 68–9; Boardman, *GO* 256–64 for Greek art and Scythians, and *Pre-Classical* (Harmondsworth, 1967) ch. 6.

375. Gold fish from Vettersfelde, west Poland, late sixth century B.C. This formed part of a hoard of Scythian objects (**263**), most of them intelligible as the decorative armour of a cavalier, either the contents of a burial (there were Scythian forays this far west) or loot. The fish may be a pectoral or a decorative frontlet for a horse, in a Scythian manner, but the relief decoration is Greek and the piece, with others of the hoard, was fashioned by Greeks in the

373a

Black Sea colonies for their neighbours. The tail tips are worked as rams' heads and the tail fin is echoed by the flying eagle shown upon it. On the body, above, a leopard and a lion attack a boar and a stag; below, Triton with a school of fish. The general scheme of attaching or translating animal forms is Scythian, but executed in an artistically unconvincing manner by Greek artists accustomed to quite a different idiom.

(Berlin, Staatliche Museen (West) Misc. 7839. Length 41 cm.)

A. Greifenhagen, *Schmuckarbeiten in Edelmetall*, *Berlin* I (Berlin, 1970) 61–2, pls. 39, 40.

373b

14. THE ALPHABET AND GREECE

L. H. JEFFERY

CAH III².1, ch. 20*b*, 'Greek alphabetic writing', offers a historical account of the Greek adoption of the West Semitic alphabet at a date not later than about 800–750 B.C., and some possible reasons for the numerous local versions which were used in the different Greek city-states for many of the letter-forms – until, by the end of the fifth century B.C., the Ionic version had become the general one. (This was probably because, some 200 years earlier, the Ionic-speaking East Greek cities had been the first to import and popularize Egyptian papyrus (paper); thus their scribes and book-merchants made Ionic the script most generally familiar throughout the country.) Figs. 104–6 in that Volume show a grid of all the local letter-forms, and some early ABCs and graffiti. This section offers some typical official, quasi-official, and private inscriptions, mainly for their content but also, in passing, for their various local letter-forms; and this same variety serves (like the ubiquitous graffiti) to remind us that in the cities of Archaic Greece the alphabet was not, apparently, the special preserve of some civic authority or closed scribal guild. As a skill, it did not need physical strength, or special tools, or long training: any intelligent child could learn it quickly. And so each local script probably preserves in its letter-forms some individual touches made, unwittingly perhaps, by whoever taught the first young literates in that small community.

GENERAL BIBLIOGRAPHY

CAH III².1, ch. 20*a* (B. S. J. Isserlin, a full histori-cal and linguistic discussion on the Semitic side); ch. 20*b* (L. H. Jeffery)
J. N. Coldstream, *Geometric Greece* (London, 1977) ch. 11
D. Diringer, *The Alphabet* (London, 1968)
G. R. Driver, *Semitic Writing* (London, 1948; revised by S. A. Hopkins, 1976)
Jeffery, *LSAG*
L. H. Jeffery, *Archaic Greece* (London, 1976) 24–6

376d

376. As the letter-names show ('ox: house: goad', etc.), the West Semitic retrograde alphabet was a final development from primitive pictographs sketched to transmit information. A profile-sketch by a right-hander usually does face left; but what convention, chance, or practical reason caused the *series* to run retrograde rather than left-to-right is uncertain. During the second millennium B.C., usage had reduced their number and shapes to 22 rudimentary signs, and their meaning to the initial sound of their names: '(lp), *b*(t), *g*(ml), etc., down to the final *t*(au), 'cross'; and, since a spoken consonant forms a potential syllable (*b*', *g*', *d*', etc.), the list *as recited* formed a brief but effective syllabary; any spoken word would be represented, roughly but intelligibly, by some combination from these simplified signs. (**a**) shows the Phoenician formal alphabet as lettered on stone, from the inscription on the ruler Ahiram's coffin (**136b**) at Byblos, about 1000 B.C. (**b**), distinctly nearer to early Greek forms (**c**) typologically, shows the lettering on fragmentary bronze bowls from Cyprus,

dedicated to the god Ba'al of Lebanon (about 800–750 B.C.?); compare here the near-Greek shapes of *kap, mem, nun, tau*. Herodotus says that long ago 'Phoenicians with Cadmus' had settled in the Boeotian area, and had taught the Greeks 'many sciences – in particular, letters' (*grammata*, literally 'scratches' – on sherds, wood, wax, etc.?), and that these letters were also called '*phoinikeia*', 'Phoenician things', by the Ionians (*sic*) then living in that area. (Euboea, offshore from Boeotia, certainly spoke a form of the Ionic dialect; and '*phoinikeia*' for 'letters' is attested in inscriptions from Ionia (Teos) and Crete (Doric!). If the alphabet was taken over in Greek territory (but see below), any of these three (particularly Euboea) sound more likely than landlocked Boeotia.) As for the date: by the start of the eighth century at latest, the good prospects offered to any ship-building peoples for trading and settlements caused some contact, however irregular, between Greeks and Phoenicians in the Mediterranean–Aegean area. A plain Semitic sherd (**d**) showing part of a Phoenician graffito

has been found on a locally made vase at Pithecusa (Ischia), where a Euboean colony had settled by the eighth century or earlier (cf. **378**); and conversely, an eighth-century Greek sherd with part of a Greek graffito has been identified among the Greek pottery excavated by Sir Leonard Woolley in the early Greek trade-depot based at Al Mina on the Syrian coast (**e**). Apparently, the Greeks learnt only the essentials – the retrograde alphabet itself (cf. **377**), and how to combine these sounds to spell out Greek; for lines *consistently* retrograde, like the Phoenician, are very rare (cf. **378**): their earliest inscriptions, once beyond the first line, maeander back 'ox-plough-wise' (*boustrophedon*, cf. **381**). Then, during the sixth century, they settled into continuous left-to-right, as still practised today. This script had two great merits; it was not the guarded monopoly of some hieratic caste, and it was simple – any intelligent child could copy these signs and learn their names by rote. The first Greek learners may well have been the children of Greek traders in settlements such as those at Al Mina and Tell Sūkās on the Syrian coast, who learnt it, in or out of school, among the children of their fathers' Semitic business-partners – a far cry from the old aristocratic Greek model of the wise centaur Chiron, tutor of the boy Achilles in riding, shooting and playing the lyre.

((**a**) The alphabet of the inscription on the sarco-phagus of Ahiram.)

R. Dussaud, *Syria* 5 (1924) 135–57 – the inscription; for the sarcophagus see **136b**.
((**b**) The alphabet used on a bronze bowl from Cyprus, Mouti Sinoas (N.E. of Amathus).)
D. Diringer, *The Alphabet* (1968) fig. 14. 18b; E. Gjerstad, *Swedish Cyprus Expedition* IV.2, 436–7.
((**c**) Local Greek versions.)
((**d**) Ischia Museum. 3 cm × 2.2 cm. After Buchner.)
P. K. McCarter, *AJA* 79 (1975) 140–1; G. Buchner, *Parola del Passato* 33 (1978) 138, fig. 5.
((**e**) Oxford, Ashmolean Museum 1982.889. 3.9 cm × 3.2 cm.)
J. Boardman, *Oxford Journal of Archaeology* 1 (1982) 365–7.
Cf. also on the derivation of the alphabet: R. Carpenter, *AJA* 37 (1933) 8–29; R. M. Cook and A. G. Woodhead, *BSA* 63 (1959) 175–6; A. Millard, *Kadmos* 15 (1976) 130–44; W. Johnstone, *Kadmos* 17 (1978) 151–66.

377. This ivory writing-tablet (late eighth century B.C. ?) was found at Marsiliana d'Albegna in north Etruria, in a grave. Probably it came originally from the Euboean colonial area of Naples and Pithecusa, much further south (cf. **378**), for along the top it bears the Greek alphabet in its local Euboic letter-forms, which the pupil would copy in the wax that filled the central tray: αβγδεϝϝϙηθι κλμνξοπ *san qoppa* ρστυχφψ. Like its Semitic prototype, this alphabet runs retrograde (cf. also **378**); and many early Greek inscriptions do start from right to left, but, if further lines are needed, they normally continue *boustro-phedon* (cf. **381**), and finally settle for con-tinuous left to right, the easiest way for the

378

379 a

379 c

379b

right-handed majority. (The letters which follow *tau* are Greek additions to the Semitic. ʋ is probably a doublet, developed from the semi-vowel *vau* to express the Greek full vowel *u*. The origins of *phi, chi* and *psi* are uncertain; *psi* is mostly confined to the Ionic cities, and some Doric islands lack all three (e.g. Crete, Thera). *Omega* may be simply a broken form of *omikron*.) Already clear here in early Euboic are the prototypes of many Latin letter-shapes: C, D, F, L, P, R, S, X; even the Euboic 5-stroked *mu* still survived (as M') for the initial letters of names in aristocratic Roman families, as their tomb-inscriptions reveal – just as, much later, many English tombstones show ffoulkeses and ffolliots still holding to their old spelling.

(Florence, Museo Archeologico. 8.8 cm × 5.1 cm.)
G. Buonamici, *Epigrafia Etrusca* (1932) 101–3, pl. 1.i; Jeffery, *LSAG* 236f., no. 18, pl. 48.

378. This big wine-bowl, now famous as 'Nestor's Cup', was found in a grave on Pithecusa, the pioneering Euboean colony of the early eighth century in the Greek west. Dated about 725 B.C. by its style (Late Geometric), it carries a joke-poem which is scratched on it in three separate lines (1 trochaic and 2 hexametric) – not, as was usual, in a single line continued in a spiral round the pot. Such deliberate separation may possibly imply a *skolion* ('zigzag') here. This was a song composed on festive occasions after supper, which got its name because each singer might stop at a 'cliff-hanger' line-end, tossing a myrtle-spray across to another diner, who had to cap the line *impromptu*. Here we have: 'Nestor's highly potable cup am I [a comic reference to old Nestor's huge goblet, *Iliad* XI.632–7]. | Whoever drinks *this* cupful, straight upon him | desire for fair-crowned Aphrodite'll seize' – the last thing to be expected of the aged and respectable Nestor, and (so Hansen, below) an unexpected bonus for the unlawful user, because lines 2–3 parody the solemn formula of a primitive criminal law: 'Whosoever commits (crime *X*) shall receive (penalty *Y*).' The letter-forms look more compact than in other eighth-century examples, and punctuation is abnormal before the seventh century. A later song, inspired by a big and obviously 'antique' pot, and incised on it for a joke, to compliment

three witty diners? But the stratification would seem to forbid a date below the late eighth century; and certainly the symposium, the traditional evening club-meeting of ancient Greece, had long been recorded in poetry and art before Plato made it his background for a Socratic dialogue set in the late fifth century B.C.

Νέστορός : ε[ἰμ]ι : εὔποτ[ον] : ποτέριο[ν] : ὸς δ'ἂ(ν) τõδε π[ίε]σι : ποτερί[ο] : αὐτίκα κ̃ενον ἱμερ[ος : ηαιρ]έσει : καλλιστε[φά]νο : Ἀφροδίτες.

(Ischia Museum. Height 10.3 cm.)
CAH III².3, 100, fig. 16 for a drawing of the inscription, and p. 99; G. Buchner and C. F. Russo, *Rendiconti* (Accademia Nazionale dei Lincei) Ser. 8, 10 (1955) 215–34; Jeffery, *LSAG* 235f., no. 1, pl. 47; P. Hansen, *Glotta* 54 (1976) 25–43; R. Meiggs and D. M. Lewis, *A Selection of Greek Historical Inscriptions* (Oxford, 1969) no. 1.

379. Inscriptions on pottery, particularly graffiti, are prominent among our earliest datable Greek writing. Very often they are only owners' names on portable pottery – one of the first and most practical uses for a non-hieratic, freely-taught script. (a), a sherd from a plain pot, incised retrograde before firing, was excavated in a Late Geometric context at Lefkandi in Euboea, and may be as early as about 750 B.C., or little later; 'I am Aischrion's.' The unusual, long zigzag *sigma* is spasmodically attested from the late eighth century onwards in other places over a wide area, such as Attica, Boeotia, Sparta. It figures also in the archaic alphabet in Phrygia, a script clearly derived from the Greeks through their colonies in Asia Minor. (b), a fine graffito incised retrograde on a two-handled Subgeometric cup of about 700

B.C., now broken, was found in Rhodes: 'I am the kylix of Qoraqos.' (c) is from the important mass of modest local Attic pottery, similarly inscribed, which was found high up on Mount Hymettus, in a small precinct to Zeus Ombrios ('rainy'). Dating roughly between 700 and 500 B.C., the many graffiti on these cups (mostly now in sherds) are often statements of ownership, mixed with occasional casual obscenities and some aspiring attempts at the alphabet. Archaeologists, noting that in such inscriptions virtually all the identifiable names are masculine, infer that, in the hot Greek summer, boys or men in company – out and about (unlike the women) from their schooldays onwards, what with life in the Agora, long public meetings, and, perhaps, long daily journeys to work – might well carry their own marked cups about, to use at any chance-met well or stream.

(a) Αἰσχρί[ονος vac.?]

(Eretria Museum. Letter heights 1.2–2.7 cm.)
L. H. Jeffery in *Lefkandi* 1 89f., no. 101, pl. 69b.

(b) Ϙοράϙο ἠμὶ ϙύλιχς

(Copenhagen, National Museum inv. 10151. Height 6.8 cm.)
C. Blinkenberg, *Lindos* 11.2 (Berlin, 1941) 1003ff., no. 710; Jeffery, *LSAG* 347, no. 1, pl. 67.

(c) [- - -κ]αὶ τάδ' αὐτὸς ἔγ⟨ρ⟩αφ[σεν]

(Athens, National Museum. Width 8.9 cm. After Langdon.)
M. K. Langdon, *Hesperia* Suppl. XVI (1976) 20, no. 30, fig. 8, pl. 5; Jeffery, *LSAG* 69, no. 3.

380. Sherd from the rim and shoulder of a flat-lipped clay bowl (*dinos*), excavated at Smyrna. Little remains of the decoration, except for part of the maker's painted signature: Istrokleës me (?'made', or 'painted'): 'Ιστροκλέης με [—]; *or* μ'έ[γραψε]. About 650–625 B.C. The heights of *epsilon* and *sigma* are exaggerated by extra strokes, perhaps to fill the width of the rim. The uncontracted ending of the name (-έης) shows that the line was metrical – the normal practice in early dedications, epitaphs and (as here) artists' signatures: the reason being (partly at least) to fix the names of those concerned in the mind of the reader; Istrokles no longer ranked as an anonymous workman, but advertised himself thus as a master-craftsman. Such signatures by pot-painters and marble-sculptors are among our earliest datable Greek inscriptions; they are much rarer among the surviving (mostly small) early bronzes, however fine the work may be. This pot-painter's name, 'Glory of the Istrus', suggests that his family had some connexion with, or at least knowledge of, the great northern river Istrus (Danube): by the seventh century this was an area which Greek traders from Miletus, at least, had already reached and tapped, as an Eldorado, for not only gold, but slaves, grain, honey and wax, cattle, hides and dried tunny.

(Izmir Museum. Width 12 cm.)
L. H. Jeffery, *BSA* 59 (1964) 45, no. 1, pl. 5a.

381. The indigenous Minoan population of Crete, though overrun by Mycenaean and then Dorian incomers, preserved the tradition of its early rulers, Rhadamanthys and Minos, as great law-givers who continued their statutory duties as judges in Hades. Indeed, parts of Greek codes and single laws have survived in several

381 1

381 2

cities, inscribed on the stone walls of the chief temple: at Gortyn, Cnossus, Lyttus, and here at Drerus. This wall-block from the temple of Apollo Delphinius, inscribed in archaic lettering *boustrophedon*, may be Europe's oldest surviving law against tyranny, about 650–600 B.C. 'Thus it pleased the city: when a man has been *kosmos* [literally, 'orderer, arranger': a title of magisterial authority, whether it means here any member of the Board of *kosmoi*, or only the president], he shall not be *kosmos* again within ten years; if he is, he shall himself be liable for double the amount of all fines which he exacted in judgement; he shall be accurst, useless [lose all civic rights?] for life, and all his actions as *kosmos* shall be null and void. Oath-takers: the *Kosmos* [= the whole Board?] and the *Damioi* [another high-ranking board?: cf. *demiourgoi* elsewhere], and the Twenty of the city [= representatives of the voting population of this oligarchy?].' Obviously, if immediate iteration of this office were allowed, tyranny could emerge unperceived from the continuous prolongation of a supreme position for which the holder was legally accountable only *after* its expiry. None the less, in the seventh and sixth centuries Greek tyrannies did displace aristocratic control in both mainland Greece and the Greek cities of Asia Minor – some short-lived, others lasting into the third generation. A Cretan law of about 500 B.C. starts: 'We the City, five from each tribe'; so the 'Twenty' here *may* represent the standard three Dorian tribes plus a fourth, Eteocretan; for we must remember that several of the fragmentary laws found here at Drerus were in Greek script but an unknown language, presumed to be that of an autochthonous Cretan element still surviving on the island.

ἆδ' ἔϝαδε πόλι. ἐπεί κα κοσμήσει, δέκα ϝετίον τὸν ἀϝτὸν μὴ κόσμεν. αἰ δὲ κοσμήσιε, ὄπε δικάκσιε ἀϝτὸν ὀπέλεν διπλεῖ κἀϝτὸν θιοσόλοιον, ἄκρηστον, ἦμεν ἆς δόοι, κ'ὄτι κοσμήσιε μηδὲν ἦμεν. Ὀμόται δὲ κόσμος κ' οἱ δάμιοι κ' οἱ ἴκατι οἱ τᾶς πόλ[ιος].

(Neapolis Museum.)

CAH III².3, 237, 241; Jeffery, *LSAG* 311, no. 1a, pl. 59 and *Archaic Greece* (London, 1976) 189f.; Meiggs and Lewis, *op. cit.* no. 2.

382. Marble Doric capital, a grave marker from Corcyra. The Classical Greek view of death and immortality was complex and deep-rooted, as may be seen from the various grave-goods which, throughout the Dark and Archaic Ages, Everyman buried with his dead, and then covered with as fine and lasting a marker as his means allowed. Standing stones (stelae) on the mounded graves of heroes are occasionally mentioned in the Homeric epic: cf. *Iliad* XI.369–73: 'But (Paris) . . . . . drew his bow against (Diomedes) shepherd of the people, son of Tydeus; he propped himself against the stela on the man-made mound of Ilus son of Dardanus, an Elder of the people long ago.' The column of this Doric capital in Corcyra originally stood on such a mound, a sophisticated version of the tall, rough stone markers of an earlier age, saying: 'I am the stela on the mound of Xenares son of Mheixis.' Stela, normally denoting a shaft rather than a column, seems to be used here in its basic sense of a 'standing marker'. The fine lettering suggests

382

be the Asiatic type called *sagaris*, traditionally wielded by the Amazons. It bears a dedication: 'I am the sacred property of Hera-in-the-Plain: Qunisqos the butcher dedicated me, a tithe from his works.' It was found at Sant'Agata in south Italy (Calabria), not far from the locality of the rich and powerful Greek colony Sybaris, and the Greek letter-forms (about 525–500 B.C.?) are typical of those Italian colonies which, like Sybaris, were settled in the eighth and seventh centuries B.C. by Greek emigrants from the villages of Achaea, the narrow strip of land along the north coast of the Peloponnese. Most of these colonies far outstripped their small metropoleis in size and wealth. In fact, the Sybarites were known for their brilliant cavalry as well as their luxury, but Greek humour popularized an image of languid, lounging, Ouida-type riders, who got blisters even on rose-petal couches, and taught their chargers to dance to the flute after regimental dinners, thus giving to the men of Croton, their perpetual border-foes, the chance for some most unsporting military ruses. In 510 B.C. the city was flooded and destroyed by the engineering skill of the Crotoniates. 'Butcher' may be literal, that is, some rich retired bourgeois: or – it is suggested – a citizen who served as an official bearing this title for the sacrifices of cattle to Hera. Possibly, he was both.

Τᾶς Ηέρας hιαρός ἐμι τᾶς ἐν πεδίοι. Ϙυνίσϙός με ἀνέθεκε ὄρταμος ϝέργōν δεκάταν.

(British Museum, Bronzes 252. Length 16.5 cm.)

H. B. Walters, *British Museum Catalogue of Bronzes* (1899) no. 252; Jeffery, *LSAG* 253, no. 8, pl. 50; M. Guarducci, *Memorie . . . Soc. Magna Grecia* 9–10 (1968–9) 47ff.

a date not before the mid-sixth century B.C.; typologically, the flattish, spreading echinus of the capital would indicate one in or near the seventh century, but pious conservatism might well retain the old shape on a funeral column. Corcyra was a colony of Corinth, and so the epitaph, cut retrograde on the abacus, is in the Doric dialect and local script of the metropolis, though the line itself is a Homeric hexameter, following the normal convention for early Greek epitaphs.

Στάλα Ξενϝάρεος τοῦ Μhεῖξιος εἰμ' ἐπὶ τύμ(β)ōι

(Corfu Museum 3. Width of abacus 76.5 cm.)
Jeffery, *LSAG* 233, no. 13, pl. 46.

383. This small bronze axehead, evidently a symbolic one to represent the real thing, may

384. This official seat of dark (Laconian?) marble stood in the Stadium at Olympia. The inscription which proclaims its owner is cut in the typical retrograde script (and terse phrasing) of Sparta – handsome, precise, slow to change (i.e., hard to date closely: here, possibly some years after, rather than before, the mid-sixth century): 'Gorgos, Lacedaimonian, *proxenos* of Eleans.' *Proxenia*, official protection of the stranger, arose from the ancient custom of the *xenia* (mutual guest-friendship) formed between the heads of two old families in two cities; in Classical times, the man in City *A* who was the *proxenos* for all visitors from City *B* was probably the head of a family which already had old, reciprocal ties of *xenia* with a similar family in B. As a *proxenos* Gorgos must have been high-born – possibly of the royal family surnamed Agidae, where the feminine form (Gorgo) is attested (cf. Hdt. v.48). Wealth was needed as well as breeding, for the post was unpaid, and the strong Greek tradition of *philotimia* (self-respect) required a man, as host, to represent his city handsomely. This seat obviously carried the privilege of *prohedria* (front seating at public events), particularly impressive here, since the Olympics in Elis, to Zeus, rated highest of the great athletic festivals – above those at Delphi (Apollo), the Isthmus (Poseidon) and Nemea (Zeus again). Founded officially in 776 B.C., they superseded a much older cult – traditionally, the Funeral Games held for the Lord Pelops, who had given his name to the Peloponnese ('Pelops' island'), but was said to hail originally from Lydia in Asia Minor.

Γόργος Λακεδαιμόνιος, πρόξενος Ƒαλείōν.

(Olympia Museum. 42 cm × 31 cm.)
E. Kunze, *Olympiabericht* IV (1944) 164–6, pl. 67; Jeffery, *LSAG* 190, no. 15, pl. 36.

384

385. Those buried in the cemetery of a Greek city were, normally, its own citizens; but there were always exceptions. This fine marble base-block is from an Athenian cemetery which lay immediately outside the Piraeus Gate of the city. On its top a polygonal cutting still survives, which once held the foot-plinth of a big standing marble statue – probably a *kouros* (see **330**), the Greek embodiment of athletic young manhood, for more elderly men were usually shown seated. Lines 1–2 give the Greek epitaph: 'This (is) the memorial of Tu?ṛ [*c*.4], a Carian, son of ?Skyl[ax].' Line 3 is in Carian, a script of which some letters were

385

obviously derived from the Greek, though the origin of others is still enigmatic. (It is also attested in Egypt, for by the start of the sixth century B.C. Greeks and Carians were serving as mercenaries in the Pharaoh's forces, and occasionally wrote names or remarks on Egyptian monuments: a famous Greek inscription at Abu Simbel in the Sudan records a mercenary army's journey south with the Egyptian forces to subdue an insurrection: cf. *CAH* III².3, 50, fig. 6, and here, **240**.) This Carian text in Attica appears to read (so Ray, below): 'tomb of Sak'qur', i.e. 'of ?Skylax', *or* 'of (some patronymic name formed from Skylax)'. Possibly this Carian was one of a ruling family on some ambassadorial visit – or an Athenian's brother-in-law, for in Attica hereditary citizenship was through the father alone (many aristocrats had non-Attic or even non-Greek mothers), until in 445 B.C. Periclean Athens passed the notorious Citizenship Decree, which required the mother also to be Attic. This sculptor's signature, 'Aristokles m[ade it]', occurs on other Attic sculpture-bases; on lettering, this one should be *c.* 525 B.C.

Σῆμα τόδε Τυρ[*c.* 4]‖Καρὸς τõ Σκύλ[ακος].|
(Carian text)
['Α]ριστοκλῆς ἐπ[οίει, *or* —οίεσεν].

(Athens, Kerameikos Museum. 22.5 cm × 43 cm.)

M. Treu, *Glotta* 34 (1955) 67–71 (Carian text); L. H. Jeffery, *BSA* 57 (1962) 126f., no. 18 (Greek text); F. Willemsen, *AM* 78 (1963) 125–9 (the definitive archaeological study); M. Meier-Brügger, *Kadmos* 18 (1979) 83f.; J. D. Ray, *Proc. Camb. Phil. Soc.* N.S. 28 (1982) 83f., fig. 4.